CW00695896

THE SILENT S

Two Years in Antarctica and the Story of the
First Winter Occupation of Alexander Island

Cliff Pearce F.R.G.S.

'In the darkening twilight I saw a lone star hover,
gemlike above the bay'
(Last diary entry of Sir Edward Shackleton, South Georgia,
Jan 4th 1922)

To Tom

With best wishes

Cliff Pearce

Nov 16 2007

The Book Guild Ltd
Sussex, England

First published in Great Britain in 2004 by
The Book Guild Ltd
25 High Street
Lewes, East Sussex
BN7 2LU

Typesetting in Times by
Acorn Bookwork Ltd, Salisbury, Wiltshire

Printed in Great Britain by
Antony Rowe Ltd, Chippenham, Wiltshire

A catalogue record for this book is available from
The British Library.

ISBN 1 85776 845 0

*Dedicated to John and Brian with whom I shared that
first winter on Alexander Island*

Cliff, John, Brian
40 years on!

CONTENTS

APPENDICES

SKETCH MAPS

LIST OF PHOTOGRAPHS

All photographs were taken by the author except where indicated. The photographs accompanying the dedication and on the inside back cover were taken by Jackie Pearce.

ACKNOWLEDGMENTS

Getting to Antarctica in the sixties was a rare opportunity for adventure and I therefore acknowledge my good fortune in being selected through the Crown Agents to join the Falkland Islands Dependencies Survey. Similarly my return to Antarctica in 2000 owed much to the Committee of four from the BAS Club who masterminded the 'Marguerite Bay 2000' cruise on the *Lyubov Orlova*.

The first person who read an early copy of the manuscript was Peter Holt, a former colleague of mine in the world of education. It was he who acted as a major spur to completing the work when he wrote to me, 'I found your tale absolutely absorbing. It mustn't be lost. Somehow, it must be published'. As Peter was outside the world of polar cognoscenti, I took encouragement from the fact that the book might have a more general appeal and so I pressed on.

Keith Holmes, who served as a geologist at Stonington Island in 1965 and 1966, and whose retirement has been largely committed to archival work on a variety of Antarctic centred projects, also read the manuscript. Not only did he show great enthusiasm for the work, but he provided me with specific advice and information, especially concerning the husky dogs, and in particular the history of the husky sledge dog Moose. When many of us went to Stonington Island, Connecticut for a reunion in 2001, his wife Christine, an experienced writer, added her encouragement.

Howard Chapman, one of the five sledgers who struggled south across the Marguerite Bay ice to reach Fossil Bluff, provided me with a copy of his diary of that dramatic journey which enabled me to improve the chapter 'Struggling South'. He also gave me permission to use his photographs.

Alan Cleps of King's Lynn encouraged me too by patiently scanning and printing my forty year old slides and proving that they still had a story to tell.

Other slides were kindly provided by my Antarctic contemporaries Maurice Sumner and Brian Taylor.

Dr John Shears of the British Antarctic Survey kindly gave me much of his time in updating me on the present situation at Fossil

Bluff and he made it possible for me to choose from the BAS photographic records.

I have had other major help from BAS where my primitive sketch maps were transformed into cartographic masterpieces! All of the maps were prepared thanks to Janet Thomson, Head of Mapping and Geographic Information Centre, British Antarctic Survey, and executed by Peter Fretwell in 2002. They are reproduced by permission of the Survey.

To all of these patient and supportive people, I acknowledge my debt and extend to them all my grateful thanks.

My family has been important in their support for me. My daughter Katherine, and twin sons Adrian and Martin, all very widely travelled themselves, have kept up their interest in this long project. Adrian has read every chapter, and his love of polar literature has not only added to my library but provided me with good insights and advice on content and construction.

I owe a special word of thanks to my wife Jackie who has been closely involved in each stage of the work. Her immense patience in reading and rereading sections of the book, suggesting changes or in discussing the minutiae on points of grammar, the subtleties of words, or phraseology has, I am sure, enhanced the final work.

Without the encouragement and support of them all the book would not have reached publication. I thank them sincerely.

INTRODUCTION

In February 2000, together with my wife Jackie, and one of my sons, Adrian, I joined an Antarctic cruise on the Russian ship, *Lyubov Orlova*. The cruise, 'Marguerite Bay 2000', had been organised by a Committee consisting of George Kistruck, the late John Tait, Adrian Apps and Keith Holmes, all of whom had served in the Antarctic many years before. The main objective of the itinerary was to reach Marguerite Bay. In the course of this cruise some, or all of us, were able to visit seven of the old bases located along the Antarctic Peninsula and its off-shore islands, and to pass close by others. Because of the ice conditions we failed to reach Stonington Island, our prime objective, in Marguerite Bay. At Rothera Station on Adelaide Island, Britain's only existing base on the Peninsula, I took the opportunity to look in the archives to see what information existed about the earliest days of the establishment of Fossil Bluff, on Alexander Island in 1961. There was little except a geological report written by Brian Taylor.

Back at home in Norfolk, I dug out my diaries and wrote a synopsis of the day-to-day life of the three of us who, in 1961, had lived at this most unusual base on the edge of Alexander Island. It overlooked the Silent Sound, the great ice filled rift named after King George VI. Copies of that simple diary were sent to Rothera, and to Fossil Bluff.

The re-awakening of interest and the nostalgia engendered by this exercise, caused me to look again at a manuscript which I had worked on at the hut during the long dark winter of 1961, and which I had abandoned after the sun returned and I had more pressing matters to occupy my time. Not until I retired after thirty six years in teaching did I have the time to return to it.

How we found ourselves at Fossil Bluff during that first winter was part of the continuing development of British work in Antarctica centred on the Falkland Islands Dependencies Survey. Although there had been private expeditions to explore the Antarctic Peninsula in the 1920s and '30s, the British government really took an interest during the Second World War when German raiders were at work in the

South Atlantic, and there were strategic reasons to have a presence south of Drake Passage. Thus, a small military force, under the name 'Operation Tabarin', was assembled, and early in 1944 bases were established at Deception Island and Port Lockroy, with a total of fourteen men! Two years later, in July 1945, following the end of the war, Tabarin was renamed The Falkland Islands Dependencies Survey (FIDS), and responsibility was transferred to the Colonial Office. Although for a few years it was administered by a committee in London, after 1949 the Governor of the Falkland Islands assumed responsibility for the Survey, with a permanent headquarters and secretariat in Stanley. The men employed by the Survey naturally were called Fids. The Falkland Islands Dependencies Survey name was retained until June 1961 when the Antarctic Treaty came into force and the British Antarctic Survey assumed responsibility for Antarctic research.

During the eighteen years up to 1961, approximately six hundred men worked for the Survey. They came from all types of backgrounds, predominantly military or naval early on, later coming almost entirely from civilian backgrounds. They all brought particular skills to their work whether it be in running and maintaining diesel engines, operating radios, building huts, or flying aircraft. Many Fids were scientists, pursuing research in the worlds of geology, glaciology, geophysics, biology, and medicine. There were also surveyors and meteorologists, mountaineers and general assistants (who were often responsible for dog teams). Cooks too were employed, though this duty was most commonly shared by all base members. The number of bases operating throughout the year during the eighteen years ranged from two to eleven, the average being about seven. The bases were all very small; during this period, the average number of men on each base was under seven. Most Fids were aged between twenty and forty, the huge majority were single and all were men. The normal contract was for two years of service in the Antarctic, consequently most were away from the U.K. for two and a half years.

In the intervening years since 1961, when the Falkland Islands Dependencies Survey evolved into the British Antarctic Survey massive changes have taken place in the nature of Antarctic exploration. The number of permanent British bases, at various times totalling sixteen, has dropped to two, with two summer bases. Exploration has become based on highly qualified scientists using modern sophisticated equipment and techniques in the setting of large, superbly equipped bases. The use of aircraft for transporting personnel to the bases, for placing survey teams in field areas, and for aerial photography is an excellent example of cost effectiveness in the use of time for research. It is now possible to travel from England to Fossil Bluff in four or five days; in 1960 many of us spent over one hundred days based on the *Kista Dan* without reaching our destination; some returned home to try again in 1961.

Since the 1950s, few personal accounts have been written of life on the bases, yet these were extremely important in laying the foundations for the respect in which Britain is held in this field of work. Much of this story was written during the winter at Fossil Bluff when for several months John, Brian and I established a creative oasis in a sterile wilderness with our various interests – painting, geological research, or writing. It was a time when my memory of the events was sharp. My diaries and my researches, mostly from polar books collected over forty years, have been used to give the story a historical perspective. My hope is that readers will enjoy this contribution to the history of the work of the British in Antarctica.

UNITS OF MEASUREMENT

All measurements are given in Imperial Units, as used in 1961.

Distance:

39.4 inches	= 1 metre
1 foot	= 30.48 centimetres
1 yard	= 91.44 centimetres or 0.9144 metre
1 statute mile	= 1.6 kilometres

Thus, mountains of 1,000, 2,000, 3,000 feet identified in the text would now be given as 304.8 metres, 609.6 metres and 914.4 metres respectively.

Temperatures are given in Fahrenheit. To convert to Centigrade, deduct 32, multiply the remainder by 5 and divide by 9. As examples, 50°F = 10°C, 32°F = 0°C, 0°F = –17.7°C and –40°F = –40°C.

1

Southwards

Mine is a story of escape. I had spent the years from five to twenty-three in the sheltered confines of the world of education at school and university, then – armed with my BA degree in geography and economics and a Diploma in education, I took up a teaching post at Stevenage in Hertfordshire. I soon realised that this was a mistake; an appalling prospect of another forty years in education opened up before me. I had to do something different.

My first escape route was to follow up an advertisement for a job in Saskatchewan – 'No weaklings need apply', ran the text provocatively. I was not successful. However, I soon spotted an advertisement for the Falkland Islands Dependencies Survey, who were looking for meteorological assistants to man their bases in Antarctica. At that time (1959) there were eight such bases thinly distributed along the Graham Land peninsula, (now called the Antarctic Peninsula), and its off-shore islands, as well as a base at Halley Bay on the Weddell Sea coast. Between five and nineteen men wintered on each base, a total of seventy-eight. This looked a really exciting opportunity to escape and, in due course, I was interviewed at the Crown Agents in London and appointed on May 15th 1959.

My headmaster was not amused and warned me of the dire consequences of losing my annual increments and of having to start my career all over again. My colleagues were much more positive – many of them already ground down by many years in the classroom. The pupils too were helpful with their knowledge and advice – 'Mind the bears, sir,' suggested one; 'I saw an Eskimo on the telly last week, sir,' offered another; 'It's dark there, what d'yer want to go there for?' asked a third.

I smiled at these comments, of course, because, apart from the obvious errors, I was not too sure myself. I knew that the Antarctic was cold and uninhabited; I knew that no land animals lived there; I had recollections of pictures of auroras, tales of heroism, and innumerable subconscious images of icebergs, ice cliffs and glaciers. I had also recently followed enthusiastically the reports of the Trans-Antarctic Expedition, so that by the time I had read the official accounts by Sir Vivian Fuchs and Sir Edmund Hillary, I was desperately keen to go south.

I therefore made my escape after one year of teaching. I reported to the Air Ministry, very close to where I lived in Stanmore, late in July and for the next eight weeks I studied the tasks relating to the work of a meteorological assistant. Finally I put my training into practice with ten weeks of working at London Airport. For much of the time there hardly a cloud crossed the sky, so that I suffered great frustration through not being able to put my newly found coding skills to the test. It was that glorious summer of 1959 ...

I boarded the polar vessel *Kista Dan* on December 18th and we sailed in the early evening. I was truly excited at last to be a fully signed up member of the Falkland Islands Dependencies Survey, a real 'Fid', and to be on the way to unknown adventures and experiences. The Survey started its work in 1944 and had been responsible in the intervening years for much of the exploration of the area jointly claimed by the governments of Britain, Argentina and Chile. On board I joined geologists, surveyors, meteorologists, biologists, doctors, geophysicists and others who would contribute to furthering our knowledge of this little-known part of the world.

By the time the *Kista Dan* had left Southampton on December 18th, the two other expedition ships, the *RRS John Biscoe* and the *RRS Shackleton*, were already beginning the task of relieving the bases, having sailed much earlier. As the pack ice breaks out from the Antarctic shores, the bases on the South Orkneys and South Shetlands can be reached in December; most of us on board the *Kista Dan* were destined for the southern bases, which can only be reached in February or March.

Our initial excitement at our departure had rapidly diminished by the time we reached the English Channel, for we soon ran into distinctly rough seas which had most of us in our bunks for a considerable time, especially as we progressed slowly across the Bay of Biscay. I shared a tiny four-berth cabin deep down in the bowels of the ship with geologists Arthur Fraser and Brian Taylor, and with diesel/electric mechanic Bob Harkness – who as an experienced seaman shamed us landlubbers by never being sea-sick and never missing a meal!

2

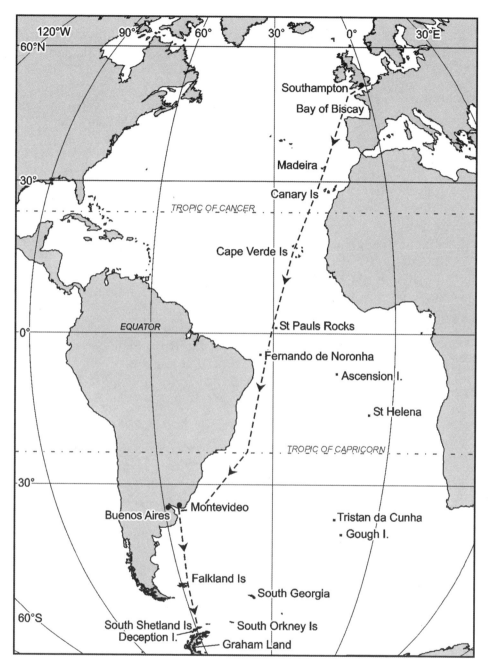

120°W 90° 60° 30° 0° 30°E
60°N

Southampton
Bay of Biscay

Madeira

Canary Is

TROPIC OF CANCER

30°

Cape Verde Is

EQUATOR

0°

St Pauls Rocks

Fernando de Noronha

Ascension I.

St Helena

TROPIC OF CAPRICORN

30°

Montevideo
Buenos Aires

Tristan da Cunha
Gough I.

Falkland Is

South Georgia

60°S

South Shetland Is
Deception I.

South Orkney Is

Graham Land

THE ATLANTIC: SOUTHAMPTON TO GRAHAM LAND
Nominal scale at the Equator 1 : 100 000 000

Eventually we reached less disturbed waters, and as the seas calmed down so our spirits rose. The more we progressed south, the more we felt the warmth of the sun on our white, wintered arms. Life became truly relaxing and we sunbathed, or swam in the small canvas pool on deck, or read, or leaned over the foc's'le, alert for flying fish or dolphins. Away from the hubbub of home life, the only noises to break the great oceanic silence were the sound of the engine – a steady industrious chug – and the swish of the water as the bows of the ship sliced through it. It was a wonderfully peaceful existence; halcyon days of blue skies broken, from time to time, by light warm winds and puffy white clouds, whilst an occasional island held our interest for a day as the first hazy mass transformed itself into mountain ranges and settlements. The houses, people and animals all became slowly discernible as we approached, and as slowly, faded into an amorphous obscurity behind us. Madeira, Santo Antao (Cape Verde Islands), Fernando de Noronha; how we would have loved to have set foot ashore on these magical places!

We crossed the equator with due ceremony and moved on towards Montevideo, arriving in the estuary of the River Plate on the evening of January 12th 1960. The excitement of seeing a new country for me has always been great, and the fact that I was seeing a fragment of a new continent made the day particularly memorable. As I wrote in my diary:

Today has been really exciting. The first unusual thing we noticed was the greenness of the sea – a khaki green. It indicated that we were in shallower waters. Then we saw some flies, a dragon fly, a moth and a butterfly – all wonderful sights after twenty-five days. Gradually a long low barrier of sand became faintly visible on the horizon. A humming bird flew out, and we saw a falcon. In the water there were sharks and later we saw many sea lions. All afternoon we followed the sandy coastline, many settlements could be seen and at eventide we came by a really large town.

What a wonderful sunset it was. The sun turned golden, then red as it dropped beneath the horizon. A bronze mist hung over Uruguay. The entrance to the Plate Estuary brought a remarkable calm to the water ... sea lions were playing in the darkening seas. I had a gin and Martini then watched a Blue Star freighter flash a courtesy call to us late at night.

It is wonderful to realise that we are in Uruguay, SOUTH AMERICA!

The next day, most people were on deck early as we moved into the harbour. Sir Vivian Fuchs and Alfred Stephenson came on board, for they were to visit some of the scenes of their earlier pioneering work on Graham Land. Sir Vivian was the current Director of FIDS; Alfred had been a surveyor with the British Graham Land Expedition 1935–37. We spent two crowded days seeing as much of this fascinating town as time permitted, whilst two aircraft were loaded on board the ship and the water tanks replenished. We made the most of the heat of Montevideo for it was certain to be our last contact with really warm air for two years, and our hours of enjoyment on the beaches, where the sand burned our feet, remained long in our minds.

On January 18th, we moved into the harbour of Stanley, Falkland Islands, the headquarters of the Dependencies Survey. Stanley has always been important as a port of call for expeditions going south, and it has been here that the members of expeditions busy themselves with last preparations for their sojourns across the other side of the Drake Passage. It was a busy time for us too, for our stay was to be as short as possible and we had stores to load from barges onto the *Kista Dan*. The South Atlantic weather, which had been kind to us until now, began to show us the teeth which have given the latitudes of the forties and fifties the epithets 'roaring', and 'furious' – and we still had the 'shrieking' sixties to come. All morning winds of fifty to sixty knots lashed the sheltered waters and sent spray over the sides of the barge and onto us as we worked below. The giant petrels which abound in Stanley Harbour loved it, and wheeled gracefully around or bobbed up and down on the churned-up water whilst we watched enviously. We had plenty of good weather, however, and in between being made welcome by the Governor, Sir Edwin Arrowsmith, attending pleasant parties, and traipsing over the peat fields to the beaches, we collected our issues of polar clothing.

Clothing for life in the Antarctic had inevitably been well researched both in the laboratory and – more importantly – in the field. We were well provided for both in terms of quantity and quality. We were amazed at first by how much went into our kit bags; however, we later appreciated how little was superfluous to our needs.

We had several types of footwear. Leather boots were provided for skiing, and a warmer type, the Greenland boot, was issued for long-distance ski marching. We were also given a thick-soled vapour barrier boot made of rubber. This boot proved particularly versatile and was extremely warm in use around the base, especially during the summer season when the sun made snow conditions wet, though it was liable to cause considerable sweating. We were also provided with mukluks, a knee-length canvas boot with a wire mesh insole which was for use in very cold weather. In my second year I soon realised the great insulating properties of this boot, which kept our feet warm in temperatures below minus 35°F. The large size of this boot enabled as many as three or even four pairs of heavy socks and a pair of linen inners to be worn, if necessary.

Underclothes naturally included sets of long underpants ('long johns') whose value was immense, and vests. The vests varied in style, but the wide open-mesh string vests proved to be particularly warm and hard-wearing. We had ample shirts and jerseys, and as an overall protection against cold, windy weather each man had a set of windproofs comprising trousers and an anorak made of ventile material. We later had the opportunity to compare our anoraks with the highly coloured, very photogenic anoraks worn by Americans on board the icebreaker *USS Glacier*. We had made a comment to an American scientist about his desirable-looking anorak, but he assured us of their inferiority. In demonstration he held the sleeve of his anorak to his mouth and blew through it, something that could not be done with ours, much to our satisfaction. There was considerable variety in the types of head wear, from ear muffs and wolverine fur hats to balaclavas made of angora wool. My balaclava never failed to keep my head warm, and I always preferred it to the more fashionable types. Gloves too varied in their style, from mittens to woollen gloves and to large capacious leather gloves with linen liners into which we could stuff our already gloved hands. Lampwick harnesses were provided to secure these gloves to our person, as the careless loss of a glove could lead to the loss of fingers! We were certainly well pleased by the time we had our goggles, towels and pyjamas to complete our outfits; we had no fear of the Antarctic cold.

Everything was now on board. The hatches were secured, the aircraft crates relashed, and a cage full of clucking chickens – destined for

Deception Island – appeared in a corner of the deck. The departure time was announced. I spent the last day tramping over the area around Stanley, making the most of the greenery and life of the island. So we departed the little town on January 23rd. As we waved goodbye to the little cluster on the jetty – Fids office girls and well-wishers – our minds turned to the things we were now leaving behind for two years: the trees and the grass, fresh food, newspapers, female company, the theatre, television and so on. It was indeed hard to realise that all of these things were gone for the time being. We were really going south at last!

2

Landless Latitudes – and Land

Around the sheltered waters of Stanley harbour and in many of the embayments of the Falkland Islands, the hulks of dozens of ships lie in various attitudes of partial or complete submergence. The rusty ironwork, the swinging, broken cables, creaking doors, lapping waters and littered decks bespeak a sorry end to ships whose outlines conjure up in the mind pictures of billowing sails and straining rigging, sounds of hoarse voices carried from poop deck to main mast, and august figureheads braving their way through huge seas with indomitable seamen. Most of the wrecks represent the culmination of lost battles round Cape Horn, when battered, leaking or dismasted, the vessels struggled gamely to this refuge – but struggled no more.

We made a boat journey out to one such vessel lying miserably at the edge of the water in Sparrow Cove, the *Great Britain*, which had been launched in Bristol in 1843. At the time of its launch it was the largest ship afloat, the first to be built of iron, and amongst the first to be driven by propeller. After many years of carrying passengers, mostly from England to Australia, the ship was transferred to cargo duties. In May 1886 she set out from Stanley to go round the Horn, but after several weeks of battling she was forced back to the Falklands, where she ended her days as a store ship. Eventually she was towed to Sparrow Cove in 1937, where she had rested in an increasing state of dereliction for over twenty years. (The *Great Britain* was later taken back to Bristol, where she has been restored.) Hundreds of other wrecks lie either around the shores of the islands, or more numerously in the uncharted depths between, or south of Cape Horn and the Falklands. A glance at the *Great Britain*, a look at some of the other hulks, a reading of Commodore Anson's tremendous efforts to get round the Horn in 1741, all imbued in us a deep respect for the Drake Passage, and we mere trippers about to make our first crossing wondered exactly what to expect, though we had a ship with a powerful engine, the alert presence of radar and radio antennae, and the knowledge that modern ships were crossing these waters regularly.

The *Kista Dan* moved slowly away from the Falklands and we watched our last direct contact with civilisation fade. We moved into the Drake Passage, the 600-mile stretch of sea between South America and Antarctica. These latitudes between approximately 56°S and 63°S are virtually devoid of land around the entire Southern Ocean. Prevailing westerly winds therefore have an uninterrupted effect on the seas here, building up a huge swell on even the calmest of days. With the passage of a depression, gale force winds from other sectors produce waves athwart this swell, rendering the seas completely chaotic. We soon had a foretaste of unpleasantness when the ship rolled lazily into the swell, and most of the items on the saloon tables rapidly slid off. We were extremely lucky, however, and our anticipation of rough seas did not materialise; we had to wait until our northward voyage in 1962 for a taste of several 'nights of terror'!

Most of us spent much time on deck constantly on the lookout for the things we had come south to see, the magnificence of the albatrosses and the giant petrels, the splendour of our first whales, and the immensity of the icebergs moving sedately northwards.

The furious fifties and the shrieking sixties, therefore, to our surprise, greeted us without fury and without shrieking and we approached ever closer to the land. On the third day of the crossing we glimpsed our first Antarctic land, the snow-mantled peaks of Smith Island, the low cloud and miserable day giving it a bleak appearance. It was not long afterwards that the outlines of Deception Island hove into view, and later in the day we sidled past Pete's Pillar and Cathedral Crags, and entered into Whalers Bay. It was here that the hard work started in order to prepare for our tasks in Marguerite Bay in the weeks ahead.

This work involved unloading the aircraft from the ship, assembling them and flight-testing them. In Montevideo, the huge crates had been loaded onto the deck of the *Kista Dan*, and now at Deception Island they were opened. Two aircraft had been obtained from de Havilland, Canada, a Beaver and an Otter. Both were single-engine high-wing planes which could be readily adapted to take off from land or ice; the Beaver also had floats which enabled it to take off from water. The Beaver was a small plane, able to carry up to six passengers or equivalent freight, depending on whether or not floats were in use – their weight would naturally cut down the payload. Beavers had already been used by several other nations in the Antarctic, and had proved their worth as speedy reconnaissance planes. The fact that it

10

could be carried on the deck of the *Kista Dan* made the Beaver available for ice reconnaissance, an attribute that was to be sorely needed in the two months ahead. The Otter was much larger and was capable of carrying 1500 lbs of freight. It had been used on the Trans-Antarctic Expedition and at the bases of other nations, for example at Ellsworth Station, an American base, in 1957–58.

All hands were now committed to unloading the Otter, which was to be assembled on the airstrip; the Beaver could be assembled on deck. There were considerable difficulties in landing such large objects ashore when no proper landing tackle existed, and it was all down to 'Fid power'. On deck, one party unwrapped the fuselage from its cocoon of silvery padding, which with the crate had protected it on its long journey from Canada to Montevideo and southwards. Whilst this was being done, a shore party constructed a raft. Huge beams were wrested from the derelict whaling factory and placed across four pontoon floats which had been thoroughly secured together by an iron girder framework. Decking was then lashed to the structure and a solid raft was ready to await the fuselage – and, of course, the calm conditions desirable for such a delicate operation. The weather was kind, and within a day the raft was towed out alongside the ship, whose derrick lifted the emergent chrysalis gently into position. The ship's boat, a small red vessel, took the strain and slowly but surely the load was towed across the still waters of Whalers Bay.

Now came the most difficult part, for we no longer had the help of the ship's derrick, or any other mechanical aid. Fortunately, however, we had plenty of Fid power, thirty of us, of all shapes and sizes, crowded around the landing zone. First a line was thrown from the pontoon to the shore and pulled in. Next a ramp was placed in position, leading from the raft to the beach, while a rigid tow bar was attached to the base tractor. Very slowly, with men holding the plane back and watching intently for any deviation from the tracks, the Otter came to the land. Once this huge task was safely accomplished, it was a comparatively easy matter to unload the wings and other parts.

Soon the airframe fitter, Pete Bates, and the engineer, Tom Sumner – both on secondment from the RAF – were able to begin the real work. Within three days a call went out for all hands to man the wings. It was an interesting operation as each wing was raised up prior to being secured to the fuselage. Fid power really came into its own that day, with a score of Fids taking up their position under the

11

wing, each in a different attitude. Tall Fids took the weight on their shoulders, short Fids took the weight on their finger tips, others in various contortions and discomfort completed the line. Once the wings were secured the Fids clambered down and Tom continued his work on the engine, whilst Pete saw to the air frame. By February 3rd all was ready, and we watched with a sense of satisfaction as Flight Lieutenant Ron Lord took the plane down the runway which had been previously rolled out on the volcanic ash as the snow had cleared. The bright orange plane lifted itself up and flew around the island; the first stage of the assembling was complete.

Work now commenced on the Beaver, which had similarly emerged from its cocoon on the deck of the ship. The Beaver was lifted onto its own floats, and a mere four days after the Otter, it was lifted over the side of the ship and onto the water. This time Flight Lieutenant Paddy English was the pilot and he soon had the aircraft skimming across the water before it, too, took to the air and made a test circuit round the island.

The work was done; the ship could now move southwards in the knowledge that both planes were ready to support us as necessary – the Beaver on board the *Kista Dan*, the Otter at Deception Island. It was not long before they were called on to work ...

3

The Kista Dan *is Beset*

We had high hopes of reaching Marguerite Bay as we moved through Neptune's Bellows, Deception Island, early in February. My kit bags and a large trunk were safely stowed in the hold and I and my four colleagues were looking forward to getting to Horseshoe Island. At the Argentine Islands, however, which we reached next day, we had our first intimation that conditions might be difficult this year. Our newly assembled Beaver was off-loaded onto the water, and after cruising around in the brash ice until a sufficiently long strip of clear water could be found, it took off, flying southwards for an ice reconnaissance. From the air, Sir Vivian Fuchs and the mate of the *Kista Dan* could see large areas of ice extending from the Graham Land coast far out to sea. Occasional leads offered some hope for advance, especially as the major part of the break-out season was still ahead of us, but our optimism was somewhat dampened by the extent northwards of the ice, whose edge proved to be only a few miles south of the Argentine Islands. We on board discussed again our chances of reaching our appointed bases; Adelaide Island (where a completely new base was to be erected), Horseshoe Island and Stonington Island. On the one hand the extent of the ice was inordinately vast, on the other – in its unpredictable manner – the whole lot could suddenly blow out to sea and break up in a few days at any time during the remaining weeks of the summer season.

The Beaver aircraft on board again, the crew weighed anchor and we moved from Meek Channel. Our stay had been brief and busy, but we saw something of the magnificence of the Argentine Islands. Their beauty is, perhaps, in their lack of extremes. The scenery is not based on the grandeur of the rocks or glaciers; indeed, the islands are too small to sustain glaciers, though each has an icecap. Small in area, the islands are separated from one another by fairly narrow, deep, channels. Along these channels, sparkling blue in the sun, myriads of icebergs and bergy bits drift aimlessly, as though – like stateless persons – they had lost their homes and would spend the rest

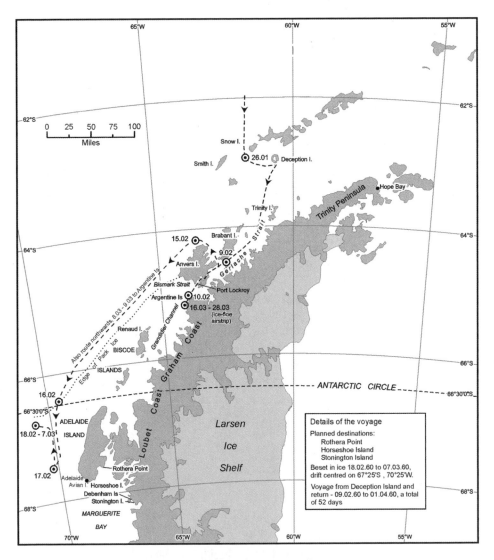

The map contains the following labels:

65°W   60°W   55°W

62°S

0   25   50   75   100
Miles

Snow I.

Smith I.

26.01   Deception I.

62°S

Hope Bay

Trinity Peninsula

Trinity I.

Brabant I.

15.02

9.02

Anvers I.

Gerlache Strait

64°S

Port Lockroy

Bismark Strait

Argentine Is   10.02

16.03 - 28.03
(ice-floe airstrip)

Also route northwards, 8.03 - 9.03 to Argentine Is

Grandidier Channel

Renaud I.

BISCOE

Edge of Pack Ice

ISLANDS

Graham Coast

66°S

ANTARCTIC CIRCLE

66°30'0"S

16.02

66°30'0"S

ADELAIDE

18.02 - 7.03   ISLAND

Loubet Coast

Larsen

Ice

Shelf

17.02

Adelaide I.   Avian I.   Horseshoe I.

Rothera Point

Debenham Is.

Stonington I.

MARGUERITE

BAY

68°S

70°W   65°W   60°W   55°W

Details of the voyage

Planned destinations:
    Rothera Point
    Horseshoe Island
    Stonington Island

Beset in ice 18.02.60 to 07.03.60,
drift centred on 67°25'S , 70°25'W.

Voyage from Deception Island and
return - 09.02.60 to 01.04.60, a total
of 52 days

VOYAGE OF MV *KISTA DAN* 1960

of their days wandering about until, worn down through age and the rough usage of life, they return invisibly to the elements that gave them their birth. Such sculpturing of ice by the forces of nature on a scale, and with a beauty of infinite dimensions, truly inspired awe in all of us. Between the isles and islets, beneath towering ice cliffs, the seals sunned themselves on the ice floes and penguins hopped up for a rest from their submarine pursuits. Other birds too created interest, for it was an otherwise inanimate landscape. We watched the blue-eyed cormorants of Uruguay Island perched on their northern cliff, the adult birds sweeping over the sea, seeking out food for their young. The predatory skuas would sweep down onto the greasy slivers of seal blubber rejected even by the huskies, and the little white sheathbill, a land bird who never seems to fly unless it has to (though it is known to migrate hundreds of miles each year), runs in to pick up the leavings. Occasionally tiny black Wilson's petrels fluttered nervously over some morsel in the water, or an arctic tern screeched noisily overhead – having completed its 10,000-mile journey from the north polar regions. Amongst the rocks – clear of snow for a few months – bright green clumps of moss appeared, only to disappear all too soon under the next cover of snow. Over all the transitoriness of summer life and activity, Graham Land stood, a few miles away, massive mountains, huge glaciers, unchanging ... proud!

Frustrated by the ice to the south, we moved northwards; a red ship, a blue sea and an endless panorama of snowy mountains, rock outcrops and evil-looking glaciers whose crevasse-ridden snouts pitched into the sea an assortment of bergs which made the *Kista Dan* look very diminutive. South of Anvers Island we headed westwards towards the Bellingshausen Sea. Speedy progress through mirror-calm water was soon slowed as we entered the porridge that is called 'brash ice', and stopped as we hit the first sizeable ice floe. To have wasted hours battering away at the ice would have been pointless when there were good possibilities of open routes further to the north. So back we went, turning north again, and passing through the Neumayer Strait, en route for the Schollaert Channel.

Next morning when we awoke, we were making full speed down the west coast of Anvers Island. Occasionally we brushed through a belt of loose, light pack, dismembered from its parent body and now rising up and down with the swell of the sea, its mass gradually

15

decreasing by its own attrition and the comparative warmth of the water. Often alongside these trails of ice we would watch several whales swimming around, their monstrous backs breaking the surface before disappearing into the depths of their cold, dark world. We who watched had great sympathy with these gargantuan creatures, many of whose great carcasses would suffer the ignominy of being pulled up onto the factory ships, or taken, bloated, through their home waters to the flensing knives at South Georgia; even as we watched, the whalers were engaged in their foul business.

What a detestable place the Bellingshausen Sea can look on such a day as this! The cloud was low and grey, a monochrome of gloom; snow fell continuously and visibility was down to a mile or two. The swell lifted the ship rhythmically up and down, and a light gusty wind blew the crests of spiteful waves in fine mists up and over the fo'c'sle to deter even the hardiest of the whale watchers and the bird spotters. An occasional berg loomed up, its steely mass towering into obscurity, and we slipped furtively by, a discreet token of respect to the rightful owners of these featureless waters. It was good to join the others in the warmth and friendliness of the saloon.

A second day passed; the same murk, the same walls of moving ice; the same gloomy nothingness. Something was different, though, for we crossed the Antarctic Circle, 66°32'S at Longitude 69°00'W, and entered the regions which experience the glory of twenty-four hours of sunlight on at least one day a year, yet have to bear the gloom of sunless winters. The circle now to our north, we knew that we were advancing towards the pack ice separating us from Marguerite Bay. We were therefore not surprised when, later on during the same day, we were able to discern a white band on the cloud to the south-east. 'Ice blink', as this phenomenon is called, is the polar warning system of the imminence of pack ice. Soon we entered the fringes of it, heading generally towards Adelaide Island, our immediate destination. The loose nature of the pack did not, at this time, impede us, but when we retired most of us were wondering what was in store for us.

The next day was the first of several days of patient navigation through pack ice of varying nature. Sometimes the ice was broken up and open and we pushed steadily through it, leaving an avenue of dark water in our wake; sometimes the floes were larger, heavier, and more closely packed together, and only by patience and the strength of the bows could slow progress be made.

February 17th. We have only covered approximately 20 miles the whole day but we have kept going surely. Adelaide Island has appeared on the horizon and, as I write, we are about 25 miles north-west of Cape Adriasola. The pack consists of large floes varying from three feet to fifteen feet thick and separated from each other by very narrow channels of broken ice. It is these leads that the Captain heads for, he has been up in the crow's nest almost continuously for the past thirty hours. Sometimes the ship is brought to a complete standstill and we go back a hundred yards for another run. It is a peculiar landscape (sic), great white expanses with narrow black lines indicating leads. Great towering bergs, which have toppled over, dot the scene. Much of the pack ice is rotten at this time of the year. The underside is an orange colour and is honeycombed with holes.

We made disappointing progress next day. The sun shone on Adelaide Island wonderfully and invitingly, but we finished the day in almost the same place as we had started from in the morning. At 8.00 p.m., however, we came across a stretch of open water and the Beaver was lowered onto the water.

February 18th. It was touch and go whether there was sufficient room to take off, but things went OK. The sun fell below some altocumulus clouds illuminating them golden. The ice floes and bergs reflected intense white light and the ship was reflected in the still open waters. And the little orange aircraft on which our hopes of finding a route must be centred, took off.

It seemed that open water could be seen near Adelaide Island but that the Marguerite Bay ice was firm. We raised our glasses to the birth of a son, (Prince Andrew), to HM the Queen on the 19th. At that time we were struggling through ice which was now being subjected to pressure arising from strong winds. Indeed, the winds later increased to gale force, and as we peered through the portholes we could see that visibility was down to a few yards; snow was being hurled against the side of the ship and for the first time on the voyage we could see the floes being pushed over one another in crumpled rafts. By the Saturday, our progress was down to a crawl – a fly in a bowl of treacle – each movement being made with immense difficulty from one icy prison to an equally recalcitrant mass of ice a few yards further on. The blizzard had packed the huge floes closer together and piled another foot of snow onto them. Yet we did move; albeit slowly, and gradually becoming slower and slower.

This day was considerably brightened for us by the appearance of an emperor penguin, which must have hopped up from the water through one of the increasingly rare gaps in the ice. It stood some way off, erect and still, over three feet in height, a personification of dignity, curiosity and hardiness, the delicate tones of orange around its neck emphasising the lack of colouring in its own environment. These are the most truly Antarctic penguins of all, their whole life being spent well to the south; appearances to the north of the Antarctic Circle are very rare. They spend summertime swimming in the polar sea in search of food, then during the cold dark days of winter they muster in the rookeries in their thousands, producing offspring who have to survive low temperatures and strong winds that no other creature could endure. Small wonder is it, therefore, that the number of survivors during the early weeks of life is small. One of these rookeries is known to exist on the Dion Islands in Marguerite Bay; fortunate indeed are those from the bases who have made the winter journey to witness this supreme fight against cold and inhospitality. Our solitary penguin gave us a few minutes to admire it, then disappeared below. We were, however, well favoured, for during the succeeding days when there was all too often little of interest to see, it reappeared and stood watching us, as if wondering if we would ever move from our present position.

We wondered too, for Sunday February 21st saw the end of our immediate progress towards Marguerite Bay. A combination of forces began to tell on us. Our previous efforts had taken us well into the belt of pack ice; a series of gales caused the pack to close, and we were surrounded by heavy pack ice, with a mere yard of open water around us. The ship was unable to move forwards or back, and it was decided that we should move sufficient ice to give the ship a short run so as to enable it to charge its way through. Fid power was in its element in such circumstances and most of us climbed out onto the ice carrying long poles. We all began poling lumps of ice along the side of the ship, a task which brought no sign of improvement. Eventually, seeing the futility of the exercise, we turned our back on the ship, put three poles in the ice as stumps, and improvised a game of cricket with a shovel and a beer can. An expression that was popular at the time aptly summed up our predicament, the ice 'was bigger than all of us'!

The weather now turned nasty. Winds far in excess of gale force shrieked across the ice, gusting to 100 knots from time to time. Though conditions in the blizzard did not enable us to see what was happening, the movements of the ship gave great cause for concern. Two huge floes at the stern moved together, nipping us and lifting us out of the water. By breakfast time next day, the list was four degrees, followed by a sudden lurch later which took the angle to twelve degrees. More movements pushed the ship about, finally settling us down at a list of ten degrees. For several days we lived at this angle, and we had to grow accustomed to annoying little difficulties: plumbing troubles, unusual sitting positions and odd attitudes taken by the furnishings – the window blind pulleys and the curtains leaning out into the room, for example. It was peculiar in bed at night for the list caused us to lie at angles not conducive to comfort, and one false move could cause us to roll onto the floor. The next day dawned brilliantly sunny, one of those days to remember the polar climes by – an exhilarating combination of cold, calm and sparkling clarity, when one's instinct is to be out in the pure air all day ... But we were beset.

For the first time we were able to see the true nature of our new environment: a fantastic vista of pure white ice. All around, the floes had been squashed together, closing the leads which had enabled us to come to this position. The edges of the floes were crumpled all round with great thicknesses of ice and snow; nothing but a pure white vastness. We ventured onto the ice, glad to stretch our legs and to survey the suddenly tiny ship, ensnared and completely helpless. All around the canted ship, ice was piled up unevenly, so that in places we had hardly to step down from it to be on the ice. At the bow the pressure had dented the one-inch-thick plates sufficiently for the ice-strengthening ribs to be discernible; they were only twelve inches apart, half the normal spacing. The local strength of the shell was thought to be sixteen times greater than on normal ships, a source of encouragement to us all. Another aspect of the design which we appreciated was that the hull was shaped so as to avoid being nipped in ice, the rounded bottom causing the ship to be uplifted, as had happened to us! We were well aware of the fate which befell Shackleton's ship *Endurance* in the Weddell Sea in 1915, when the pressure of the ice stove in its sides so that it eventually sank.

The first novelty of the situation soon wore off. We roamed the ice and photographed the ship with considerable interest, but it would have been good to hear the engines turning and to feel that we were on the move. Several days passed, days on which there was no apparent movement of the ice itself though we were part of a massive drifting movement which, by February 24th, had taken us to 67°55′S 71°02′W. We idled away the time, thinking that our stay would be too brief to do anything of constructive value. Indeed, there was little to do anyway. One by one, however, the trunks in the hold were opened and new books appeared, a couple of models were started – of the ship and of a Nansen sledge – and records and record players passed from cabin to cabin. The continual passage of depressions moving eastwards across the Bellingshausen Sea gave much cloudy, mild weather – even with some rain – which made conditions outside miserable. Mozart's Clarinet Concerto gave me some intense moments of nostalgia as I listened whilst looking through the porthole. Outside, I could discern nothing in the great horizonless expanse of ice and sky except an iceberg whose massive structure and prominent lines reminded me of the Royal Festival Hall back in London. Our evenings were spent in playing games, gossiping and drinking, sometimes far into the night. The *Kista Dan* was not a very large ship; as time passed we became more and more conscious of its smallness.

Seven days went by; our second Sunday came. The environment remained unchanging but our drift continued slowly to the south and west. On this day a strong easterly wind arose, so our hopes of progress increased. It was not to be, however, for the wind backed to its usual direction and the only difference was the appearance of a narrow lead between two floes, of no use to us in our predicament. We now began to hear news of two icebreakers in the area, the *San Martin*, from Argentina, and the *USS Glacier* from America. The *San Martin* had been trying to effect the relief of the Argentine base on the Debenham Islands when it too was caught by the ice and sustained some damage to the propeller. The *Glacier*, on routine support work for the US Antarctic programme, was on its way to render assistance to the *San Martin*. It was highly probable that the *Glacier* would come to our assistance, should the need arise.

We had been stationary for nine days; thirty-two frustrated Fids, Sir Vivian Fuchs and Alfred Stephenson, and the crew of the ship. Tension arose. Inevitably in the evenings gossip was well lubricated by beer, and nightly parties stretched deeper and deeper into the night; there was noise, frivolity and a variety of minor disturbances.

Sir Vivian was not happy. On February 29th a notice suddenly appeared on the saloon noticeboard:

THE BAR IS CLOSED UNTIL FURTHER NOTICE

If it becomes apparent that reasonable hours are being kept, and the ships company is not kept awake by constant noise, reopening of the Bar will be considered.

V.E.F. 29.2.60

Inevitably this had a somewhat demoralising effect; there was no real evidence that the late-night drinkers were disturbing anyone but themselves, and the headmasterly tone of the note was inappropriate for such a group at such a time. Perhaps it was a rare insight into the stressful position in which he found himself.

The second Monday, Tuesday and Wednesday passed, slowly. Sometimes we all clambered out to collect blocks of ice for the water tanks, or to indulge in snowball battles or aimless peregrinations. One brilliantly sunny day, I climbed the mast to the crow's-nest, sixty feet above the water level. The immediate scene was as it had been all of the time, yet I still gazed around in incredulity. Beyond the ice – which formed the horizon in all directions – the 9,000-foot peaks of Alexander Island could be seen far away to the south, a breathtaking panorama made the more attractive because of its inaccessibility. To the east, Adelaide Island stood clear and so tantalisingly near: three or four hours from our present position. The icebergs stood uncompromising and grand; the pack ice threw back the intense light of the sun. We had some apprehension about the icebergs, for one near us had been visited and was marked with a flag placed on top. A day or two later this same berg had trundled away to the south, moving through the pack with an ease which would have caused terror on the *Kista Dan*, had its path been towards us. The enormous volume of the submerged portion of the berg – perhaps ninety per cent of its volume – left trails of open water in its wake as it moved, the only open water we saw for days.

March 2nd, the eleventh day on which our engines had been stilled and our movement had been dictated solely by the drift of the ice, proved to be a day of drama. A steady fifteen-knot wind from the south-east blew all morning and just before lunch the ship suddenly lurched, as the port side floe eased, freeing us from our list at last.

21

For several hours all returned to quietness, during which time we once more collected ice blocks for water. In the early evening, however, the movement of the ice began to make itself felt in an alarming way. These events were described by Sir Vivian Fuchs in a press message to London:

... On March 2nd, the long awaited south east wind moved hundreds of square miles of ice, the enormous forces crushing the thickest floes and raising tumbling ridges of ice that advanced over the surface like the slow moving front of the lava flow. At first the movement loosened the *Kista Dan* allowing her to return to an even keel and sink back into the water from which she had been raised four to five feet. The propeller, locked by floes forced under the ship was freed and no damage to rudder or screw was found. Soon the milling ice was again careening the ship to one side or another, sometimes as much as 16 degrees. At the same time huge blocks rose surging to the surface only to be driven under adjacent floes, or once more beneath the ship. As the larger floes closed in, the congested mass of snow, slush, and brash was squeezed from between them like toothpaste, carrying the ship in its viscous flow, only just in time to escape the closing ice. Sometimes intense pressure built up before she was squeezed clear and mounds of snow and ice began to rise along her straining sides. When all was over and movement ceased the scene over several acres was like a battlefield with smears of blood red paint rubbed onto the ice from the ship's sides, the slush darkened by the churning of bilge oil discharged in the last days, and everywhere a scatter of boxes and tins and rubbish thrown over the stern and now stirred by the turmoil in the ice. We hoped that all this movement would free us from our predicament but a change of wind has caused the ice to grip us again and we have to wait for further movements unless the U.S.S. icebreaker *Glacier* which is in the area is able to reach us in the coming days ...

So March 4th, 5th and 6th came and passed, the news of the movements of the *Glacier* being the main interest. The ice relented a little on the 4th, and in the evening a little knot of men peered enthusiastically over the foc's'le as the ship moved along a narrow lead that had appeared. Such luck was too good to last; the wind veered to the north and the pack, very gently but firmly, closed together. It must

22

have been very much like this in 1898 and 1899 when the *Belgica*, under the command of Adrien de Gerlache, (and with Roald Amundsen and Frederick Cook on board), was trapped near this area for a full year. They were completely at the mercy of the temperamental ice, lacking the benefits of modern radio and the other comforts of life which we on the *Kista Dan* so much appreciated. The *Belgica* drifted to the south-west for what must have seemed an eternity of bleak uncertainty before the Bellingshausen gave up its victim and the expedition was able to sail home.

On March 5th we heard that the *Glacier* had finished with her commitments to the *San Martin*, and the plume of smoke that we saw on the following day proved to us that modern radio had come to our aid, even if the wind had not. All day we watched the plume of smoke, then a vague outline of the ship, then a funnel, then the superstructure getting closer and closer. An hour after our first sighting, a bright orange-coloured helicopter hovered over us, then eased gently onto the ice; direct contact had been established. The ice swarmed with camera-bedecked Fids as the pilot – suitably clad in Kodachrome colours – alighted onto the ice.

By the evening the huge grey ship was right alongside us, ploughing a way through the ice with enormous force, whilst we watched dumbfounded as the monster encircled us. How small the *Glacier* made us feel! How the ice yielded to her supreme strength! How puny our own valiant efforts looked when this ship seemed to possess the power to walk over the ice if it had to! We drew comparisons between the two ships, bearing in mind the fact that the *Kista Dan* was a passenger and cargo-carrying, ice-strengthened ship, whereas the *Glacier* was, first and foremost, an icebreaker, the newest and the largest in North America.

The *Kista Dan* had a gross tonnage of 1,238 tons; the *Glacier* 5,800 tons. The little red ship had one engine of 1,700 h.p.; the huge grey ship had ten engines each producing 2,400 h.p. (though the commander bemoaned the fact that only seven were working at that time!). Our expedition ship had a total complement of under 60 men; the naval vessel had a crew in excess of 220 men. With respect to the ice, the comparison was one between a shovel and a bulldozer, though the *Kista Dan* undoubtedly had advantages in other circumstances.

The break-out effectively began the next day, fourteen days after we had become beset. The roar of the engines signified that the *Glacier* was under way. However, huge blocks of ice thrown back by the screws prevented movement by the *Kista Dan*, whose bow was pushed aside, or backwards, by the weight of the ice thrown back! Attempts were made to tow us out but soon the cables broke, and we had to progress slowly along the leads made by the *Glacier*. We suffered some good-natured ridicule from our rescuers – a friendly, tall, thin, buck-toothed, gum-chewing flower of American manhood leered down at us contemptuously and enquired, 'Say, you guys, how the hell d'yer get in here?'

The *Glacier* trundled on, a soulless epitome of modern efficiency. Sometimes if the ice proved a little troublesome even for her, liquid ballast was moved from port to starboard tanks in a minute or so, and the ship rolled and broke the offending ice. If we, behind, had trouble when the lead closed too quickly, the commander patiently came back and reversed the propellers, thereby spewing the ice away from our path. We progressed five or six miles that day. The churning of the ice gave us a chance to see the underside of the ice. The thickness varied tremendously, but was generally over ten feet, and frequently in excess of twenty feet. As huge chunks rolled over, it was possible to see the diatomaceous underside, a honeycomb of decayed ice which often fragmented on impact and floated to the surface to add to the sluggish brash which often hid the water through which we were, at last, moving.

That evening the two ships tied up together and we went on board. Immediately one felt the incredible impersonality of the ship, inside and out, a huge network of cold metal, grey paint, booming tannoys and machines. Yet we all enjoyed the courteous hospitality of our kind hosts, some of whom returned to the *Kista Dan*. The *Glacier* being a naval ship was 'dry', so many of the Americans were pleased to enjoy the facilities of the *Kista Dan*, which was certainly not dry! Many private trading arrangements were made which came to fruition on the next day when the *Kista Dan* took on several thousand gallons of water. Whilst the hoses were being secured from ship to ship, a number of 'fishing rods' suddenly appeared, and the trading was completed; the Americans had highly coloured anoraks and special commemorative mugs ('Operation Deep-freeze', '*USS Glacier*' etc), and maps which we coveted, whilst we had many things, mostly in bottles, which they coveted!

Gradually the ice floes became noticeably thinner, and less compact, and both ships increased speed. A slight swell could be discerned, and its effect increased as we neared the edge of the ice. The helicopters, which had been floe hopping, a technique by which the pilot reconnoitres suitable routes through the ice then rests his craft on an ice floe, to which the ship is steered, now rested on deck outside their hangars. Last messages passed between the two ships, and the rescue was over. On March 8th, in the evening, the *Glacier* increased its speed and gradually widened the gap between the two ships as it rolled its way towards the northern horizon. What a fine ship it was, what a magnificent demonstration of icebreaking it had given. As we too moved northwards we had plenty to thank the US Navy for; they had made a timely appearance.

4

Frustration and Failure

Two days later we arrived back at the Argentine Islands, which we had left twenty-five days earlier with such high hopes. Even getting back to the Argentine Islands had its difficulties; the Bismarck Strait was blocked with ice, so the ship took the long way round, up the west coast of Anvers Island then, via the Schollaert Channel, we entered the Gerlache Strait. In the brilliant sunshine we enjoyed watching large numbers of seals on the ice floes, and large packs of killer whales on patrol. On the evening of March 10th, we met up with the *John Biscoe* and, next morning, we moved past Wiencke Island into Flandres Bay and through the Lemaire Channel before reaching the base.

On the previous afternoon Sir Vivian called us together in the saloon to outline the problems (about which we already knew!) and future plans. The original plans for the Marguerite Bay area had been straightforward:

A new base (Base T), was to be established on the south-eastern side of Adelaide Island and occupied by six men to carry out a programme of geology, surveying and meteorology. The material for the hut and all necessary supplies were on board.

The six men at Horseshoe Island (Base Y), were to be relieved and five of us on board, myself included, were to reoccupy it in order to continue the meteorological programme.

The base at Stonington Island (Base E), was to be reopened. It had first been closed in 1950 after ice conditions prevented its relief in the previous year, and had caused some of its occupants to spend three years there. It reopened in 1958, only for it to be evacuated, by air, a year later. Now it was hoped to install seven or eight men to carry further south the programme of survey and geology.

27

In the light of our experiences so far, and in view of the lateness of the season – the captains like to have their ships well to the north by early April – Sir Vivian had to make alternative plans. There was no hope of getting the ships to any of the three bases, so the plan to establish Base T was postponed indefinitely. Base Y was to be evacuated by air and four men taken in, with the hope that they could sledge to Base E and start their work there. The men displaced from Adelaide Island were to occupy Wordie House on the Argentine Islands, others of us unable to get to Horseshoe Island or Stonington were to support the work at other bases, whilst some chose to go back to the UK and return a year later.

The first part of the plan started at the Argentine Islands. Dogs, men, food and equipment were unloaded and the men from Base T were installed in the Wordie House on Winter Island. This hut had been built in 1947 when the hut built by the British Graham Land Expedition in 1936 was found to have been washed away; it had been occupied until 1956, and stood about a mile from the main hut on Galindez Island. During these operations we had what some thought to be an amusing incident. Brian Taylor and I were working on the scow (a type of barge) with a Danish crew man, placing boxes in a cargo net. The net was suddenly jerked upwards by the man on the donkey engine, and two boxes fell overboard. In trying to save another box from disappearing, Brian was caught in the net and flung into the sea between the scow and the side of the ship. The sea temperature was 28°F, and the scow was moving, so we had to act quickly. Fortunately the two of us still on the scow were able to pull Brian out before his big boots and heavy clothing weighed him down. He now became a member of the Antarctic Swimming Club, to the amusement of all – except perhaps himself!

The next day a variety of events contrived to epitomise what life for us Fids was like during that remarkable summer of 1960: a mixture of hard work, humour and accidents. The work really was incredibly hard. Forty forty-five gallon drums of avgas (aviation fuel), each weighing 400 lbs were loaded onto the scow and taken ashore, where fifteen of us manhandled them onto the rocks and pushed them up to the store. It was a cloudy morning, during which sleet gave way to rain as the seasonal warmth was increased by the wind. As we worked, the wind increased to gale force; the drums had to be unloaded, however, so we continued until we all became bitterly cold and absolutely soaked, the water streaming under our anoraks and

28

percolating to all sorts of uncomfortable places. The journey back to the *Kista Dan* in the little red 'jolly boat' was difficult; the wind buffeted the boat, thin ice made progress slow and the rain stung our faces. Charlie Le Feuvre, a hairy, bearded, bedraggled, West Country hard man, decided to act as 'tour guide' for his passengers, the butt of his jokes often being Pete Bates, the airframe fitter, noted for having the coarsest vocabulary on the ship.

> *March 12th.* We circuited the ship and had great fun – Charlie Le Feuvre being 'guide'. As we passed under the sewage outlet from the fo'c'sle he said, 'Here we have the back end of old Bates' cabin. If he shits now, we will get it!' Of course everyone roared with laughter.

The accident followed after lunch. The *Kista Dan* was anchored with her stern towards Galindez Island, the stern being secured by a hand line and the bows held by an anchor in the middle of Meek Channel. The *John Biscoe* was anchored in mid-channel some distance away. The gale increased in intensity, soon reaching above fifty knots and gusting erratically in its various directions. The changing wind caused the *John Biscoe* to swing round on its anchors so they could not be lifted. The gale then dragged the ship towards the firmly held *Kista Dan*, where a feverish attempt was made to cast off the lines and move away. It was to no avail; the gale was too strong. Before anyone could act, the *John Biscoe* bore down towards the deck of the *Kista Dan*, where many drums of avgas were standing and the Beaver aircraft was resting. There was a protracted grinding noise as the bows of the *Biscoe* rasped the port side. With a great crash the projecting wing of the Beaver was hit; torn from the fuselage, it fell onto the deck and toppled slowly into the water. Its fuel tanks ruptured and a fine spray blew back over the bridge, a danger to all. Splinters of metal littered the deck, which now became alive with men frantically rushing around with ropes and wires trying to secure the rest of the plane, which had been pushed to the starboard side of the ship. Even as this was being done, the fury of the gale had pushed the *Kista Dan*, now freed of its holding lines, across the channel towards some dangerous ice cliffs. Nothing could stop the ship from hitting the cliffs; the best chance rested in the hope that the rocks supporting the ice cliffs sloped deeply and vertically under the water. As we hit the ice cliff, masses of ice and snow fell onto the fo'c'sle deck, and the ship twisted broadside on to the cliff face. The depth of the water, and the fact that the scow could be used as a fender to keep the ship off what rock projections there were, enabled us to wait for calmer conditions ... but we had lost the use of our aircraft.

The next morning dawned under a canopy of soulless grey stratus cloud. It was another time for review. The safety factor in flying had gone, for we had only one aircraft still remaining, the Otter, and that was at Deception Island, 200 miles to the north. At that time the dangers inherent in flying were at their worst, as it was getting towards the end of the season, with no other ships and certainly no other aircraft within any possible range for assistance should anything happen to the Otter. It followed, therefore, that the number of flights to Horseshoe Island must be kept to the bare minimum. On this day the *John Biscoe* sailed south in order to seek out a suitable landing strip, on the ice, from which the Otter could operate. A few days later the *Kista Dan* also sailed south to join the *John Biscoe* at the edge of the fast ice. We did not have far to go, for the edge of the ice was only four or five miles south of the Argentine Islands in Penola Strait.

The usual seasonal ice regime off the coast of Graham Land is one of development during the winter, followed by break-up and dispersal during the spring and summer months. The break-up may begin at any time during August, and usually starts in the north, working southwards, so that more often than not, the Marguerite Bay ice clears in March, sometimes earlier, sometimes not at all. The winter temperatures and winds determine the thickness and extent of the ice, and periodic break-outs during winter do occur. Sadly, less than two years before our experience with the unyielding ice, it had broken up in Marguerite Bay on May 28th 1958, carrying three of the Horseshoe Island base team with it. They had been on a sledging journey to an emperor penguin rookery on one of the Dion Islands, some forty miles distant. During the following month, nine of the fourteen dogs which had made up the two teams succeeded in getting back to the base; the men were tragically lost. The most unusual conditions of 1959/60 accounted for the great northward extent of the ice at such a late time in the season; during the ensuing days, however, those with responsibility for the ships, the aircraft and the men must have been mindful of the treachery of the ice.

All was now ready at Deception Island, and pilot Ron Lord made his first attempt to fly to the ice on March 16th, though he was forced to return due to bad weather. Better luck prevailed the following day.

March 17th. A lot of activity and interest today. The morning dawned fine and sunny and cloudless. The Otter set out from Deception Island early on, and it had arrived at the fast ice by 11.00 a.m. Ron Lord made a fine landing on the ice which tends to be a bit slushy. We were soon out on the ice with cameras and we had a field day. Graham Land stretched magnificently along the eastern horizon. *The Kista Dan* sparkled red in the white ice ... Well, the Otter was loaded up with three chaps who were going (indirectly) for Stonington and it took off from the ice at 3.00 p.m. Shortly afterwards the cloud moved in and unfortunately, when only 45 minutes from Horseshoe Island, it had to turn back.

So yet again the plans were stalled. A day of strong winds passed with the Otter sitting on the ice and all of our eyes watching the landing strip. Two days later, however, although conditions were far from ideal, a successful flight was made; three men and food supplies were taken in, and the six men who had wintered at Horseshoe Island were brought out.

More flights had to be made. The men from Horseshoe Island reported that man food was running very short and that dog food was almost non-existent; it was vital to take in more supplies if the wintering party were to survive. Since there were more dogs on the base than could be supported, the decision was taken to bring fourteen of them out by air.

Once more the weather determined our course of action over the next few days, culminating in the near loss of the Otter. Days of wind and snow followed; Graham Land disappeared into misty obscurity and the Fids from *John Biscoe* and *Kista Dan* spent the time traipsing over the ice to each other for socialising or for film shows. At one stage a massive iceberg bore down on the *Kista Dan* and the captain, Kai Hindberg, was quick to move his ship to a safer part of the ice edge. Ominously, the continual winds began to tell on the holding strength of the ice, which began to develop faint hairline cracks. As we retired on the 22nd, most of us were mindful of the fifty-knot winds of the day, and of the fragile Otter being buffeted about on the ice.

Next day our fears were confirmed. When we awoke, much of the ice front had broken away and was beginning its drift. Huge cracks and narrow leads had spread out in all directions, and the aircraft was completely isolated on an island of ice whose area was visibly diminishing in size as the floes abraded each other. Most of us thought the worst; to our eyes, the moving airstrip looked pitifully small and we visualized an attempt to hastily dismantle the plane and haul it on board, a task which would have been extremely difficult and dangerous. However, matters were not quite beyond redemption. Hopping from one floe to another, a reconnaissance party found that, away from the broken edges, there was still solid ice. Ron Lord climbed into the cockpit, started the engines and paused for a short time. Then he applied full power, the Otter surged forward, sped over the floe and lifted off just in time to avoid the dark waters below, and landed again a few hundred yards further onto the ice. The Otter had been saved, and as we watched the former airstrip drift away, we could see the empty fuel drums and other rubbish marking the scene of some more of the anguishing moments which characterised that season.

It took a further six days for three successful flights to be made. An unsuccessful flight was made on the day after the near disaster; the Otter had to return when it was only fifteen miles from Horseshoe Island. Cloud had made it impossible to see the mountains. March 26th was the one-hundredth day on which I had been on the *Kista Dan*, and we had not achieved anything by way of furthering the programme. On that day, however, the Otter recorded its second successful flight when it took in supplies to Horseshoe Island and came out with eleven husky dogs on board. Two days later the Otter flew south once more, taking a fourth man in to winter and carrying large quantities of food for men and dogs. On its return from the base, it brought three more dogs and a collection of geological specimens. Whilst the weather was holding, the Otter crew rapidly refuelled on the ice and took off for its home base at Deception Island.

The use of aircraft in this season had been a great disappointment. Conditions meant that the Beaver and the Otter had not been used for the purposes for which they had been planned, only for emergency work, and the Beaver had been severely damaged. Yet they had shown their potential. They covered in a few hours distances that the ships had taken weeks to cover, or had failed to cover at all, and, given proper airstrip facilities, they had the potential for extending the work of the survey ever southwards. Of course, for much of the time the two types of transport are complementary, for the ships can carry massive quantities of cargo but are restricted by the ice; aircraft can carry relatively little cargo but they can access areas far away, over the sea, the ice or the land. Certainly the relief of the men from Horseshoe Island, and the removal of some of the dogs, could not have been accomplished without the Otter, so there was a measure of success.

The immediate work was completed and nothing now remained to do, apart from the final visits and deployments of the remaining Fids, before the departure of the ships from the Dependencies, to await another, hopefully more fruitful year. We stayed at the Argentine Islands for two more days before we left, though fifteen to twenty-feet thick ice floes near Meek Channel delayed the ship, and there were various cargoes to be transferred to the base. We finally left the Argentine Islands on March 31st and had fabulous views of the land east of Penola Strait, the Lemaire and Neumayer Channels and Gerlache Strait. However, the fates had not completely finished with us, for as March turned into April, another gale developed and the *Kista Dan* began rolling its way across the Bransfield Strait, whose black waters were seething angrily. On deck was the scow, the flat-bottomed, unpowered barge used for moving cargo from ship to shore; inside it were five diesel engines. The scow had been securely lashed to the metal rings of the hatch covers on the deck, and lashings elsewhere gave additional security. However, the rolling and twisting proved too much even for the ironwork. On the morning of April 1st, the continued agitation of the scow sheared the holding rings, and the increased movement of the scow as the ship rolled rapidly soon told on the other lashings. Desperately, in the fury of the gale, under conditions when the crew men could hardly stand upright, attempts were made to save the scow, but to no avail. A further roll took the great scow, with its five engines, sliding into the waters, from which it was impossible to retrieve.

Many of us were confined to our bunks for most of that day, as the ship pitched and rolled. Then suddenly we entered the sheltered natural harbour of Deception Island, and there was a feeling of great relief to have arrived. For myself, I had come to stay, and my 110 days on board the *Kista Dan* were over. Yet, for all its undoubted hardships and frustrations, I had seen enough, and had developed a taste for the beauties of Graham Land, to make me yearn for the days, within a year, when once more I would be going south.

5

Winter at Deception Island

Deception Island is a sea-breached volcanic caldera. The encircling rim of mountains project upwards to a highest point at Mount Pond of 1778 feet on the eastern rim, with the second peak, Mount Kirkwood, reaching 1505 feet on the western rim. The breach in the volcanic rim, named Neptune's Bellows, faces south-east and is approximately 600 yards wide. The ocean-facing sides of the island are generally precipitous ice cliffs or lava rock faces, with occasional embayments or low-lying headlands which often are the sites for huge rookeries of Chinstrap penguins. The inside of the crater consists of a large bay, Port Foster, with a secondary smaller embayment called Whalers Bay. The main bay is approximately six and a half miles long by three and a half miles wide. The inside coast is generally more gently sloping than the outside, and occasional areas of undulation, or flat plains, afforded ample suitable spaces for the three nations then maintaining bases there.

Many of the higher parts of the island have permanent snow cover, though during the summer time the heat of the sun quickly denudes the snow from the ash near sea level and gives the island a bleak, dismal appearance, especially when the cloud is low. In 1960 the island was a dormant volcano, with reports of occasional eruptions; voyagers in the 19th century had given graphic details of fires along the whole of the southern and eastern coasts. We were made aware of the origins of the island in a variety of ways. The beaches of Whalers Bay, Fumarole Bay and Pendulum Cove steamed persistently, with off-shore waters being remarkably warm. We found temperatures in shallow water along a distance of several hundred yards in Whalers Bay to vary between 90°F and 120°F (the highest mark on our thermometer). Subterranean activity fluctuated considerably too; the *Antarctic Pilot* recorded that in the twenties, the heat of the water in Whalers Bay was sufficient to blister the paint off whale factory ships at anchor there. In Fumarole Bay, circular fumaroles ejected steam and sulphurous gases continually. In winter time it was possible to

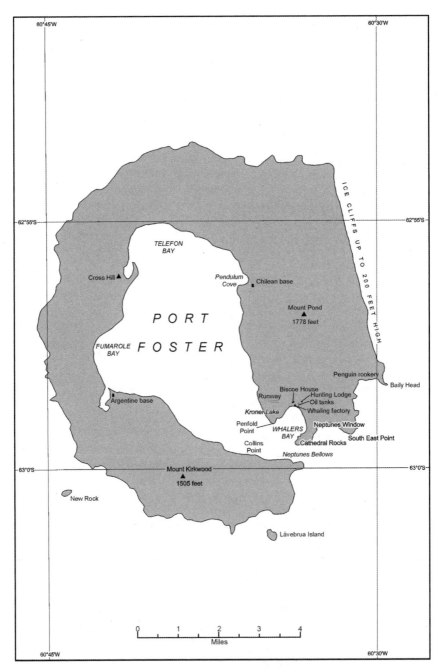

DECEPTION ISLAND
(coastline from 1956 records)

observe sea water steaming a few yards from sea ice. The volcanic origins also accounted for the loose ash covering the island which, during strong winds, was blown everywhere, so that our clothes and hair often became covered in the clinging dust.

Massive evidence of the volcanic nature of the island came after we had left when, early in December 1967 – after months of tremors had been felt – an eruption occurred, causing a large new island to appear in the northern part of Port Foster. A much larger eruption happened in 1969, with fissures opening up near Mount Pond. Vast amounts of ash were ejected, and a lahar rushing down the mountain side went through the base hut, whilst other nearby streams of ash and mud took away the cemetery, the jetty and other fixtures. All three bases (Argentinian, Chilean and British) had to be evacuated.

Man, too, had added to the desolation of the landscape. As the search for seals extended into the unknown waters of the Southern Ocean in the early and mid-19th century, so Deception Island, with its amazingly sheltered harbour, was discovered. Fur seals were in such abundance here that rich pickings were to be had for those who ventured south, so much so that the fur seals were hunted to the verge of extinction. After years of protection, numbers gradually increased on the sub-Antarctic islands, though rarely did one visit us during 1960. (In February 2000, however, whilst on a cruise to these areas, we were delighted to see thousands of fur seals throughout the South Shetlands.)

Following reports from the captains of the sealers, whale companies sent their ships south, where there were great rewards to be gained from harvesting huge numbers of whales, especially with the advent of the harpoon gun. Early in the 20th century, therefore, whaling stations were opened on South Georgia and on some of the South Shetland Islands, the station at Deception Island being the largest. For many years the huge carcasses were towed into the bay, to be dismembered and fed into the vats where the oil was collected. The whalers had built a large wooden factory for their work, and six or seven huge oil tanks. The factory had been abandoned in the thirties and suffered the ravages of time. The factory itself was a shambles of wood, iron, chimney stacks and machinery, broken, rusty and jumbled. The oil tanks were long since derelict, having been made unusable early on in the war, to prevent them from having any value to the South Atlantic German warships thought to be in the area; explosives and gunfire shots had peppered the structures with great

37

holes. Nearby were abandoned waterboats and a vast quantity of bleached whale bones. The cemetery stood silent amongst the ash, a mute testament to the men who were lost from ships at sea, by accident on land or even, in the case of one former base member, by suicide. Certainly the whole prospect was one of man-made dereliction and decay set in an environment of natural devastation.

Permanent bases on the island first originated from a naval operation, Operation Tabarin, which sought to establish a British presence in this area during the Second World War. Two bases were established in 1944, Deception Island and Port Lockroy. Two years later the Falkland Island Dependencies Survey assumed responsibility for the bases and for the future development of the survey. One of the still habitable whaling huts was occupied by five Britons. Since then, (up to the time of the 1967 volcanic eruption already referred to), Britain had always maintained a base there, though the original hut was destroyed by fire in September 1946. The strategic position of Deception Island, at a time when territorial considerations were important, led the Argentine and Chilean governments to initiate visits by their naval ships to the island, in order to establish or reinforce their claims to a slice of the territories. Always, at this time, the base leaders had to issue formal 'protest notes' from HM Government, establishing the precedence of Great Britain in its claims. In 1952 shots were fired by Argentinians over the heads of a British landing party at Hope Bay, where a base was to be re-established after it had been burned down some years before. Since then, however, and more particularly since the Antarctic Treaty came into force in 1961, inter-country cooperation has ensured harmony between the many nations carrying out programmes of research throughout the continent.

The main base hut, Biscoe House, was undoubtedly the best accommodation in use by the Survey, for it was roomy and comfortable. It was built by the whalers, probably as their hospital, but it had been neglected for several years after the whaling station closed down. Successive generations of Fids had wrested the rooms, one by one, from their dereliction and had made them most comfortable. A wide corridor extended down the centre of the hut, its walls adorned with collections of skis, fishing rods, snow shoes and ropes. Opening onto the corridor were rooms for a good kitchen, radio room, meteorological office, bunk room, bathroom, battery and coal store. Facing these rooms, across the corridor, were the diesel/electric workshop, a food store, general workshop, bar, dark room, battery and electrical shop, base office and a small bunk room. Above all of these rooms was an extensive loft which was used for storage purposes and as a dog room. The hut was by far the most commodious of the Graham Land base huts, but it had some disadvantages with respect to heating; when some of the cold north-easterlies were blowing, the temperature in the corridor would approach 0°F. Year by year improvements had been made within the hut, and these improvements were often assisted by fortuitous accidents. A whaler, the *Southern Hunter*, had gone aground in Neptune's Bellows on the last day of 1956, and had been abandoned. Resourceful Fids soon collected some good furniture, including some fine tables, bunk chests and armchairs. During our own year the base was made more comfortable in a variety of ways, foremost of which was the redesigning of the bar carried out by Paddy English, so that we had a small room in which we could feel quite at home on festive occasions, and which served admirably to host a large number of visitors from ships and from the other bases on the island.

Before 1960, the complement of the base was usually five or six men who carried out continuous meteorological programmes, though in some years geologists, surveyors and biologists had been based there. As a result of the prevailing ice conditions in 1960, it was decided to establish the FIDS air base there. The four RAF men, together with Fraser Whyte and myself – who had been destined to go to Horseshoe Island – increased the base complement to eleven.

It was to be eight weeks before we were all in the main base. Because the air group had very specific tasks to carry out in order to prepare the Otter and Beaver for the spring and summer programmes, and because it was felt that more than doubling the number of men in the main base would put undue pressure on the facilities there, the six of us were to occupy Hunting Lodge, a hut built by and for the Falkland Island Dependencies Aerial Survey Expedition in late 1956. This hut too, though much smaller than the main base, was extremely comfortable. For six days whilst the *Kista Dan* remained in the bay, we worked incredibly hard to get cargo ashore, and to haul supplies up to Hunting Lodge. From the holds of the *Kista Dan* massive quantities of supplies and materials were disgorged. There were two years' supplies for Stonington Island and Horseshoe Island, boxes and boxes of foodstuffs, coal and building materials deposited on the beach for us to store away in the massive oil tanks which provided such excellent storage facilities. Also, there was a vast amount of supplies to support the aircraft, including, of course, hundreds of drums of aviation fuel.

After the *Kista Dan* had left on April 7th, the six of us settled down to work to get the hut back to order, (it had been unoccupied for three years), and to sort out the mountains of supplies. The lateness of the season generated a sense of urgency and necessitated hard work; this fostered a good team spirit which sustained us for several weeks. However, there were undercurrents of dissension amongst the RAF team. Paddy English and Ron Lord were flight lieutenants, whilst Tom Sumner and Pete Bates were from the other ranks; a small Antarctic base is not the best environment for men of such differing temperaments to be thrown together. Paddy enjoyed his rank – even appearing in full uniform occasionally – whereas Pete Bates was very down to earth with his attitude and language; it was not conducive to long-term harmony. Additionally, of course, none of us were engaged in the job for which we had signed on; Fraser was a radio operator with no radio, I was a meteorologist not involved in meteorology, and the airforce men had not come south merely to haul cargo about interminably. A degree of frustration was therefore inevitable.

A base routine was established. We took weekly responsibilities for cooking, in which Paddy and Ron excelled in producing exotic dishes; we did water duties – keeping the tank filled up – and 'bog' duties – taking the bog bucket down to the beach to empty it every day – and we all contributed to a big clean-up each Saturday. After several weeks we were able to start the process of getting the aircraft ready. On its last call of the season on May 6th, the *John Biscoe* brought a new wing for the Beaver, so Pete and Tom were able to fix it. We also spent time picketing the Otter securely – it had to stand outside during the whole winter – and we built a lean-to shed for the Beaver by using timbers from the old whaling station. There were also some memorable experiences.

April 18th. Looking from our newly constructed porch (Paddy's work), it was quite eerie to look towards the cemetery. The wind was sweeping the snow into a kind of shallow fog. Stark stone monuments and crosses rose from this fog, and the accompanying moan of the wind made an unusual impression on us. What a place to die in and be buried in, completely forgotten by the rest of the world.

On April 26th I offered to take on, a day at a time, meteorological observations at the main base. I was immediately made to realise that this modest task had its own dangers when a full gale developed during the day and increased its strength into the darkest of nights.

April 27th. What a night met. duty it was. After midnight, winds increased to 35–40 knots and they stayed that way until my watch finished at 3.00 a.m. Gusts of 51 knots were recorded twice ... I was very worried about the walk back to our hut. I decided to risk making the journey. Visibility was about 10 yards. I stumbled from one drift to another, the great winds blowing right into my face. I planned to go to two tanks, well remembered landmarks. In the terrible conditions I missed them, however. I stumbled on in the fantastic conditions until, eventually, I stumbled over some oil drums. Suddenly a door loomed up, our lavatory door. By sheer luck I had arrived in a dead straight line. 10 yards to the left and I would have missed the hut completely. My 3.00a.m. 250 yards was rugged in the extreme; 40 knots, 17°F, 10 yards visibility! Thankfully I made it and clambered into bed.

We had just about sorted ourselves out in our unusual circumstances when a radio message arrived from John Green, the FIDS Secretary in Stanley, instructing us to move to the main base. Our first six months with the Survey had made us somewhat sceptical concerning the planning abilities of some of those in charge, and this confirmed our scepticism. Pete Bates had a linguistic field day! There were great advantages, however, as Fraser and I could significantly help with the radio schedules and meteorology, and the air group could benefit from the full support of the whole base. On May 31st, therefore, the move was made.

We now came under the leadership of Ian Jackson, whose enthusiasm for work – and quiet example – resulted in a huge amount of moil and toil: anything from digging out aircraft or shifting stores of timber to innumerable other unromantic tasks. He had already spent one year at the base, so he was well experienced to meet the problems in store. Flight Lieutenant Paddy English was in charge of the flying programme, so it was logical that he had been in charge of us when we were based at Hunting Lodge. The rest of the base members comprised the usual varied types of humanity that would be expected on a base down south. The radio communications were in the care of Frank Fitton (now with help from Fraser). Frank was also in charge of the dogs at the base. We had eleven husky dogs and Puta, a mongrel with lots of red setter in her. Fraser Whyte came from Scotland. He cherished dreams of a 'nice quiet life' – an aspiration which always eluded him as he would good-humouredly pick up a shovel and wade into a snow drift which had built up in front of the Otter, or elsewhere. Fraser loved strong winds and would wander down to the beach on the stormiest of days to watch the fury of the waves dashing themselves out on the cinder sand. When he returned to the hut he would usually engage in some amusing repartee with Ron, describing in his broad Scots accent 'the snow on the McHills'.

Mike Tween kept the diesel engines in perfect running order throughout the year; how much we wished for his skill and ingenuity a year later when our engine failed us and we had no spare parts available (or in truth, skill!).

The meteorological staff comprised four of us, Ian, Roger, Brian and myself. I had trained with Roger Matthews and Brian Westlake on the course in Stanmore, so we already knew each other. Roger combined his role as senior meteorologist with an equal ability to play the accordion very well, forming an entertaining trio with Frank and Ron. Brian followed the weather with an incredible enthusiasm, giving minute-by-minute reports not only on the exact time of the commencement of precipitation, but also the exact type of snow crystal being precipitated, as well as the height and type of the clouds above us. His eyes were always focussed on the thermograph trace in the met. office, his mood and spirit being inversely proportional to the height of the air temperature. He also took on the role of ice observer, a task which involved a daily return trip of two miles to Neptune's Window, at a height of 700 feet.

I had lived with Paddy English, Ron Lord, Tom Sumner and Pete Bates for eight weeks before we moved into Biscoe House. Ron, when he was not piloting aircraft, was a great character. He gave us endless pleasure when he dressed himself up in a bowler hat, suave black suit and rolled umbrella. This outfit was admirably suited to his small stature and great hairy black beard, and was displayed to great advantage when, later in the year, an Argentine oil tanker, the *Punta Ninfas*, anchored in the bay. Being a picture of sartorial elegance, Ron went on board and 'inspected' the decks, prodding the dirty rails and greasy decks with an air of authority. The Argentine crew were, naturally, speechless! Tom Sumner, the one married man on the base, was always calm and affable. He was a master technician, and when his work on the aircraft engines was finished he could turn his hands to anything from the base sewing machine or typewriter to the tractor or water boilers. Pete was the airframe fitter and base comedian with a predilection for lewdness. He looked on his secondment to the Antarctic as just another posting; he disliked it immensely and being forty something years old, he regarded most of us younger men with a degree of contempt, more especially those who had been to university. Pete went home after a year.

So the eleven of us settled down together for the last six months of the year. We had come from all walks of life and social backgrounds, there was a twenty-plus age span from twenty-five upwards, and a variety of skills, personalities and habits. Some smoked a lot, others didn't smoke at all; some drank large amounts, most were more moderate consumers. With such diversity it would obviously be naive to pretend that we lived together in perfect harmony. Yet, apart from occasional rows, we generally managed to work well together and to enjoy some very good times.

Each of the FIDS bases – apart from representing British interests in the Antarctic, an important function at that time – carried out specific programmes of work. On some bases, the sledging bases, the work involved considerable travel, with an accompanying amount of adventure and excitement; Hope Bay and Stonington Island stood supreme through the years for their pioneering sledge journeys over the length and breadth of Graham Land. Deception Island was a 'static' base, like most of the other island bases, but work there had already contributed significantly to our knowledge of the Antarctic. The main programmes of work for us in 1960 centred on the meteorological work and on the preparation of the aircraft which would open up new areas of exploration and research for the Survey.

Four of us shared the meteorological work; synoptic observations were made every three hours round the clock throughout the year. Whatever else was happening on the base, the fortnightly progress report which was sent by radio to Stanley always commenced, 'Met. continues'. At each three-hourly observation, the duty meteorologist took readings of temperature, pressure, humidity, wind speed and direction, visibility, cloud types and heights, precipitation and any special phenomena. These were coded and sent to Stanley at 0900, 1500, and 2100 hours local time. Stanley received this information from all the other weather bases – a total of six in 1960 – then later broadcast a collective report, which we received and plotted on weather maps. We were thus able to derive some idea of the weather systems influencing Graham Land and its surrounding seas. During the spring and summer seasons, Stanley sent out weather forecasts to assist whaling ships operating in the area and for the benefit of our aircraft, a service which became extremely important. Information was also made available to the South American and South African weather services to supplement observations from their own stations.

If the weather permitted, that was if the cloud base was above 3,000 or 4,000 feet, it was worthwhile to send up pilot balloons. By following the ascent of these balloons with a theodolite, it was possible to derive the direction and speed of upper air winds; these were also transmitted to Stanley as a supplement to normal weather messages. The record ascent, which we were able to follow, reached a height of 39,000 feet. At Halley Bay and at the Argentine Islands, much more sophisticated techniques using radio-sonde ascents enabled accurate measurements to be made on a daily basis, not only of upper air wind speed and direction, but also of temperature, pressure and humidity at different levels.

At the end of each month, many hours were spent in working out the meteorological statistics. All the charts had to be analysed and the daily record of weather observations had to be copied onto forms for punch cards which were used by the meteorological office. Part of the work included observations of the sea ice movements and the nature of the ice. Cumulative knowledge of the patterns of behaviour of the ice was important in an area used by more and more ships (including, much later on, tourist ships). Deception Island is strategically placed in this respect for it commands a fine view of the Bransfield Strait, along whose waters great belts of pack ice move annually. Brian made the daily observations when possible, and would draw sketch maps to indicate changes in the ice distribution, the sort of pack ice, and the number of icebergs. In Whalers Bay he took sea temperatures (away from the hot, volcanic spots), and would record the gradual development of the ice, which in that year reached a thickness of three feet in Port Foster. We saw some gigantic bergs. During

October we all watched the movement of a tabular berg some three to four miles in length, probably over two miles in width, and approximately a hundred feet above the sea level. With 900 feet of ice below the surface, its volume was immense. It made an impressive spectacle moving slowly north-eastwards, a huge flat white mass with its sides riddled with water-eroded caves which reflected brilliant blue light. However magnificent we thought it to be, it really was small when compared with the huge sections of ice which broke away from areas such as the Larsen Ice Shelf during the eighties and nineties and which had lengths in excess of 100 miles.

Deception Island suffers a most unpleasant climate. It combines all that is worst of the elements, including rain, snow, drizzle, high winds, low clouds and extremely variable temperatures. The island is far from rugged in the classical Antarctic sense of bitter coldness and fierce blizzards; indeed, Deception Island is sub-Antarctic, which makes its climate transitional between the mildness of the north and the colder, more settled, weather of the south. A never-ending succession of depressions come in from the South Pacific/Drake Passage on their eastward passage. Such depressions bring low cloud – we often reported 8 oktas of cloud at 100 feet – with warm temperatures resulting from their passage over the sea, and consequently with torrential rain in summer time. Fortunately, the winter brings more settled weather, especially when the high-pressure systems extend to the north. Then come a few days when the muggy, mild, unsettled weather gives way to calm conditions with clearing skies, and the sun sparkles on the snowy hills, whilst the air temperature falls towards 0°F, and sometimes further still. On such a day the water quickly freezes and, if the cold persists, the island is blessed with sea ice which greatly increases the range of travel with the dogs, besides dramatically enhancing the beauty of the island, a beauty unseen by the summer visitors. Our climatic extremes in 1960 ranged from +47°F to –4°F in temperature; our highest wind gust reached 72 knots.

The other main part of the programme centred on the two aircraft, the Otter – which had already proved itself – and the Beaver, whose usefulness had been temporarily terminated in Meek Channel. The work here was inevitably carried out by the RAF team and is described elsewhere. The two aircraft added considerably to our shared interest, especially when base members were taken up for an occasional flight. The planes, because they were exposed to all weathers, acted as a focus for snow drifts and provided all of the base members with considerable shovelling practice.

Most of the other tasks on the base were a necessary support to facilitate the programmes. The diesel engines supplied the base with the power needed to light the hut and to keep the radio working and the instruments running. Radio communications were made daily with Stanley for the transmission of weather messages, and for receiving traffic from headquarters and other bases. Frank and Fraser would often indulge in 'hamming' which provided news and interest for all. Inter-base schedules were regularly held, when we contacted friends and colleagues at other bases and exchanged news. For several days in July we followed with great interest the aftermath of a crevasse accident which befell a member of the Hope Bay base at work down the eastern side of Graham Land. His sledge had broken through a snow bridge and he had fallen seventy feet, injuring himself in the process. During the following days we were able to learn about the progress of the rescue and his subsequent removal back to base. On Tuesday evenings a BBC programme, *Calling the Antarctic*, was broadcast from London, when news, topical talks, music and recorded messages from our families brought a breath of home into the hut.

Work was far from over when our commitment to any particular part of a programme was finished for the day, for we had to live, and that relied on a great deal of organisation and commitment. We had to do, by hand, many of the things that are carried out so easily in a normal house. Snow had to be collected every day for the water tanks, a tedious job if the snow was fresh and uncompacted, for a bucket of snow usually produces considerably less than half its volume of water. Furthermore, the amount of water used is considerable when eleven men need to wash themselves and their clothes frequently, and the debris of eleven meals, three times a day, has to be cleared. (Two years later, an enterprising Fid with a theory that there should be ground water in plenty, dug twenty-two feet down through the ash at the hut and struck water! A pump was installed and a reliable flow of warm water was secured – too late for us, unfortunately.) The hut had to be kept clean too, and this was a regular Saturday morning event, when the kitchen and corridor were scrubbed, the rooms swept and all areas restored to order.

All too soon the dreaded moment arrived when one was faced with cook duty for all meals for all men for a complete week – breakfast, lunch and dinner for eleven men for seven days, twenty-one meals to be prepared, starting on that awful Sunday! There was a huge assortment of tinned foods from which we could choose and a surprising number of varied and extremely palatable meals were forthcoming. Most cooks had specialities; Ron and Paddy excelled in oriental dishes which, to my taste, were excruciatingly hot but which won general acclaim; Fraser's *métier* was cakes, the recipes often being culled from the side of baking powder tins; Brian mastered the art of making brandy snaps. Occasionally we sampled seal liver, a change made more tasty because of its freshness; we also used penguin eggs in cake making – they were unsuitable for frying because the albumen stayed gelatinous and did not turn white. Besides preparing three meals a day, bread had to be baked regularly, and was invariably first-class. There were exceptions to the high standards, however; early on I produced six dwarfed loaves like concrete bricks which reminded me – as I threw them away – of the need to allow time for the yeast to ferment. Mike put his bread in the oven one day, then went for a ninety-minute flight! We also cooked cakes or pastries every day for tea, so that after a few weeks our culinary efforts were well received.

> *June 23rd.* Only two more days of cook! Today I served up kippers for breakfast, Vienna steaks, mash and cabbage for lunch, and fried ham, chips, mash, peas and tomatoes for dinner. In between I successfully baked six loaves, quite a relief after yesterday's flop. Being base cook is hard work. All day long one must be constantly thinking well ahead, or washing up etc. It's hot work, too. Yet it's quite rewarding so long as the results turn out OK!

Techniques varied too. Ian liked to wash up persistently so that the kitchen was always spotlessly clean and his day finished early. On the other hand, Ron produced magnificently exotic dishes, though the sweet often had to be dished out in plates on the floor because every inch of table space was occupied by odds and ends of garlic, pimento, sultanas and curry, not to mention the number of plates and dishes and cutlery used. The meals he cooked, of course, were always superb!

So the chores were done, each and every person taking turn to cook, clean the rooms, fetch the coal, empty the latrine buckets and collect snow for water. It really was an egalitarian society, and the result was that the base ran smoothly and was distinctly comfortable.

Despite the work and the base duties, we had plenty of leisure. After all, we wasted no time in travelling to work and we had none of the normal activities of home life which occupy a lot of time. Almost all of our leisure activities had to be self-provided, and on a coastal base there is always plenty of interest outside the hut.

After the last ship had departed there was still time to make boat trips before ice formed. We had three useful dinghies, the little fleet being used to enable us to catch seals for the husky dogs, to travel around the shores of Port Foster (we would never pass out through Neptune's Bellows), and for maintaining the lighthouse at Collins Point. As the gales of May arrived and the air temperatures dropped, often below 15°F, conditions for boating became unpleasant and the boats were hauled ashore for the winter. The oars, engines and life jackets were put away and the boats turned over, until the time came when maintenance work could be undertaken. Pete took on responsibility for the care of the boats, giving one of them a fine new coat of paint and carrying out repairs on another.

During the transitional time between the boating season and the time when travelling on the sea ice became possible, our interest turned to the wildlife of the island. Penguins were, of course, daily visitors until the chinstraps moved north. Even so, often during the winter months groups of gentoo penguins would toddle along the beach, or scoot rapidly on their bellies, propelled by their feet and flippers. We also took an interest in birds. The small, delicate Wilson's petrels flew north early on, but pintado petrels (cape pigeons), terns, giant petrels and skuas stayed on until May. Dominican gulls and sheathbills stayed throughout the winter and occasionally a snow petrel appeared – usually when there was pack ice around. The sheathbill is a true land bird, depending for its food on scavenging, our 'gash' heap being a particularly rewarding source of nourishment. It seems to prefer not to fly, rather it scuttles across the snow as fast as its legs can carry it. Not having webbed feet like the petrels and gulls, the sheathbill often had to watch enviously as some morsel of food in the water was gobbled up by others!

Four types of seal would appear on the beaches. The Weddell seal was the most common, often coming ashore to sleep. The main enemy of the seal is the killer whale, and the number of scars on many of the seals testifies to some terrifying encounters. One Sunday morning, Frank and I killed a seal which lay dying at the water's edge. A gash in its neck from the throat almost to the nape of the neck, and penetrating the blubber deeper than an inch, had been opened, presumably by the sharp teeth of the orca. Crabeater seals, with their long pointed heads, came into the bay frequently, and we saw many leopard seals. Leopards are definitely seals to be respected. They have tremendously strong jaws, and some of those we caught measured over nine feet in length. They are attributed with having considerable speed when moving over the land, though none of us on the base was willing to put this fleetness of movement to the test! The leopard is the terror of the penguins, and we would often watch groups of them on the beach watching anxiously whilst the lithe form remained motionless just off-shore, hoping for a quick meal. The fourth type of seal visitor was the elephant seal, whose huge pachydermatous mass would lumber out of the water, slowly, clumsily and harmlessly. It was unfortunately necessary for us to hunt seals in order to feed the dogs, a task that none of us enjoyed. The elephant seal, however, was spared, for a number of dogs at Signy Island and Admiralty Bay had died during the year and there was a suspicion that their deaths might be related to elephant seal meat.

Occasionally, a little fishing was undertaken, for these waters abound in notothenia, a prehistoric-looking fish with an enormous head and a large percentage of bone, as we found out one day when we sampled it for lunch!

All of this wildlife provided interest for the photographer, and the base had a darkroom in which we spent many hours in developing and printing our efforts.

For the more energetic base members, the main active types of relaxation during the winter months were skiing or dog sledging. There were some excellent ski slopes near the base, the best run being in excess of 700 feet downhill, though only the most proficient were confident on this slope, and most of us tumbled a good part of the way on many occasions. Generally snow surfaces were poor, because of the wetness of the snow or the unevenness or iciness of the surfaces. Even so, on several days of each month we took to the slopes. We first learned to ski on a small nursery slope which terminated amongst the huskies. On one occasion Ron, a veritable bundle of flapping clothes, ended his run by running into Max's chain, which rapidly became twisted around the heap of flailing arms and skis. Max, a huge long-haired husky, thought this an act of extreme friendship, and rewarded Ron's efforts to extricate himself by showering him with enthusiastic licks.

The dogs enabled us to travel to the Argentinian and Chilean bases, where we were always warmly welcomed, usually returning to base with a selection of wines or fresh meat, and usually having partaken of a delicious meal including fresh eggs.

Actually we had chickens of our own, Ian having obtained them from Stanley. Whilst we were on board the *Kista Dan*, the six chickens laid eggs regularly. This promising start ended soon after their arrival at Deception Island; a most disappointing development. After several luckless months, Fraser offered to bring his psychological powers to work, so Ian handed them over to him. Fraser's first diagnosis of the problem was that the chickens needed something to interest them, so he installed a huge bowl in which ash and titbits of food were mixed up. The chickens took great delight in this, and scratched away happily each day but laid no eggs. He made them warmer by installing a paraffin heater, to no avail. He thought that perhaps they were missing the sun so he installed lighting which simulated daylight lighting hours, again without effect. Sadly we concluded that the experiment was not working, and three of the chickens appeared as the main dish of our mid-winter's day celebration on June 21st.

Once the days began to lengthen, we resorted more and more to outdoor pursuits. Most of us went on sledging trips, when for a week or so the dogs would haul the camping equipment round the island, and we would enjoy a spell away from the base. Often the weather would be persistently cloudy and windy and many days were spent idling the time away tent-bound. Yet Mike and I were extremely fortunate in October to enjoy a week of almost unbroken weather when we travelled round the outside rim of the island below Mount Pond. Each morning we would peer out through the tent flap to view the magnificence of Livingstone Island, twenty-five miles away, or to see the great icebergs moving sedately along, or simply to look at the sea; often we paused to think how fortunate we were to be the sole witnesses to such incredible beauty.

Our indoor leisure hours were spent in diverse ways. Photography was very popular, the record players were overworked, and there was plenty to read, especially polar books, which were a source of inspiration and fascination. The new bar, designed by Paddy, was always much in use. We had a beer ration of two or three cans a week but this had been substantially increased by large quantities of private supplies, and was often supplemented by Argentinian and Chilean wines.

The great festival down south is the celebration of mid-winter's day, after which one can look forward to lengthening days and to the increased interest and activities of the summer months. We had a great feast including shrimp cocktail, asparagus, chicken – freshly killed and processed! – tongue, pork, ham, sprouts, peas and new potatoes followed by Christmas pudding and brandy sauce, mince pies, cheese straws, biscuits and coffee – all accompanied by much wine and followed by spirits. We all smartened ourselves up for the occasion and there was a very good spirit of camaraderie. In the evening we joined the other bases in gossipy radio schedules.

The winter months passed: June, July, and August, bringing accompanying changes in the landscape, clothing the island in deep, white snow, providing scenery that the transient summer visitor can never know. We looked forward to the new season and the richness of the experiences that would come our way.

February 22nd 2000 was an intensely nostalgic day for some old Fids. For on that day, eight old-timers returned there whilst based on the *Lyubov Orlova*, a Russian cruise ship which had taken thirty-five ex-Fids and lots of friends and relatives to Marguerite Bay. Our experiences at Deception Island spanned the years from 1956 to 1965; John Smith and Jim Fellows '56, myself '60, Mike Cousins '62, John Tait and Harry Ashworth '63, Don Parnell '64 and Bernie Chappel '65.

Biscoe House stood forlorn, an enormous hole cut right through its middle by the torrent of liquid ash in 1969, and a complete corner room lacking both its walls, though the roof was still in place. The bunk room, scene of our mid-winter party, gaped open, the floor covered by a foot of ash, and with three or four bunk bed structures still remaining, mute testimony both to the good times and to the disaster. The corridor was choked with ash, as was the diesel room, which had always been a scene of perfect cleanliness and order under Mike Tween; one generator was still in its position, rusty and derelict. The radio room and the kitchen, where we had spent many hours together, were unrecognisable. Outside, the fuselage of a very old Otter – maybe the one we had helped to build – rested wingless and dead. Ash had covered much of the beach, though the oil tanks and part of the shambles of the whaling station remained. The beach steamed dramatically; there was very little snow to be seen. The cemetery had disappeared completely; there was nothing to be seen except for a solitary empty coffin resting on the flat black ash.

Don Parnell had vivid memories of the 1969 eruption when, as a radio operator at Adelaide Island, he had copied messages to London from the *RRS Shackleton* which had described the drama leading to the rescue of the five beleaguered base men on February 21st. A sequence of tremors had occurred during the week up to the day of the eruption when they became violent. The men left the base and headed towards South East Point. The volcanic cloud rose to 10,000 feet and masses of debris began to fall – pumice an inch in diameter, and larger pieces of scoria. They sheltered under a rock outcrop but the radio was damaged so that they could no longer send out messages. After taking refuge in a small whaling hut they used galvanised sheets to protect themselves and then, during a lull, they went back towards the base. They could see that the lahar caused by the melted glacier ice and hot ash had driven through the base area destroying Biscoe House and partially filling it. The width of the lahar was wide enough to take away the cemetery, tractors and other installations near the beach. The party rolled out a drum of fuel and ignited the contents so as to act as a beacon. They sheltered in the aircraft hangar for three hours before two helicopters from the *Piloto Pardo* arrived and picked up the whole party, a difficult exercise as the cockpit dome was completely obscured by ash and wet snow. The men were later transferred to the *RRS Shackleton* where Captain Turnbull was effusive in his praise for the skill of the Chilean seamen and airmen.

We reboarded the *Lyubov Orlova*, which took us into the inner heart of Port Foster. The Chilean base had been almost completely buried; the Argentinians had built a new one called Decepcion. The new volcanic island of 1967, half a mile long and 200 feet high, gave evidence of the intensity of the eruption, and added more acres of dull black ash to the snow-free ashy landscape. We left; we had plenty to think about and to remember.

6

Toscaig and Friends

One bright sunny day, Ian and Fraser decided to take the dogs on a short depot-laying journey in anticipation of a sledging trip they were to make later in the month. It was one of those days when Deception Island looked at its best; a cold south-westerly wind was blowing, and as was usually the case with such a wind, the weather was exhilaratingly clear. Drift whipped along the Kirkwood Hills and scurried across the snow-covered ground; the Cathedral Crags stood imposingly rugged. It was the first time I had seen huskies at work so I watched with keen interest: seven huskies leaping away, pulling the sledge with great enthusiasm, their tails up, legs pounding away, and a splash of snow spraying up as the sledge runners cut through the snow crust – or so I thought! The last dog was secured to the centre trace and Pete was ready to lift the picket that held the front of the trace; the dogs would soon be off; a glorious movie shot ...

Things did not go well that morning. No sooner had the picket been removed and Ian had called out 'Up dogs ... Weet', than the whole team was transformed into one huge writhing mass of dogs and fur, accompanied by a cacophony of howls and screams of pain. Flailing legs, bared teeth, torn ears, enough fur to fill a palliasse cover and dog leads becoming inextricably entangled, all produced a scene of absolute chaos. Little Val – a discreet observer – suddenly nipped in to have a mouthful from Shuna's leg; Shuna in turn was grappling with Chris's ear, and Sandra, a pint-sized little bitch, had some part of another dog. Meanwhile, in the middle, and locked in deadly combat, were poor old Nudo and Toscaig, the invariable instigator of the trials and tribulations which made learning the techniques of dog sledging such a rueful, but incredibly happy memory of Deception Island. I put down my camera and joined the others, who were breaking up the fight and calming the belligerents. A few minutes later the dogs were back in their correct positions, smartly away at the command and soon out of sight and happily on their journey.

Husky dogs had made a major contribution to the work of the

Survey over the years. Originally, some twenty-five dogs were brought to Graham Land from Labrador in 1945, and were taken to Hope Bay. Later, some dogs were imported from Greenland. The dogs were used simply to make travel possible, in order to carry out survey and geology programmes. By the mid-1940s virtually nothing was known about the Graham Land plateau or its eastern side facing onto the Weddell Sea. There had only been a few coastal surveys in the early 20th century, and not until the British Graham Land Expedition arrived in 1935 were significant journeys made beyond the coastline – especially in the southern part of Graham Land. The BGLE used dogs, most of them from Labrador, after a huge number of their sixty-five Greenland dogs had died of distemper.

Year by year dogs were introduced to the sledging bases: Hope Bay 1945, Stonington Island 1946, Horseshoe Island 1955, Halley Bay 1956. Not all of these bases were continuously occupied; however, some amazing journeys were made. In October 1947 a group of four men with three dog teams set out from Hope Bay for a 600-mile journey to Stonington Island, travelling down the eastern side of the peninsula. They were met, on that eastern side, at Three Slice Nunatak by a party of five from Stonington Island. Having met up, the nine sledgers then crossed the plateau to reach Stonington on December 28th. In 1949, Vivian Fuchs accompanied by Ray Adie (who had been on the Hope Bay to Stonington journey two years earlier), travelled 1,084 miles in 90 days on a return trip from Stonington Island to Eklund Island at the southern end of King George VI Sound, Alexander Island. Such journeys were major feats of organisation and endurance, and depended on support from other sledge parties involved in laying depots as far along the intended route as possible. The journey down King George VI Sound had actually been pioneered by the BGLE in 1936, and further explored by the Americans Finn Ronne and Carl Eklund on a journey of 1,264 miles in 1940. Eklund Island is named for this pioneer.

The dogs that were at Deception Island, and other 'static' bases, had arrived for a variety of reasons; perhaps they were unsuitable by temperament or size, or, like Max, had problems with long shaggy fur which collected ice too easily, or because they had been given honourable retirement – Spud had had a distinguished career at Hope Bay and was now ending his days more peacefully – or simply that they were born at the base and would be moved to a sledging base as they grew older. We had eleven dogs, but two more were born during the year, making a total of thirteen. For us, the dogs had two main purposes; one was to enable us to travel around the island during most months of the year, or to travel over the frozen bay during the winter, the other was simply to enhance our leisure time. The distance from Whalers Bay to the most northerly part of the island along the eastern rim was approximately twelve miles; to the farthest point of Port Foster across the ice was about six miles, so although Deception Island was a static base, our activities would have been strictly limited without the dogs. The fact that five of us were heading south for 1961, mostly to sledging bases, enabled us to get a feel for the dogs which would be useful.

Frank was the dog man at Deception, and he gave the job his full commitment. Rarely did a day pass by which did not witness the howl of delight from the dogs as he made his daily round. He had the greatest success when running the team, but the fact that we all took turns at running the dogs made it difficult for them to settle down as a team in the way that they would have done on a sledging base.

Never before had I realised the differing characters that the dogs possessed. Neither did I realise how lovable a dog could be until I had been at the base for some time; never did I appreciate the extent of my invective vocabulary until I had been out with the dogs on a few runs!

Toscaig was a handsome dog aged two years. He was undoubtedly the king dog, and exerted his position with great authority. A bigger bully was hard to imagine; a stronger or more powerful dog would be hard to come by. Nudo, a cringing black dog, had apparently once challenged Toscaig for the kingship, a battle that ended in defeat and lifelong submission; Nudo intensely disliked having Toscaig behind him in the team, snapping at his heels. The other dogs were a strange assortment; we had Bueno, a bandy-legged dog who was strong and hard-working but who liked to nip the ankles of passing men. Max and Min had arrived from Admiralty Bay. They were brother and sister but both were unsuitable for running – Max, a huge Greenland dog, had long fur which caused ice to ball up, especially on his feet, when running; he had never been properly trained and was far too excitable to run. Spud was in retirement, having been a veteran traveller at both Hope Bay and Admiralty Bay. He was at least eleven, according to his record card, but suffered from rheumatism in his back legs; he never ran, of course, but pottered happily around whilst he still had mobility. Nudo and Bueno were brothers of the two bitches, Chris and Val. These four were predominantly black-coloured, and had spent many of their early weeks travelling to a base. The *John Biscoe* had been held in the ice and it may have been that living in this restricted environment at a crucial time in their development had contributed to the crookedness of their legs. Rona, Sandra and Shuna were sisters of Toscaig and showed much of his spirit, always game for a fight, all hard-working, and all adorable animals when they were safely chained up and well away from each other.

So we had the basis for a team; four dogs and five bitches for we rarely used Max, and never used Min or Spud. After a great deal of thought by Ian and Frank a seven-dog line-up was favoured as the best combination:

```
              Bueno         Toscaig       Nudo
Sledge  |———————<———————————<—————————————<—————————►Sandra or Rona
              Shuna         Chris         Val
```

With this combination we had two good pullers immediately in front of the sledge, with Shuna safely behind Chris, for Chris would never turn on Shuna and Shuna could never quite get to Chris! Toscaig was ahead of Bueno, whom he liked, and behind Nudo, who was safe provided that he kept moving! The crucial issue often depended on the lead dog, for both Sandra and Rona disliked the black sisters in the pack, and the leader had the freedom to turn back into the pack, a sight which made every driver wince and prepare to wade in amongst the team to sort them out. One false move at the front and Rona would be onto Chris, the team would stop, and Toscaig would be on to Nudo, and so on ...

There were various recognised methods by which the dogs were attached to the sledge, of which two were the most commonly used by Fids. One was the centre trace method, under which a central trace went from the sledge to the lead dog, and pairs of dogs were then secured at regular intervals to the trace. The advantage of this system was that it gave greater control since the dogs could not move out of their position with respect to one another. The other system was a fan trace, whereby the trace from each dog was secured directly to the sledge, thus enabling each dog to have a direct pull on the sledge and to enjoy a better run because it could move freely from side to side and did not have to stay permanently behind the same dog. The disadvantage of this system was that if the dogs moved about too much, the traces became tangled, and it meant that control of the team was much more difficult to maintain. This method was popular with skilled drivers; we at Deception Island, for obvious reasons, always used the centre trace system.

I first went out with the dogs, with Ian driving, one afternoon for a run of three or four miles, which was uneventful but exhilarating. From June to October all of us, apart from the air group, went out on camping trips to gain experience. Such expeditions gave us plenty of laughs. One day Pete from the air group decided to take a pleasant walk to the shoulder of the Mount Pond ridge. He disliked the dogs and was therefore well away from them as they were being prepared for a run. A few minutes later, the dogs were straining at the trace, ready to leap away. Roger stooped to pick up a glove, and in a flash the dogs were off. There was always a flurry of sheer delight when the dogs started. The two sledge men were left standing with no hope of catching the team, whose initial speed was incredibly fast. Within a minute, the dogs had disappeared over a crest, and all sorts of gruesome images flashed into the minds of those of us watching from the hut. Pete, meanwhile, was enjoying his moment of peace and tranquillity on one of the sunny, calm days that we occasionally enjoyed on the island. Suddenly they appeared, seven wildly enthusiastic dogs pulling the loaded sledge at a prodigious speed. But where were the drivers? There was nothing for it, Pete had to stop them; just the job for someone who had renounced sledging! The dogs ran by him, but slowing as their initial energy was expended. Pete desperately grabbed the sledge handle as it passed, and slammed his foot on the brake. The two beleaguered drivers staggered along through the snow, arriving to find seven happy dogs, all pleased with themselves and licking each other joyfully, and one man looking on in disbelief at what he had done.

We often travelled with the dogs to the chinstrap penguin rookery some two or three miles away near Baily Head. The distance was short but it involved a steep climb to a ridge over 500 feet, then down the other side. One of us had to lead here, for the slope was very discouraging to the dogs and they preferred to rush back down the hill, if given the chance. If the surface was bad, with soft, wet snow, the second man had to push as well. After a long session of hard work, the ridge was reached. On a pleasant day, a pause for rest at the top would enable us to see right out over the Bransfield Strait towards the mainland. A never-ending stream of icebergs of all shapes and sizes moved sedately along. At this time they were ploughing their way through the pack ice which had been around the island since May, and stayed intermittently until September. After the pause, came a speedy run downhill to the rookery. On such a trip as this, if the eggs had been laid, we would help ourselves to as many as we could carry for the benefit of the cooks. The dogs would be staked out near the rookery and we would frequently chase away penguins whose inquisitiveness with respect to the dogs was likely to get them into danger.

Back on the dog span at the base, some of the dogs became quite expert at catching penguins. Chris was particularly adept at this, using intelligence and patience to secure an extra meal. When a penguin appeared, she would calmly sit down, making sure that there was plenty of loose chain. The visitor, penguin or bird, would invariably wander right up to her before she would pounce and claim her victim. Other dogs could never do this. Max, for example, would run around at the end of his chain in a frenzy of excitement, which was enough to frighten away all of the wildlife and deprive him of any chance of extra food.

We gradually became familiar with all the dogs and their habits. Every other day, Frank would feed the dogs their lump of seal meat, a source of concentrated goodness. The dogs thrive on this meat and we had to hunt as many seals as we could in order to keep the dogs supplied. The seal would be shot through the head, rolled over and slit down the front from throat to tail flipper. The entrails would be carefully cut round and pulled from the body in one mass, using a sharp knife and a hook. From the entrails, the liver and occasionally the heart, would be removed, for they were delicacies which the dogs loved. The task of sealing took some getting used to, but once learnt, the unpleasant job could be over in ten minutes and the dog team would then be harnessed up to tow the seal back to the seal pile.

If a dog had an infection, usually resulting from a fight, Frank would bathe the wound and carefully tend to it. Such wounds usually healed up as long as the dogs were on seal meat. All illnesses were recorded on special cards which were kept for every dog on every base. These cards also recorded details of parentage, litters of pups, sledging journeys, bad and good habits, and other remarks likely to assist the men who took over the teams.

Especially in May, and in winter time, blizzards would blow for many hours. Strong winds were a feature of the weather at Deception Island, and these winds were often accompanied by considerable snow. Under these conditions the dogs would curl themselves up and lie with their backs to the wind. Some huskies, over the years, had been buried by snow and had suffocated, so during bad weather, one or other of us would visit the dog spans to check on their well-being. We might see just an ear protruding from the snow; at our presence the ear would twitch, the nose sniff and, a moment later, an excited dog would leap up and show its delight. Huskies always seemed to show the most intense affection for everyone, an affection related to their source of food, perhaps!

On many nights, especially on calm, clear ones when the moon was full, old Spud would totter to a sitting position and start howling. Every other dog would join in, a regular, eerie chorus echoing across the stillness of the night. On some mornings, the base would be prematurely awoken by an outbreak of barking and growling. Such a noise was usually a sign that a dog had slipped its collar and was loose. The duty weather man would rush outside to intervene in the inevitable fight. Shuna, for a time, developed this skill, and she would immediately pick a fight with Chris or Val. Val, if free, would make a courtesy call on all the dogs, then visit her sister Chris, steering well clear of the other four bitches.

We had a pleasant house dog called Puta. She had strayed over from the Argentine Base a few years earlier. It was her prerogative to wander free, and she would often visit the dogs – a fact which increased the canine population from fourteen to twenty-six one day!

Frank was scheduled to go to Adelaide Island in 1961 and he was hoping to take Toscaig, Rona and the two pups, Noko and Lusk with him. We therefore decided to try again to train Max and Min, and we put them in the team as back pair. Although Frank and I did make one successful journey to the rookery, the experiment was not a success. Big Max thought the whole affair such fun that he couldn't resist running back every so often to lick the driver, much to the detriment of the smooth-running team; Min rapidly lost her original enthusiasm and kept sitting down for a rest – only to be dragged yelping by the rest of the dogs.

The year progressed and our experience with the team increased. Often journeys would be made to the Argentine and Chilean bases. On one occasion Nudo managed to free himself and enjoyed a few minutes rounding up the Chileans' flock of sheep. On another day, one of those when, because we had an audience, we longed for a perfect display of dog behaviour and control, the Chileans were treated to the spectacle of a huge fight when the lead dog suddenly turned and wrapped the trace around a radio mast, thereby bringing the team into an enormous heap, much to the delight of Toscaig, who had had no chance of getting at Nudo for some time.

By June, Noko and Lusk, pups born of Sandra and Nudo, were old enough to have the run of the base. They lived in a kennel near the hut and spent these wonderfully free days picking over the refuse heap, or playing in the snow. Often they would accompany us on walks, revelling in the snowy world. They showed intense interest in the penguins, but at this stage, one smack from a flipper sent them on their way. Their food consisted of penguin meat until they were old enough to chew the seal meat. Sometimes they would visit the other huskies, whom they soon learnt to respect. Then came the day when their freedom ended. A collar was put on them and Noko and Lusk were secured to the dog span, amid a great deal of howling. Soon they were used to their new life, and Frank started to train them, first with their mother, and later with Rona and Toscaig. To begin with they had no idea what to do; gradually, however, they got used to running and to pulling, and they would soon become part of a team, probably on Adelaide Island, where they might have ten years of work ahead of them.

The dogs at Deception Island helped us move lots of stored material about, they enabled us to travel, and they acted as a great boost to morale. Yet we were, of course, mere amateurs. On the fully organised sledging bases, the dogs were more stable in their teams, worked together for hundreds of miles, and were looked after by one driver. At Hope Bay, and Stonington Island there were dog spans for well over 100 dogs, though they were not all occupied simultaneously. On these bases there was usually manpower to drive eight or nine teams at maximum. There was also a need to provide hundreds of seal carcasses to feed the dogs and this required a lot of manpower and a lot of time.

Wherever the dogs were, however, the basic principles of dog management remained the same, and the experience learnt at bases such as Deception Island was never forgotten if one was fortunate to progress to a sledging base. During the spring months of late September, October and November of 1961, when the great white highway of King George VI Sound was beckoning to us on our man-haul trips, how we would have loved to have had Toscaig, Bueno, Nudo and Shuna – and the others – pulling our sledge, and the necessities for life, and enabling us to see something of the south. To most men who have worked with dogs, the husky is the finest dog in the world. It's a dog that works hard, plays hard and lives hard, exposed to the coldest and the windiest weather anywhere. Who wouldn't put up with that infuriating tendency to fight, when, after the combatants had been separated and thoroughly chastised, Toscaig would immediately leap up and lick you, then get his massive shoulders behind the harness and pull – as none of our other dogs could pull?

John Killingbeck arrived at Deception Island on December 11th 1960 to take over from Ian Jackson as base leader. During the next six weeks before I sailed south, I got to know John quite well; we worked together, we enjoyed many walks, we spent many hours in the dinghies. Unfortunately we couldn't do any sledging because during the height of the summer there was too much exposed ash for the sledge to run. After spending a year at Deception Island John moved to Adelaide Island, which had become a sledging base. Then suddenly, after thirty-four years, in January 1994, I received a letter from him bearing the address, 'Fossil Bluff, King George VI Sound, Alexander Island'.

Dear Cliff,

I had to write to you from your old hut … In August I received a telephone call from the Base Commander at Rothera asking if I would like to return south and be involved with the last dog sledging in Antarctica … what an offer! … The idea with the dogs is to take two teams, the Admirals (7), and the Huns (6) out into Alexander Island and to use them for a traditional field season supporting a small, but genuine survey/field programme. It is a farewell to the dogs before they leave the continent and a 'thank you' from FIDS/BAS to the generations of loyal and faithful teams.

John went on to describe the exact nature of the work he was carrying out with John Sweeny from Rothera Base, together with descriptions of the base at Fossil Bluff.

This truly was a historical journey in Antarctica. The use of dogs had been declining for many years in the face of competition from motorised vehicles – Muskegs, Weasels, Snow-cats, Skidoos, the Eliason Motor Toboggan, aircraft etc. There were, however, still two teams at Rothera used for some sledging, but mostly as a source of recreation and interest. Then, arising from the Antarctic Treaty which was ratified in 1961 (during the year I was based at Fossil Bluff), a new protocol on the environment was enacted which prohibited the introduction of non-native species and added the edict that dogs should not be introduced onto land or ice shelves, and dogs currently in those areas would have to be removed by April 1st 1994.

Thus was decreed the end of the husky in Antarctica. Their history of support for Antarctic expeditions was, in itself, a veritable history of Antarctic exploration. The first party ever to winter on the continent, led by Carsten Borchgrevink in 1899 to 1900, had seventy-five dogs from Siberia and Greenland; Erich von Drygalski took forty Kamchatka dogs with him on the *Gauss* in 1902. Nordenskjold, also in 1902, had dogs which enabled him to travel almost 400 miles, based on Snow Hill Island – his ship the *Antarctic* was held in the ice and subsequently crushed. Scott, in 1902, took nineteen dogs to 82°16′S accompanied by Shackleton and Wilson. Shackleton carried some with him on the *Nimrod* in 1909, though he was never very keen on dogs and made his epic journey to within less than 100 miles from the pole on foot with three companions. Amundsen in 1911–12, the most successful dog man of them all, landed ninety-seven dogs at Framheim and started out on his triumphant journey to the South Pole with four teams of thirteen dogs. Captain Scott also started out for the polar journey with dogs, twenty-three of them; unfortunately, however, they were sent back whilst there were still twelve men and three sledges struggling southwards. Filchner, also in 1911–12, Shirase in 1911, and Mawson in 1912 also used dogs to further their objectives. Later on in the 1930s the British Graham Land Expedition was incredibly successful with their dogs; the Americans under Richard Byrd, took in 100 dogs to Little America in 1928–30, and 145 in 1933. In the 1940s at Little America and at Stonington Island large numbers of dogs were used (the two bases were under the commands of Paul Siple and Richard Black in 1940–41). Later, in 1947, Finn Ronne used dogs at Stonington Island, in collaboration with the FIDS base dog teams. Many countries involved in the International Geophysical Year of 1957/58 still needed them; Sir Vivian Fuchs had the support of sixty dogs on the way to the pole in 1958 – the first time that dogs had reached the South Pole since those with Amundsen in 1911. During the 1960s and 1970s New Zealand, Australia and Argentina still had them on some of their bases. FIDS/BAS used them continuously from 1945 to 1994.

So the importance of dogs in opening up the continent was paramount; without them, exploration and survey away from the coast would have had to await the development of snow vehicles and aircraft, well into the second half of the 20th century.

It is hard to believe that a mere handful of dogs could cause real harm to the environment of a continent larger in area than Europe, Australia, or the USA. Even the human population of a few hundred winter residents has only a small impact; environmentalism has been taken too far – how sad that the last huskies were not allowed to live out their life peacefully at the last sledging base, Rothera.

John Killingbeck finished his letter to me on a note of optimism:

At the end of the season the dogs leave by air (in a Dash 7), for Stanley and then on to Maine, USA. From here one team is being given to an Innuit family in SE Hudson Bay and this is a reintroduction of dogs ... the older dogs will be used for breeding.

The last dogs were flown out on February 22nd 1994 and went on to their new homes in Canada. Most of them died from infections for which they had no resistance, and the breeding programme was not successful. So there are no longer dogs to boost the morale of all the men who have been touched by their exuberance and loyalty; the Antarctic is a poorer place without them.

7

The Penguins Return

Living on an island base in the South Shetlands gave all of us an interest in the diversity of wildlife, the seals, whales, and birds – both those able to fly, and those which are flightless. Of the day-to-day wildlife around the base and along the coastline, the penguin was ubiquitous and was a source of constant interest. The penguin is assumed to be confined to the southern hemisphere, their range extending from the Antarctic to the Galapagos Islands. However, as these islands just extend across the equator, perhaps there are a few of the Galapagos penguins in the north!

There are eighteen species of penguins in the world, six of which live in the sub-Antarctic or Antarctic regions. During our voyages along the Graham Land peninsula and its islands we saw a few emperor penguins near Marguerite Bay – they had a rookery on the Dion Islands – as well as great numbers of the other types: adelies, chinstraps, gentoos; and a few macaronis. Around South Georgia there were many king penguins. These birds, long since bereft of the ability to fly, are extremely attractive, with combinations of black and white, tightly packed feathers, and some species have beautiful colours around their necks – especially the emperors and kings – or coloured beaks, crests, or other adornments. They spend much of their life in the water for they feed on krill, a small type of shrimp. Penguins are marvellous swimmers; they treat water like air and fly through it with grace and speed. They also travel by porpoising along the surface of the water. Their great enemy in the sea is the leopard seal, and great groups of penguins can often be seen jumping almost vertically in the air, out of the water and onto an ice floe, in order to avoid being caught. On land, penguins are very competent at getting about. They can walk for many miles – emperor penguin rookeries are often well over fifty miles from the edge of the fast ice, so the adults have to make frequent journeys in order to feed their young. At Fossil Bluff in 1962 the base members were amazed one day when three adelie penguins – hopelessly lost – walked by the hut, which was at least 100 miles from the edge of the ice shelf, and even further from any open water. Penguins can hop very effectively over difficult terrain and they use their beaks and claws to get up steep slopes. They also paddle themselves along, often at a good speed, over the ice or snow, on their breasts, with the help of their flippers.

Deception Island has two resident species, the gentoo and the chinstrap, though occasional wanderers of other species visit the shores, especially the adelie and macaroni penguins. Macaronis have been known to breed in small numbers on the island, though we saw none in 1960. Chinstraps and gentoos breed in rookeries on the ocean-facing coasts, the chinstraps outnumbering the gentoos by many thousands. Both types are similar in height, around two feet, and have black backs from the back of their heads to their tail feathers, and white breasts from under their chins to their feet. The gentoo is the more shy of the two species, and is characterised by having a red beak and large white flashes over its eyes which meet on the top of its head. They assemble in November to lay their eggs; their rookeries are smaller, and were less accessible to us, than the chinstraps'. Unlike the chinstraps, the gentoos stayed around the coasts during much of the winter, and we often saw little groups swim into the bay and clamber ashore, especially if the fast ice had broken away. Chinstrap penguins are very slightly smaller than the gentoos. They have a more darkly uniform black and are characterised by having a very narrow black line of feathers which passes under their chin and eyes and meets up with the black body feathers behind their heads.

Our interest was centred on one of the chinstrap penguin rookeries, for its accessibility enabled us to watch the activities of the birds more closely. The rookery is situated in the area of the hinterland of a small embayment near Baily Head on the south-eastern corner of the island, within approximately two hours' walking distance of the base. Information suggests that this was one of the larger Antarctic rookeries, but estimated numbers of penguins vary considerably and we had no suitable system to count them. We estimated that there were more than 100,000 penguins here annually; there may well have been twice that number.

The rookery is based on ash, and extends from close to the shore to a rising area several hundred yards inland, reaching a height above 500 feet. During the winter months, the rookery is evacuated. Heavy snowfalls cover the entire area, obliterating the site of frozen melt streams and mantling the undulating ground into a deceptively even surface. All is white and pure, and quiet, save for the wind and the swish of the pack ice as it grinds itself out on a nearby beach.

On October 19th Mike and I set out for a week-long sledging journey, and for the first night we camped above the site of the rookery, which was still unoccupied. During the next morning eleven chinstraps arrived, with three more coming later in the day. We watched as the black and white penguins emerged with a rush from the wave that was carrying them up the beach; soon there was quite a group of them standing back from the water's edge, resting after their enormously long swim from further north. After a rest, they preened themselves so that their tightly packed feathers gleamed in the sunshine. The little band of first arrivals trekked away from the beach in a neat line, at this stage all following each other. They walked inland, crossing the packed snow, and climbed up the slopes to a prominent ridge feature. It was obvious to us that the most favoured nest sites were high up on knolls covered by only a thin layer of snow. We left the rookery to go on our travels, leaving behind the fourteen chinstrap penguins, minute specks of black and white in a vast snowfield, with two or three neat little tracks leading from the beach to the hillocks.

On our return on October 25th, the noise from the penguins could be heard a long way off, exciting the dogs as much as ourselves. As we neared, the sweet, sickly smell got into our breath. When we rounded the last hummock we saw an amazing transformation in the scene. Much of the area had become a mass of black and white penguins, with several thousand now having arrived. The high ground nest sites had been the first to be occupied, and later arrivals had spread down the hill slopes to meet up with the lower inhabitants of nearby knolls which had also been occupied. Where the snow had disappeared from the thinly covered slopes of the knolls, some of the chinstraps were busy carrying stones to place at the feet of their mates. Those penguins on the slopes well away from a supply of stones had to forgo this courtship action. Others were engaged in the peculiar swaying motions which are an integral part of chinstrap courtship. There were a great number of squabbles going on, mostly over nest sites or property in the form of stones. Down at the beach came the endless tramp of new arrivals, hundreds and hundreds surging from the water, all running up the beach to escape the next wave, which might snatch them back again. Off-shore, a long lithe body which had been motionless lifted its head and we could see the great teeth of a leopard seal. It was waiting for the inevitable moment when a meal would present itself, when the little penguin would be wretchedly jerked inside out and eaten; a sad fate indeed after such a long swim for an all too defenceless chinstrap. Yet nature is very abundant, and despite the enormous loss of life in the sea, and even more so on the land, the penguins are well able to sustain their numbers.

We left the rookery for several weeks. However, a few days after our return to the base, a group of chinstraps appeared, coming down the slope from the ridge which separated the bay from the rookery; they had climbed to a height in excess of 500 feet, and had walked two miles (a short distance by penguin standards, but one which surprised us). During our absence we knew that the numbers arriving in the rookery would continue to grow, well into November, and that, where the snow had cleared, nests consisting of shallow hollows lined with stones would be made. Later on in the month the female would lay two eggs and start to incubate them. The penguin eggs take approximately seven weeks to hatch, so the chicks would appear in late December. The intervening period was notable for many heavy falls of snow.

On December 1st we decided to go to the rookery in order to collect eggs for use in cooking. Five of us went, two of us with the dog team and boxes for the harvest. Our first view of the rookery was somewhat dismaying. Gone, of course, was the purity of the snow and the whiteness of the penguin breasts we had seen earlier. The whole area had now become fetid with excrement, pink-coloured and foul-smelling. This mattered not, for the sea would soon cleanse the penguins and return their feathers to their pristine state. What disturbed us, however, was the sight on the lower areas, where the thick snow had not yet melted, of thousands of holes with little black heads peering over the lip. Where there were conspicuous gaps in the number of black heads on view, it was because the holes were too deep, or the inhabitant was dead. Whilst the warmth of the penguin's body on the eggs was melting a hole downwards through the snow, recent heavy falls were increasing the general snow cover. The result was that a large number of birds were at the bottom of holes often at arm's length. Many were dead, others that we pulled out were extremely weak, and the eggs were often lying in a puddle of water, another demonstration of the waste of life that is characteristic of a rookery. The hill dwellers were not affected, and they were sitting on clusters of eggs that were well drained, and dry. All of the penguins had two eggs – occasionally there were three – and we helped ourselves to one egg from each nest. The penguins naturally showed their displeasure at our intrusion, and it was sensible for us to wear a glove and to expect a few hearty clumps from a well-aimed but harmless flipper or beak. We had five boxes to fill, so we collected over 300 eggs, which would be used mostly for making cakes and for other culinary experiments.

During December the warmer weather rapidly caused the snow to melt and when we visited the rookery in January things were very different. By now, most of the young chicks had emerged from their shells and were at varying stages of development. The area of previously deep snow bore eloquent testimony to the earlier disaster in the form of little groups of bones, feathers and flippers. The young chinstraps at this stage were very different in appearance from their parents. They were bundles of fluffy greyish-coloured feathers, some already losing their first down. They stood close to their mother, or father, their beady little eyes watching and their receptive mouths ever ready to receive the processed krill their parent would regurgitate! Everywhere there was great movement, noise and smell. Adults were making their way in long lines down to the water to collect krill; others were returning up through the rookery with food for their chicks. Lots of chicks moved about, lost their parents and were pecked at mercilessly; adults squabbled.

The major predator on land is the skua. This strong bird is always on the lookout for an unguarded egg, early on, and small chicks when they hatch. They have the ability to pick up a whole egg and to remove it to a suitable feeding place; similarly with the chicks. The white sheathbill is also ever vigilant, but has not the size or carrying capacity of the skua. The depredations of the birds, the deaths through neglect or disasters resulting from the snow, cause the rookery to appear desolate towards the end of the summer. The penguins spend two or three weeks in moulting and this produces masses of feathers which add to the general filth of the area. In March, a few chicks which have been born late can be seen disconsolately wandering around, abandoned and with no hope of survival.

The chinstrap survives in a tough environment, and those that survive are tough. Once the young have moulted their juvenile coats and assumed adult plumage, they begin to wander down to the beach and into the sea. All that is left at the rookery is the pervasive smell of lots of skeletons. The winter snows will clean up the place, and next spring probably more than 100,000 chinstraps will return to commence the cycle again. This is a process that goes on every year in thousands of rookeries around the Antarctic coast; it was a privilege for us to have one fairly close at hand.

8

Our South American Neighbours

We stopped for a rest and loosened our clothing to allow the cool air to get at our steaming bodies. The deep, wet snow and the steep incline made pulling the sledge a miserable task, like dragging a huge anchor across an area of quicksand. Every yard had to be won by an effort completely disproportionate to the amount of ground gained. It was September 28th, and Roger and I had just left the sea ice in Telefon Bay, which we had crossed from a camp site on the far shore. We were on a man-hauling trip, and gales, temperatures above freezing point, and interminable skies full of low cloud had already caused us to lie up for two days in wet, unpleasant conditions. Although, even now, the cloud was down to 200 feet, we had trudged on to the Argentine base, which we knew would afford us interest and hospitality far exceeding that to be derived from watching the inside of a flapping, wet tent. We pulled on slowly up the valley which separates Cross Hill from the mountain rim of the island. Slowly we reached the crest and hurried easily down the other side into Fumarole Bay, where we could once more use the sea ice as a reasonable highway. Soon we reached the meltwater stream which flows in front of the base, coming from the valley waters draining into a lagoon which still bore its winter covering of ice. Soon we were spotted by a base member, who crossed the mushy ice of the lagoon to show us the best route and to help us carry our belongings.

It was good to be inside Decepcion hut, where we were courteously welcomed by the base commander, who introduced us to the doctor and the *delegado federal*, a civilian representative on an otherwise military staff. We entered the ward room, a huge lounge whose use was the prerogative of the three senior men and their guests. We consumed orange juice, tea and biscuits; we enjoyed the luxury of a shower; we listened to music and chatted. At dinner we had an excellent Wiener schnitzel, preceded by sherry, accompanied by wine and follow by Anis. The steward – who waited on the others at all meals – offered us more meat and more wine; we were soon satiated, and

71

retired to the luxurious depths of a nearby armchair. It was just like home ...

In 1960, Decepcion was one of five Argentine bases located on the sub-Antarctic islands or along the shores and islands of Graham Land. Orcadas on Laurie Island in the South Orkneys had been continuously occupied since 1904; Decepcion was opened in 1948, San Martin in Marguerite Bay in 1951, Esperanza at Hope Bay in 1952, and Jubany in 1953 on King George Island (South Shetlands). There were others occupied during summer seasons, and some were used only occasionally. The Chileans also had four bases including Presidente Aguirre Cerda on the island, whilst the UK had eight including our base in Whalers Bay. Argentina and the UK also had bases on the shelf ice in the Weddell Sea named Belgrano and Halley Bay. Inevitably, therefore, there was much contact between the countries, with lots of ships and movement of personnel. Because all three countries had bases on Deception Island there was closer contact between them than at any other location.

Roger and I enjoyed splendid hospitality from the Argentines for several days. The doctor was able to speak English, and his desire to practise it complemented our desire to find out how others lived in the Antarctic. Almost immediately we arrived, he took us on a tour of the base. The hut was in three sections based on a circle, each section serving the different functions which, together, made up the whole. One part was for accommodation, another for cooking and storage purposes, and the third to house the scientific and radio departments. There were a few small deviations from this pattern, but the general principle remained. The hut was centrally heated, making each room extremely warm – too warm, in fact, for us, and we found it necessary to open the windows and rest on top of the blankets; even so, the atmosphere was still stuffy. The men lived in small cabins, where two men had double-tiered bunks, cupboards and a small table to share between them. The leaders had larger, single rooms to which they could retire. The central heating was a by-product of the hot water system which provided an excellent flow to the wash rooms and showers. Another refinement was a splendid WC, a fully flushing model which caused us to think back to our own primitive arrangement with some regret! A cook house was situated at the focal point of the hut, whence meals could be easily served to the different quarters where officers and men dined.

There were fifteen men at the base, which was maintained by the navy. Most of them had been posted to the Antarctic, though a few men had wanted to come back; there were certain attractive financial advantages to be derived from serving at Decepcion. Because it was a military base, the social system was inevitably based on rank, and this dichotomy between officers and men struck us forcibly. The officers were separated from the men for most of the time, and dined separately, being attended by a steward. Unlike at the UK bases, almost all of the men were married and their average age seemed to be in the early thirties, whereas Fids tended to be on average four or five years younger. A full-time cook served at the base, and this was reflected in the quality of the food and its presentation. There was a well-stocked refrigerator with a lot of top-quality meat, the basis of their diet. Vegetables were in short supply and the tins of fruit were of a lower standard than we enjoyed at Biscoe House. Good wine was enjoyed at most meals; vitamin pills were also always on offer.

The work carried out was very similar to the work on the UK base, though the system of deployment was different – each morning and afternoon the commander paraded the men and allocated tasks to them, obviously excluding the doctor and the *delegado federal*. Outdoor commitments were minimal.

The doctor was responsible for a magnificently equipped 'hospital', reminiscent of a hospital operating theatre. Illnesses in the Antarctic – apart from accidents – are infrequent, so we were not surprised to learn that his facilities were rarely called on. He made monthly medical examinations of the men and dealt with minor disorders and injuries. He was young, only twenty-six years old, recently qualified and with an interest in the psychological aspects of medicine. He occasionally spoke of 'problems of adjustment' on the base and we knew that this had resulted in strong disciplinary measures being taken; we were given to understand that one man had been confined to his room for 100 days. One of the minor ailments on the base was a persistence of headaches. The doctor attributed this to the incidence of low (barometric) pressure; our own diagnosis was that the problem might have arisen from the clamminess of the almost tropical atmosphere inside the hut. We never had this problem on the British base, nor did we have any illness – but then we had no doctor either ...

The meteorological office was maintained by one man. He was kept extremely busy for he carried out a full synoptic programme with observations every three hours, and the associated wealth of statistical processing, that four of us shared at Whalers Bay, though we had a multiplicity of other tasks to carry out that would not have come his way. His office was well-kept, and was full of diagrammatic climatological information; he was particularly pleased to show us a trace from the anemograph which indicated a wind speed of 122 knots, recorded on the same day as we had recorded a highest gust of 72 knots. We too noticed the strong winds at the base, probably accounted for by its position at the bottom of a steep valley.

In the seismological office we were interested to see the records of the seismic activity on the island, which from time to time shuddered threateningly.

The radio room was a buzz of activity. Whilst only one weather man was employed, five radio operators shared the duties. Decepcion was the centre for traffic to the other Argentine bases. Apart from this, and the traffic in sending weather reports, regular daily schedules were arranged by which men could call their families; this was a major commitment. The base also issued a daily news sheet with information culled from the news bulletins. Thus the base functioned, a sedentary organisation carrying out their programme of work, just as we did.

A short break in the weather enabled us to visit the site of a penguin rookery a mile away on the outside coast of the island. The rookery was unpopulated at that time of the year, but we enjoyed watching the great breakers plastering the rocks with a coating of hard sea ice, and protecting them, temporarily, from the rapid erosion which eats away at the volcanic ash and rock. Again, the snow was deep and we were surprised that our companions did not wear skis, which they found to be a hindrance; indeed, several times they had trekked across the sea ice to the Chilean base – a distance of over four miles – without them, arriving there exhausted after traipsing over the mushy sea ice. We formed the impression that many of the base members were not happy with their posting to Decepcion, and this was confirmed when we chatted to them, a difficult process when we only had a limited number of mutually comprehensible words. They all spoke with great enthusiasm of home, telling us nostalgically of their wives and children who had been left behind. They enjoyed the periodic film shows, but the highlight of the week came when the radio signals carried the voices of home over the ether, and over the vast distances of sea; this was their main interest.

As we trudged back across the ice to our own base, most of us pure volunteers, happy to settle for our salary of £550 a year just to be there, my thoughts returned to the men who had been so kind to us and who had so cheerily wished us 'goodbye'. My impression was generally one of comfort imported into the wilderness to an extent that the face of the Antarctic world outside might be forgotten. I thought of 'home', of 'adjustment', and of 'living together', and I wondered wherein the best solution was to be found to the problem of living and working in the Antarctic. Certainly on our own base (where its impact was very limited) and on the Argentine base, the distinction between 'officers and men' seemed inimical to an atmosphere of unity of purpose and commitment.

Relations with the Chilean members of the Presidente Aguirre Cerda base were extremely cordial, and rarely a month passed by without visits being made by members of the one base to the other. Amongst the Chileans there was always a sense of happiness and this was always expressed in their great hospitality towards us and towards the Argentines.

The Chilean base was one of four bases run under the auspices of the Chilean Air Force. The first, Capitan Arturo Prat, had been established on Greenwich Island (South Shetlands) in 1947, followed by Bernado O'Higgins in north Graham Land in 1948 and Gonzalez Videla in Paradise Bay on the mainland in 1951. Aguirre Cerda was manned by eight men: two officers, two radio operators, a cook, a diesel mechanic, a radio mechanic and a general assistant. The military structure inevitably necessitated a social organisation based on rank, but an admirable compromise was effected which promoted the happiness of all. The officers spent the whole of their time with the others, and everyone appeared to benefit from the sense of community.

The building contained a main hut, with off-shoots which produced a plan that was F-shaped. The living quarters were situated in the main part, with two men sharing small cabins, whilst the officers had a room each for themselves. A lounge served the purposes of dining room for all, a few yards from the kitchen. During the previous summer, an extension had been added, containing a 'contemporary' room for the use of the officers. This was magnificent, with plush carpets, deep armchairs, a glass table and ultra-modernistic fittings. A small guest room and WC (whose drainage was an enigma!) completed the new addition.

There was no evidence of any major scientific programme at the base, either in the buildings or in the personnel. Everyone had taken a basic course in meteorology, however, so regular observations were made. This was a time when having a foothold in the Antarctic was important to protect territorial claims, reason in itself for countries to maintain bases.

There was a barn in a wing of the building devoted to farming activities. At the start of the year the base had twenty sheep, one pig and forty chickens, which acted as a good fresh food supply. The twenty sheep lived in the barn, where they were all well fed and cared for until the inevitable day came, when one by one they came under the knife! The sheep thrived on hay, and were let out for exercise when conditions permitted. This gave rise to an amusing incident when one of them strayed away. At the time, its departure went unnoticed. Ten days later, the commander was on the sea ice, a mile or so away, when he observed in the gloom a peculiar animal the like of which he had never seen before. In his typically excitable manner, Fernando Mansilla told us how he had taken out his revolver and had crept stealthily up to the animal, not realising what it was until the very last moment, when the plaintive bleat of a starved sheep issued from the weakly mass of white wool! Soon, a great Chilean rescue party was launched, and the sheep returned to the fold. Such were the rigours of the Antarctic!

The Chilean pig was enormous and affectionate; his attractive personality, however, came to naught a few days before the feast commemorating the celebration of Chilean Independence. The forty chickens provided the base with a never-ending supply of fresh eggs, which made us particularly envious in view of our own failure in this enterprise. The wealth of fresh meat, which because of its invariability tended to become monotonous, was not equalled in vegetables, which were in very short supply; neither was the fruit supply very good. The white flour which we had on our base was very much envied by the Chileans when they visited us, and became a very good 'trade' commodity. The wine was plentiful and everyone kept in the best of health, though they, like us, had no doctor.

The course in meteorology was one of several attended by the base members; they had training in skiing but most of them considered the use of skis a painful business, they had a course in taxidermy (very

76

useful!) and they had courses in boating and first aid. In fact, they made us quite envious because FIDS at that time gave no general courses in anything. We had to do our own research on crevasse rescues, skiing, boatmanship, cooking and first aid. We were confident, however, that our self-taught techniques were quite the equal of the Chileans'. With one exception the men were all married and, as with the Argentinians, great importance was attached to the weekly contact with home, though the officers had almost daily contact with their wives. The importance of the radio contact was reflected in the high proportion of radio operators on the base. Film shows were again a regular and pleasant feature of life. They had an enormous range of indoor games, for which their enthusiasm was incredible and culminated in an Antarctic Olympiad involving everything from draughts and ping-pong to sheep-throwing and rifle shooting.

Such was the extremely happy and basically indoor existence in the Chilean base. The Chileans had no difficulty in obtaining men for their bases, for the financial rewards made their one-year stay a not unpleasant way of saving, an important consideration for married men.

The year progressed, and our visits became more frequent. September 18th is celebrated all over Chile as the day marking their independence from Spain. We had long since received an invitation to join in the festivities, so Ian, Roger and I decided to go. It was a horrible day, low cloud, snow and warm temperatures making conditions miserable. We did not want to disappoint out hosts, besides which we looked forward to much enjoyment, so we harnessed the dogs and made the journey. The sea ice looked dangerous, but we found that underlying the mushy surface there still remained good ice. We crossed it and soon reached the outer shore and made our way up a valley which led down to the base hut, using this route to avoid a patch of very dangerous ice at the entrance to Pendulum Cove. The dogs ploughed on through the deep snow, and we arrived at the base, white and snow-covered. Immediately, Fernando – the base commander – came out to welcome us, amazed that we had come on such a dreadful day, and beaming gleefully as he expostulated, 'Bravo, only the British and the Chileans would travel on such a day as this!' We picketed the dogs and went inside to greet the other Chileans and three men from the Argentine base who had arrived the previous day. Soon we were imbibing the wine and eating the food. We feasted on pork, gorged ourselves on chicken and drank, and drank ... Musical instruments appeared, which enabled Roger to take a leading part in the entertainment. A regular Bacchanalian orgy developed in an atmosphere of great friendliness. At the end of the dinner, speeches were made in which the orators, of which there were eleven, rose and spoke of fraternity and greatness, which compelled Ian, speaking for at least half a minute on behalf of the rest of us, to reply. It was all very amusing, and the festivities went on far into the night until, weak and inebriated, people tottered off to bed. It gave us plenty by which to remember our Chilean friends.

There were as many as four prolonged visits to each of the other bases, and we reciprocated the hospitality in good measure. Fernando was keen to improve his English and he spent three weeks with us. Each base became specialised in its trade items. We could offer whisky, gin, cigarettes, flour and yeast; the Chileans could offer first-class fresh meat (mutton!), eggs and wine; the Argentinians had beef and splendid wine. UK base members had an entitlement of 200 cigarettes a week, and since only three or four smoked, we had a huge surplus. Our sledges were eagerly awaited in Pendulum Cove and Telefon Bay. In the summer we had large numbers of visitors from the ships anchoring in the bay and we always made them welcome.

We always showed cooperation and helpfulness to each other. Brian and I had intermittently suffered toothache for several months. So, on January 6th 1961, we set out in the dinghy and made our way the four miles into Port Foster to the *Piloto Pardo*, a Chilean ship anchored off their base. Brian had two hours of treatment whilst I was entertained in the ward room. I then had a filling removed; the dentist prodded around and found a festering dead root, the cause of my abscess. The tooth was removed expertly; I was very grateful.

I left Deception Island later in January, and I was glad to have such memories of our South American friends; they had added to the richness of our experience.

Our visit to Deception Island in February 2000 was a time of nostalgia and sadness. The British and Chilean bases were finished, the Chilean base having been buried under the ash of the 1967/69 eruptions, whilst Biscoe House still stood, though derelict and destroyed. The Argentines had built a new base in Telefon Bay which was occupied during the summer.

The visit also made us aware of the huge changes that had taken place over the years in the balance of numbers of bases and personnel, and in their distribution. Whereas Britain now has only Rothera as its single permanently occupied base on the Antarctic Peninsula (Graham Land), with summer bases at Signy Island and Fossil Bluff, the Argentinians have as many as thirteen bases (not all occupied all the time), and Chile has seven (again, not all occupied all the time).

The British base at Adelaide Island – which we had helped to build in 1961 – is now Carvajal, a Chilean base. The welcome we had in 2000 was just as cordial as we were used to in Deception. Teniente Camara on Half Moon Island and Esperanza at Hope Bay are large multi-hutted stations owned by Argentina. Esperanza is now a full village with at least twenty-five buildings, a summer population of eighty and a school having twenty-two pupils, some of whom were born in the Antarctic. There are houses for the families, a shop, a bar, and a church dedicated to St Francis of Assisi, with a statue of the Madonna of the Snows. A few hundred yards from Esperanza stands one of the most historic of British bases, Hope Bay – starting point of many hugely important pioneering sledge journeys by Fids. Gone are the dogs and the sledges of the past; the base is now under the ownership of Uruguay, who welcomed us with characteristic South American hospitality. One of our party, Chris Brading, had been a surveyor at Hope Bay, wintering in 1959 and 1960; what memories must have been stirred by his return!

Most of the traditional work of survey and geology on the peninsula has been completed, so work in Antarctica is inevitably being based in stations concentrating on scientific programmes of great complexity. Certainly the British base at Rothera is a manifestation of this change. The number of countries involved has also risen dramatically and approaches two dozen; there are as many as nine bases on King George Island in the South Shetlands, so hopefully the fraternisation between bases which we so much valued can still flourish in these modern times!

1. The Beaver returns to the *Kista Dan* after ice reconnaissance, page 13.

Photo courtesy of Howard Chapman

2. Rescued by the *USS Glacier,* page 23.

3. Whalers Bay and Port Foster, Deception Island, page 35.

4. Meteorology at Whalers Bay, page 44.

5. Biscoe House, Deception Island, page 38.

6. Biscoe House, many years after the volcanic eruption, page 51.

Photo courtesy of BAS Archives

7. The Chinstraps trek inland from Baily Head, page 67.

8. A successful season, page 69.

9. We help the Beaver to turn, page 85.

10. Digging out the Otter, page 85.

11. The end of the Beaver . . . page 85.   Photo courtesy of Maurice Sumner

12. . . . . despite all possible help from men and dogs, page 85.
Photo courtesy of Maurice Sumner

13. Pristine Wilderness - Adelaide Island, page 100.

18. We fly from the ice, March 4th 1961, page 115.

19. Our new home at Fossil Bluff, page 116.

20. John and Brian sort things out, page 129.

21. The sun declines over The Silent Sound, May 10th 1961, page 144.

Photo courtesy of Brian Taylor

22. John and Brian set out on April 28th for the Geological Survey at Waitabit Cliffs, page 142.

23. John and Brian - frugal fare for mid-winter's day, page 151.

9

Up in the Air

By the time we had arrived at Deception Island in 1960, there had still only been a few flights in the Graham Land area. Wilkins, with Eilson as pilot, had made the very first flight in Antarctica from Deception Island on November 16th 1928 in a Lockheed Vega, using the same plane on December 20th of the same year to fly 1,300 miles in a round trip far to the south. A year later, with floats attached to the Vega, and a new pilot, Cramer, he flew from Port Lockroy over the plateau to the east coast, returning by a southerly loop in which he wanted to confirm his earlier discoveries from the previous year. Wilkins had claimed that Graham Land was cut through, east to west, by one large strait (Stefansson Strait), and by two channels (Casey and Lurabee Channels), all of which were proved not to exist by the British Graham Land Expedition in 1935.

The next series of flights was made by Ellsworth, with Balchen as pilot, from Snow Hill Island, starting on December 18th 1934; a year later, with Hollick Kenyon as pilot, he returned to fly from Dundee Island on November 20th 1935, the first of a series of attempts to reach the Bay of Whales on the Ross Sea side of the continent, in the Northrop aircraft which he named 'Polar Star'.

The British Graham Land Expedition used a de Havilland Gypsy Fox Moth to explore a large area of the Graham Land coast from Anvers Island to King George VI Sound, their first flight being made on January 27th 1935, starting from Port Lockroy.

The Falkland Islands Dependencies Survey first used an aircraft, an Auster, at Stonington Island in 1947, simultaneously with aircraft of the Ronne Antarctic Research Expedition. The Americans had brought Beechcraft and Norseman planes for their aerial surveys, and they were also based at Stonington Island at the same time. Unfortunately, nine months after its arrival the British plane crashed, though the three men on board all survived.

Five of the men who had wintered at Stonington Island or on other bases in 1947 were trapped for a third year when impenetrable ice in

Marguerite Bay prevented their relief by ship in 1949. In order to ensure that they would be relieved early in 1950, the Governor acquired the use of two aircraft, a Norseman and an Auster. Late in January 1950 flights were made from the Argentine Islands and the men were rescued.

At various times during the 1950s, Argentinian and Chilean planes made reconnaissance flights. Finally, the greatest use of aircraft of all, was made over two seasons in 1956 and 1957 by the Falkland Islands Aerial Survey Expedition, who operated with Canso aircraft from Deception Island and surveyed 35,000 square miles of new territory.

1960 marked a major innovation in the use of aircraft in the British sector of Antarctica, for when the de Havilland Otter and Beaver aircraft arrived at Deception Island in the spring of 1960 the first permanent air base was established. From then on, the use of planes would become a permanent and vital part of the work of the Survey. In this first year we learnt from some very hard lessons.

The Otter had finally flown back from Penola Strait on March 28th and was securely picketed near the runway. On April 1st, the *Kista Dan* arrived in Whalers Bay, and a few days later the wounded Beaver was brought ashore. The Beaver had sustained severe structural damage in the collision in Meek Channel. When the port wing was wrenched off there was a certain amount of twisting where it had been joined to the fuselage. We built a small 'hangar', to house the fuselage and to store its remaining wing, onto the end of the boat shed. It was put together from an assortment of aircraft crates built round a sturdy framework, and roofed in with corrugated iron removed from the whaling factory. It was small as a hangar but it could accommodate the wingless fuselage of the Beaver, and even though its tail projected outside, it gave it protection from the wind and snows of the season ahead.

The Otter too, after its exciting season, had some airframe damage which needed attention. It was picketed to face the north-east, from which direction the prevailing winds blew. There were many gales from other directions, however, and gales from the north-west and south-west caught the back and sides of the plane, inflicting undue strain and some specific damage to the airframe. Any repair work, together with the normal maintenance work on airframe and engine, was not made easier by having to be carried out in the open, unsheltered from the icy winds which blew for much of the time.

The *John Biscoe* had made a late, end of season, run to Montevideo to collect a new wing for the Beaver, arriving back at Deception Island on May 6th, when the shiny, silvery wing was brought ashore. Day after day from then on, Pete and Tom would disappear into the hangar to work on the airframe and engine. June and July passed, and the basic work neared completion. The two engineers therefore took a brief respite at the Chilean base, and whilst they were away, the rest of us dismantled the end of the hangar and removed the Beaver on August 2nd. It was towed by tractor to the airstrip and picketed near the Otter. It was a week later before further progress could be made – air pressure fell to 940 mb by August 7th, and this precipitous fall was inevitably accompanied by gales and blizzards. Eventually the weather cleared and on August 10th, the eleven of us went out to lift the wings whilst Pete secured them to the fuselage. We benefited from the assistance of Fernando, the Chilean base commander, who organised us all very effectively! The wings were on and the two planes stood a few yards away from each other, the Otter surrounded by creeping snow drifts, the Beaver above the snow, and resplendent in its different coloured wings of orange/red and silver.

The work planned for the spring was the transport from the Argentine Islands of the six men destined for Adelaide Island who had been occupying Wordie House on the Argentine Islands since the abortive attempt to establish the Adelaide Island base in March. These men, with the dogs which had been brought out of Horseshoe Island, and with food and field equipment, would be landed on the northern part of Adelaide Island, and would work southwards towards the proposed base site at which the *John Biscoe* would arrive in February 1961. They would thus have the benefit of a full summer season of valuable field working time. During August a great deal of time was spent in preparing the aircraft. The Otter had to be dug out and small amounts of damage caused by gales made good. By the 30th the planes were ready for testing, but not until September 3rd did the two planes take to the air again. This was a magical day at the base, and for me, because it was my first flight:

September 3rd. I was on duty met. so I was up early. The sky was 8/8 stratus but it soon began to break up and promised a fine day. Preparations were soon in hand for the test flights of the Otter and Beaver. By noon they were ready to go when an unaccountable 25 knot wind blew up. It lasted for 20 minutes – but the aircraft had by then been secured again. Lunch followed gloomily. The wind dropped to 10 knots; the sky cleared completely. By 2.00 p.m. we were all round the aircraft. Ron and Tom took the Otter up for a 5 minute test, then Ron took Brian, Fraser and me on board. I clambered into the cockpit next to Ron. At 3.00 p.m. we took off. We climbed steadily and soon we were admiring Deception. We climbed to 9,000 feet and flew round and round the island, and out into the Bransfield Strait and towards Livingstone Island. Visibility was 100 miles, the sky blue, the sun shining. Deception was completely white mantled, a few gashed crevasses grinning up at us. The Bransfield was $8/10^{ths}$ full of very light, loose pack, rather like pancake ice. Soon the Beaver, with Paddy, Mike and Roger, took off. Paddy brought it alongside the Otter at 5,000 feet, for a few frightening moments! Before this the Otter had momentarily spluttered due to an overheated carburettor. My heart sank! What a wonderful 95 minutes we had, how indescribably memorable and unique. Of course, everyone was cheery in the evening for the aircraft are obviously OK and many of us were thrilled by the experience.

Everything was now set for the flights to the Argentine Islands. Weather schedules were commenced with Brian Wigglesworth, the forecaster based there. Every day the existing weather was reported and assessed, and there were many delays before the flight was made. On September 8th, all was well at both ends and the aircraft were prepared. Within a couple of minutes from take-off, a thirty-knot wind sprang up and the planes could not be safely turned round to go to the runway. On the next day the planes took off, for though we had low cloud, conditions south were better. Yet, within twenty minutes the pilots reported a cloud base of 250 feet, an unpleasant state of affairs when there was nothing but icy water beneath them and they returned. Soon after they had landed, visibility at the base approached fog levels, and snow fell. No flying was possible for several days. On the 16th the day dawned clear and by 11.00 a.m. the planes were ready. First the Otter took off, followed by the Beaver, recently adorned by a penguin which Brian had painted on the side facing the bright letters which spelt out FALKLAND ISLANDS

84

DEPENDENCIES SURVEY. Soon they were gone, winging the four aviators over the sea towards Graham Land and the Argentine Islands. It was the last time we saw the Beaver.

At lunch time the seven of us left behind were congratulating ourselves at the conclusion of the digging operations, for the planes had drifted up considerably, and were planning what to do with the extra spare time we now had. Over the radio, the Base F (Argentine Islands) radio operator reported the arrival of the Otter, piloted by Paddy. It landed on the strip which had been marked out on the ice, and taxied to the island where it was to be parked. 'The Beaver's just coming,' he went on, then 'What's that? Somebody's said it's through, hold on ...'

We held on ... 'Yes, it's through the ice,' came the fateful words. 'They're trying to get it out.'

They tried, but it was hopeless. The little plane had crossed an isolated patch of weak ice, and one ski had broken through; the other followed, and soon the plane was sinking up to its wings, which supported the fuselage and prevented it from sinking. Pete had already alighted from the plane, farther down the runway, but Ron could only get out by crossing to the other side of the plane and forcing the door, for his own was already caught by the ice.

Determined attempts were made to pull the plane clear. There were twenty Fids on hand, and two dog teams, all desperate to help. Even after removing the wings and lightening the plane by taking out its cargo and fittings, the attempt failed. The skis were trapped under the ice and every tug simply pulled them along under it without releasing the plane. Reluctantly, the Beaver had to be abandoned, though it hung on the ice for several weeks before it was gently dropped through a weakened patch, into the sea below. It sank in Meek Channel close to where it had first lost its wing on March 12th. In its entire flying career the Beaver flew four times, twice from the *Kista Dan* on ice reconnaissance, once from Deception Island on a test flight, then finally its one-and-three-quarter hour flight to the Argentine Islands, a total air time of approximately six hours fifteen minutes.

On the next day there was a long radio schedule with SecFids, John Green in Stanley. The Adelaide Island scheme now had to be abandoned and the Otter would fly back to Deception Island as soon as possible. The implications of this inevitable decision were demoralising for those six men at Wordie House whose whole year would now prove unproductive, with no survey work possible, no geology, no exploration of Adelaide Island from north to south, nothing but sitting it out for perhaps five months when the ships, hopefully, would arrive. We coined a phrase earlier in the year when we were gripped in the Bellingshausen sea ice which had a real application at times like these: 'The Antarctic is bigger than all of us.' It certainly was!

It was several days before the Otter could return to Deception Island. By the 24th, a sense of urgency was creeping in, for the edge of the ice at the Argentine Islands had broken back to the end of the runway, and there was concern that the plane might not get off at all. On the 28th, however, the weather improved and the four airmen clambered aboard the Otter and returned to their home base, where once again it took its place on the open airfield. This was the end of the first summer of air operations; a great disappointment in that one aircraft was lost and the other had succeeded only in carrying out a very limited relief of Horseshoe Island. The Otter would have to await the moment when it could help to prove the value of aircraft in furthering the work of the Survey.

This proof came in the following season. It was conclusive proof too. Not that flights were not made before then. The Otter could be used as an ice reconnaissance plane, and flights were made when the *RRS Shackleton* was approaching the island in late November, and when information was required about the ice in the Hope Bay area.

The main flights of the summer were made during February and March 1961. By this time, a new Otter had arrived on the *Kista Dan*. Flight Lieutenant Bob Bond, and Roy Brand, respectively pilot and airframe fitter, had also arrived to replace Paddy English and Pete Bates. As soon as the new aircraft was ready, Bob took a few flights to familiarise himself with it.

By February 9th, an airstrip had been found on the ice piedmont near the southern end of Adelaide Island, and the two Otters were flown down from Deception Island. Soon after, the decision was made to fly in the supplies to a new base at Fossil Bluff whilst awaiting the break-out of the ice in Marguerite Bay, and a reconnaissance flight was made down King George VI Sound, across the bay and to the south. The site for Fossil Bluff was determined, and the following day, the first of the airlifts was undertaken. Food was the first to be taken in, followed by a building party to construct the hut as the parts arrived. Progress was splendid; in the three days following the reconnaissance, the two planes totalled fourteen flights, each return journey taking some five hours. This excellent progress was maintained right up to the last flight, the twenty-seventh, when three of us (John Smith, Brian Taylor and myself) flew in to winter at Fossil Bluff on March 4th. Carrying their loads of 1500 lbs, the two Otters showed that, given reasonable weather, they could increase the scope of the Survey tremendously within a few short weeks.

When they finally flew back to Deception Island in mid-March, they carried out other work, laying depots on the eastern side of the peninsula in order to help the sledge teams from Hope Bay who were operating in that area. The second season of flying ended; it had been an unqualified success and we who had witnessed all of the difficulties at close hand were very pleased.

On February 12th 2000, the *Lyubov Orlova* sailed past Jenny Island in northern Marguerite Bay on its way to Rothera Point. It was a most beautiful, cloudless day, with Adelaide Island and Pourquoi Pas Island sparkling white. Suddenly, overhead there appeared a twin-engined Otter returning from the south, perhaps from Fossil Bluff. It was red, and emblazoned on the side in black it carried the words BRITISH ANTARCTIC SURVEY. Later that evening when we had anchored off Rothera Base, we watched as, at 11.20 p.m. another plane arrived, having just come from the South Pole! Both aircraft landed on a crushed rock runway, approaching 1,000 yards in length and equipped with all the necessary landing lights and navigational equipment. They were then able to taxi to the crushed rock apron and move into the very large hangar close by. We visited the airport next day and looked with interest at the number of Otters and Dash 7s and other aircraft which are now used by the Survey. What a contrast to the volcanic ash of our 'airport' in 1960!

Over the years the British Antarctic Survey has developed its fleet of aircraft, and the ancillary services, in keeping with the role they now have of taking scientists out into the field in all directions. An advanced base at Fossil Bluff is used during the summer time. Also, it is now possible to fly staff for the base into Rothera, from the UK via Stanley. The days of spending 110 days on board a ship trying to get to a base – as I had done – are long since gone!

10

Summer Comes to Deception Island

The newly hoisted flag hung limply on its pole. The cloud hung grey and uncompromising over the factory. It was November 17th 1960, a November day reminiscent of home. I carried out the 6.00 a.m. observation, then wandered down to the jetty, a crude but efficient structure of oil drums and timbers which now rode gently up and down on the easy swell. A dog stirred and dragged its chain, a giant petrel glided hungrily over the water. Little broke the silence. Then suddenly, as through a London fog, the bass note of a ship's horn echoed round the bay. A few moments later, a grey ship with frosted outline moved through Neptune's Bellows and turned into Whalers Bay. It was the *RRS Shackleton*, the first relief ship of the year, whose arrival marked the onset of the summer season. The summer really had not yet arrived and the rails and masts and aerials bore a considerable weight of ice, a testimony to the inclement wind and the icy moisture through which the ship had sailed. As the long rattle of iron against iron indicated that it had dropped its anchor off-shore, some base members emerged; we all knew that from this moment on our settled routine would be interrupted, and that nothing would be the same again.

The length of a summer season for bases around the Antarctic coasts was generally directly proportional to their extent northwards. In the Dependencies, the South Orkneys (Signy Island), South Shetlands (Admiralty Bay and Deception Island) and Hope Bay were usually relieved between mid-November and mid-December. Bases further down the Graham Land peninsula (Argentine Islands and Port Lockroy), together with Halley Bay in the Weddell Sea, were usually relieved by mid-January. The bases in Marguerite Bay (Adelaide Island, Horseshoe Island and Stonington Island) generally had a brief open season in late February or March (or not at all!), during which time feverish activity ensued before the ships hurried away to avoid the grip of the ice. In that the visit of a relief ship inevitably entailed turmoil on the bases, everyone, whilst delighting at the prospect of mail, a passage home, or transference to another base, looked forward to the departure of the ships. Only after they had gone would the base be able to settle down once more to its own routine and its programme for the year's work.

Deception Island, because it was in the north, and because it was the focal point of the Antarctic work of three countries, suffered the trials and tribulations of a five-month summer season, during which time a multitude of ships came and went with great frequency, in keeping with Deception's classification as 'port of entry' to the Dependencies. The *RRS Shackleton* was the first arrival of the season, and soon we could see the decks lined with new Fids. I thought to myself of the days of hustle and bustle ahead, and lots of work, when the base hut would be filled with strangers, with many eyes peering into every corner. These days, however, would eventually culminate in the arrival of the *John Biscoe*, which would take me south again.

Unloading started immediately, and went on for most of five days, until the ship left on the 21st. The amount, and variety, was extraordinary. The basic base requirements included masses of boxes of food and drink, boxes of nutrican for the dogs, fuel supplies – anthracite, oil, and gas cylinders – and various other supplies and pieces of equipment. There were also four lamb carcasses and a huge flank of beef, so we immediately dug a large freezer cupboard into the huge drift at the back of the hut to preserve these valuable commodities. Needless to say, the most delicious steaks and lamb chops appeared on the menu for a great many days.

The largest element in the unloading schedule, however, was for the aircraft. Apart from additional steel work, there were hundreds of bags of sand and shingle and tins of cement for the base of a properly designed hangar, and there were hundreds of drums of aviation fuel, each drum containing forty-five gallons. There was also a new Otter aircraft (which had to be treated with particular care!). It came in a huge crate, with separate crates for the wings. There was also a vast stock of timber and two new diesel generators, each weighing over a ton. We had two tractors to assist the work on land, but the vast majority of the work was carried out by heaving Fids. We worked incredibly hard and for incredibly long hours, and with an incredible variety of invective and oaths. Yet most of us saw the amusing side of it and I have rarely laughed so much in my life.

The main work during the summer was the erection of a proper hangar to house the aircraft. The first Otter had already aged considerably under the onslaught of ground winds equal, perhaps, to many hours of flying time. A new diesel shed was also to be erected, and new diesel generators installed. Furthermore, the air contingent had a new section of airstrip to prepare and a new Otter to assemble, whilst the rest of the base had the normal routine work to conduct. To help in this work, two steel erectors (Pete Secker and Ben Hodges), and a carpenter (John Collings), moved ashore, the rest of the labour supply coming from the base members, the number of which never exceeded fourteen. For several weeks, the deep snow prevented any preliminary excavations for the hangar or diesel shed foundations; on November 30th Ben Hodges looked for the hangar girders and found them eighteen inches below the surface. On the same day John Collings dug down nine feet through a drift which had built up where he was to work.

Although the snow was melting quickly, there was no chance of work commencing, so Pete, Ben and John were able to enjoy the other aspects of base life. These pleasantries would soon be foregone as the melting snows revealed the huge piles of wood and steel and other equipment which had been unloaded from the *Kista Dan* earlier in the year. Pete went out with the dogs, who marked his initiation with a huge dog fight which caused him to utter in a strong cockney accent full of horrified disbelief, 'Just look at the f...ing blood.' Back at the base, thoroughly exhausted, he announced his retirement from dog driving! Ben Hodges interested himself in everything, and when he and I went out fishing in the boat, we sat in the sun under the Cathedral Crags, lifting the notothenia out of the water two at a time, and he made the remark, 'I wish my mates could see me now' – a thought that I had had many times during my first year. (Ben became so enamoured of the Antarctic that I think he spent more than three winters and ten summers running his dog team, as a general assistant and as a refurbisher of bases such as Port Lockroy, which later became a museum.) John Collings too made the most of the delay by boating or walking, or in using his skills in making things for the hut, a small drying cupboard being particularly useful for protecting our developed films.

At the first opportunity the foundations for the hangar were marked out and squads of base workmen reported for the long job of digging the holes for the foundations. The two tractors were pressed into service, and day after day, loads of sand, shingle, cement, steel and water were moved. It became a real construction site; some wag thoughtfully suggested that we construct an observation platform for the use of visitors! Pete and Ben energetically led the way and the great steel stanchions were put into position. Every day, a handful of base men reported for work but it was a very fluid labour supply, with men running off to do the meteorological observations, carry out radio schedules, fill the water tanks, cook meals, or carry out the many other jobs necessary to keep the base operating. Every two weeks, Pete and Ben had to leave the job themselves, for they also took their turn as cook. The short labour supply was spread even more thinly when John Collings was able to start his job of building the generator shed, for he too needed a team of diggers and general labourers. Gradually, both buildings took shape, and Fraser, Brian, Roger and I, all that remained from the old base team, were able to talk quite knowledgeably of such unlikely things as 'podgers', 'sticks', and 'clints' which we had seen in use in the hands of the steel erectors! Often Pete and Ben would return from the hangar after midnight and, as often, John would be out on the diesel shed soon after 6 a.m. to make a start. The days flew by and frequently, as we labourers lifted our servile eyes from our work, we would see yet another ship move slowly through the Bellows.

The British Antarctic fleet comprised four ships, though one of these was *HMS Protector*, a Royal Naval net layer whose helicopters often assisted Fids to undertake work in inaccessible places such as islands or highlands. The *Protector* was assigned to these southern areas each summer for strategic reasons. The *RRS Shackleton* was usually the first to arrive in the area to relieve the northern bases. Often it would leave the UK in September and sail by way of the mid-Atlantic islands of Ascension, St Helena and Tristan da Cunha before reaching South Georgia and the Falkland Islands. The *RRS John Biscoe* tended to depart a month later, calling at Montevideo and the Falkland Islands before commencing work in the Dependencies. It was used to relieve Halley Bay in the Weddell Sea, and the more southerly bases of Graham Land. Unlike the *Shackleton*, the *John Biscoe* was capable of working in areas of pack ice, though it was not an ice-breaker. The *Kista Dan* was chartered from a Danish shipping company – Lauritzen Lines – and was used in Marguerite Bay and the Weddell Sea.

Whenever one of these ships arrived, there was great excitement and continuous comings and goings from ship to shore, and from shore to ship. On the *John Biscoe* and *Shackleton* the base members would enjoy film shows. When the *Protector* arrived we were grandly entertained to a gastronomic buffet with the officers, followed by pleasant conversation, liqueurs and a film show. At the time of our visit the officers were elated at the success of a party from the ship which had recently made the first ascent of one of the twin peaks of Mount Paget on South Georgia.

Argentine ships were to be seen frequently; there were four of them during the 1960–61 summer. The *San Martin* was a large icebreaker used for relieving the southern bases both in the Weddell Sea and in Marguerite Bay. Earlier, in the previous season of 1959–60 it had found the same Bellingshausen pack ice which had trapped us in the *Kista Dan* just as impossible to get through, and the relief of the Debenham Island base had been effected by helicopter. The ship also had two Beavers on board in case air operations were necessary to relieve the men at Belgrano – Weddell Sea – who had not been relieved during the previous year. After a successful summer season the planes went to Esperanza, where both were lost during the year, one crashing shortly after take-off and the other being destroyed during winds which gusted to over 130 knots. Such were the difficulties – in which we had shared – in keeping aircraft in the Antarctic in the open.

A large oil tanker, the *Punta Ninfas*, anchored in the bay whilst it took on water from a well originally dug by the whalers. On Boxing Day 1960 we enjoyed a football match against their team, though the result reflected on the standard, though not the spirit, of Deception Disunited and we lost 9–2. The *Bahia Aguerre*, a large provisioning ship, arrived but was forced aground by a strong gale. A tug boat, the *Chiriguano*, tried to pull her afloat, but this proved impossible until some of her oil was transferred to the *Punta Ninfas*.

The Chileans used three ships to carry out their relief programme, the *Yelcho*, *Piloto Pardo* and *Lientur*, a tug. The *Piloto Pardo* was a fine ship, similar in general design and use to the *John Biscoe*, where Brian and I had benefited from the excellent dental surgery on board.

The arrival of all of these ships often brought an influx of visitors to the base. From the FIDS ships, this meant an augmentation to the meagre labour supply; catching the new Fids full of enthusiasm for a few days helped considerably to advance the progress of the buildings.

Visitors from foreign ships, though welcomed, often resulted in a cut in our work force, for one or other of us had to show them around the base and entertain them in the bar, just as we enjoyed similar courtesies when visiting their bases and ships.

The arrival of the ships naturally brought about changes in personnel. Only Ron Lord and Tom Sumner of the old base members were staying to share the aircraft duties with Bob Bond and Roy Brand. Ian Jackson, Paddy English and Pete Bates were returning home; Frank Fitton was going to the new base at Adelaide Island, Fraser Whyte to the Argentine Islands, and Brian Westlake to Signy Island, whilst Mike Tween, Roger Matthews and I were bound for Stonington Island, though as things turned out, I went on from there to Fossil Bluff.

There was a natural resentment amongst the few remaining 'old guard' as new men arrived and started making rapid improvements to 'our' hut. Water pipes appeared along the walls of the kitchen, a well was initiated under the hut, and talk of a 'ski lift' was briefly in the air. However, the natural enthusiasm waned, especially as everyone began to realise just how much work there was to be done. We soon grew to know the new arrivals, and spent a few very happy weeks with them whilst awaiting our own transfer. Led by John Killingbeck, the new base members added a great surge of effort to keep the work going that was already well under way.

We celebrated Christmas in style, with fourteen of us round the suitably decorated table for dinner. It just happened to be my turn on cook. We had a good larder at this time, so we enjoyed a sea food hors d'oeuvre and asparagus followed by turkey with various trimmings, baked potatoes, peas, sprouts etc. Christmas pudding and brandy sauce followed. We also had plenty of wine. Our tea was provided by individual enterprise; Fraser made some ice cream, Paddy cooked some mince pies, Ray McGowan baked a fruit cake; it all made for a very convivial occasion. Five officers from the *Punta Ninfas* joined us in the evening, participating fully in the food, drink and tobacco.

The buildings began to take shape. By mid-January, the foundations of both hangar and diesel shed were completed, and a framework of iron girders began to appear. Before the diesel shed itself could be built it was necessary to install the generators in their final

94

position. The two engines each weighed two and a half tons and they had to be moved from the beach up the 120-yard slope to the proposed site. Tom adapted the tractor for winching purposes, and we managed to get steel rollers under the engines. By a very long process of winching each engine along the baseboard of an Otter crate, both were ready for lifting onto their plinth after two days of work. Fortunately we had Pete Secker, for he put up a 'stick', a latticed framework for lifting heavy weights. This device completed the lifting process quickly and safely. In the middle of our efforts fifteen Chileans arrived on a social visit; fortunately they soon registered our inability to socialise and disappeared!

The arrival of the *Kista Dan* in early January caused a brief stoppage to the building operations. All day on the day of its arrival in the vicinity of the island, gales raged and made it inadvisable for the ship to enter through the Bellows, where funnelled winds could have damaged the new Otter crates stowed on deck. Late in the day, the gales eased and it became certain that the ship would soon come in. I walked up to Neptune's Window, a large gash in the Cathedral Crags from where the Bransfield Strait could be viewed. A mile away, under the still glowering clouds, the proud little red ship wallowed along through the waves which were still breaking over it. My mind went back almost a year, to the days I had spent on board when the ice proved victorious in preventing our attempt to reach Marguerite Bay. I wondered if the same thing might happen again in the coming months, though this time it was to be the *John Biscoe* that would take up the challenge. The next day, the weather conditions ameliorated, and the task of unloading the new Otter went ahead. The experience gained from last year enabled us to manage the job with comparative ease and soon the fuselage and wings were ashore.

Later on in January, we learnt that the *John Biscoe* would soon be starting on its second voyage of the season. We who were now to leave, started packing and preparing for our departure from Deception Island. I felt distinctly sorry, though I was very pleased to be going south. After Frank had left, I looked after the dogs. They continued to give us all great pleasure. Occasionally I would take a break from helping the builders, harness up Bueno, Sandra and Shuna to a small sledge which we had, and go for a run. The rookery was full of interest at this time, for there were many young chicks. On the way I noticed that several crevasses had opened up close to our normal route, and I mused on the incredible luck which seemed to preserve visitors to the island. The ships disgorged men who rambled everywhere, with no precaution at all, and without ever consulting the base members, who generally develop an awareness of where dangers lie.

The tempo of packing speeded up, last trips were made in the boats, and last walks taken to favoured spots. On January 21st the *John Biscoe*, newly painted red, entered the harbour. The next day I moved on board and looked landwards to the base. Cloud made it look dismal. The dogs barked as feeding time approached, at 3.00 p.m. I knew that someone would be taking the temperatures, that some men would be at work on the building, that the water tanks would be filled, dinner cooked, and coal buckets refilled. For whatever else happens and amidst the excitement of arrivals and departures, someone would always be carrying out the work which kept bases such as this continuously occupied.

11

To Marguerite Bay

A group of us sat in the 'Fidary' (the saloon), of the *John Biscoe* as it lay at anchor in the small natural harbour of Port Lockroy, Goudier Island. In the comfortably appointed room, whose armchairs, seats and tables provided a pleasant centre for sea-going Fids, we chatted about the voyage of the *Kista Dan*, which had, in the previous year, been unable to carry out the work that the *John Biscoe* was now about to attempt. Someone purchased a round of cans of beer, and distributed them, interrupting the game of darts that was in progress. It was a pleasant atmosphere in which to recall the amusing aspects of earlier voyages, and to muse on the prospects for the season ahead, though we already knew, from an aircraft reconnaissance, that open water extended down the coast of Adelaide Island as far as could be seen from its northern point. We felt distinctly cheerful at the prospects. Travel on board the FIDS ships was a very comfortable matter. Two men shared well-appointed cabins with washing facilities, wardrobes and a small table (except on the *Kista Dan*, where four of us shared a very small cabin deep down in the ship). There was sufficient seating for private gatherings, should one wish to listen to music or pursue other occupations away from the Fidary. Bathrooms, showers, a comfortable dining room and the Fidary were all conducive to making the many months of travel a pleasant experience. Each Fid took a turn at carrying out the minor chores – serving the meals or cleaning out the communal rooms (and the cabins) – but except at times of loading and unloading, everyone had considerable freedom to enjoy the ever-changing environment from the deck.

Whilst we chatted, the launch had taken a party ashore to visit the base hut. Port Lockroy was one of the first two bases opened by FIDS in 1944. Its first commander (as they were then called), was Lieutenant Commander James Marr, who had been the boy scout chosen to go with Shackleton on the *Quest* Expedition of 1921. In its early years the base carried out a programme of meteorological observations, but as the number of bases increased, it became a base for conducting geophysical work.

We had moved from Deception Island earlier that day, though the murk had hidden the impressive scenery under a pall of cloud, and our main interest was in watching the occasional penguin break through the motionless waters of the Gerlache Strait. Port Lockroy, too, did not reveal its beauties as it had done in the previous year when the glistening ice faces which surround the bay, and the tiny Goudier Island, which bears the base hut, had sparkled as a jewel. Now, only glimpses of the Sierra du Fief, the towering mountains behind the island, peeped through the cloud, while in the bay lumps of ice – growlers and bergy bits – loitered aimlessly around, awaiting the wind which would send them on their way.

The next day too, as we made our passage to the Argentine Islands, cloud veiled the splendours of the coast, and most of us stayed within the warmth of the ship. As we approached Meek Channel (of infamous memory!) a great berg could be seen completely blocking the entrance. We therefore had to turn north to circumnavigate Uruguay Island, along some tortuous channels whose reefs occasion-ally scraped the hull of the ship. Eventually, we anchored at the scene of the previous year's collision, and at the point where the Beaver had made its last landing. Several days were spent at Base F, for we had to collect all the dogs, personnel and equipment for Base T, the new base to be established on Adelaide Island. The party who had wintered in Wordie House on the Argentine Islands, and whose programme had been frustrated when the Beaver was lost, were naturally delighted to be back on board, and once more on target.

Ice still blocked Stella Creek, the best passage to Wordie House on Winter Island, and this necessitated many boat journeys along a narrow passage separating Galindez Island from Skua Island. Most of the Argentine Islands are ice-capped, and the ice cap of Galindez Island terminated in an abrupt ice cliff well over 100 feet in height, which directly overlooked our narrow route. Every time as we crept by, anxious thoughts were directed up to some of the ice pinnacles, which must fall down sooner or later ... but fortune was with us, and the evacuation of Wordie House was accomplished safely.

By the time that the *John Biscoe* was ready for departure, the ship looked like one of the early pioneering polar vessels. Every nook and cranny of the hold was filled; the decks were loaded with sledges, timbers, boats and vast quantities of fuel, and every gangway and deck provided berths for a great many dogs. We already had nine dogs on board; by the time we had picked up forty-two more from Wordie, there were fifty-one huskies (plus three puppies) who made an incredible noise as soon as they heard the axes cutting up the seals, and more especially as the odours wafted towards them, and they each received their portion, howling delightedly. Everywhere we walked, a bundle of fur leaped excitedly around, hoping for a pat. If one stood on the foc's'le, there was a good chance that Bass, or Worthy, or Guinness, or Taurus – Bill Tracy's dogs – would rudely intrude into some reverie engendered by the passing scenery, by using whoever was standing there as a lamp post! How the bosun, whose clean decks were a delight to the eye in normal times, loved the huskies!

The attempt to reach Marguerite Bay was on. We left the islands on January 28th, and Captain Johnston took the ship out via the French Passage, then southwards down the west coast of the appropriately named Biscoe Islands, a few miles off-shore. We had a good run crossing the Antarctic Circle the same day, then we sailed through Matha Strait to Hanusse Fiord, which separates Adelaide Island from Liard Island and the mainland. There was a possibility of calling in at the unoccupied Detaille Island base in this area in order to check on its condition. Captain Johnston anchored the ship overnight near some pack ice, which gave us some concern after the previous year. However, there was no problem and, although we were unable to reach Detaille Island on the next day, we were able to speed down the full length of Adelaide Island. We didn't mind the presence of a great deal of low cloud, which enabled us to see little but the wall of the ice piedmont which covers the whole of the western coast of Adelaide Island. No indeed; most of our eyes were watching gratefully the black waters ahead, whose openness after two years made all the preparations by FIDS staff in Stanley and London worthwhile.

Towards evening the exciting panorama of Marguerite Bay unfolded as the cloud lifted. That there were still several miles of ice we knew from the men at Stonington Island (those who had been flown to Horseshoe Island and who had sledged down to Base E in the spring). That we had reached so far, so early, gave plenty of time for the remainder of the ice to break out. I stood on the deck with Jim Wilson, a diesel mechanic from the Cheviots who, like myself, enjoyed many hours outside just watching. Twice he had been scheduled to winter in Marguerite Bay, and twice he had returned north to winter at Admiralty Bay. Now, at last, as he was on his way home to England, he was able to see the magnificent landscapes that had eluded him. He wanted to come back, so he did – in 1962. What fantastic scenery it was too, a world of incredible beauty, seen by so few, but never forgotten. Jagged mountain ranges and smooth snow fields; black rock, pure white snow; cruel glaciers, blue light; a whole world perpetually dormant except for its wildlife.

We rounded the southern point of Adelaide Island and headed towards the Leonie Islands, beyond which, at Rothera Point, the new base was to have been built. Twelve miles from our destination we reached the fast ice and anchored for the night, close to the black screes of Jenny Island. As the sun declined, the light on the cloud intensified into a sunset of supreme glory silhouetting the shadowed lands to the north beneath a sky of rose and pink and purple and bronze. On the next day:

> *January 30th.* I was on met. today so immediately after breakfast I went up to the bridge to do the observations. Today has been perfect with the sun shining all day, temps. reaching 41°F and no wind. After an early bash at the ice it was decided to wait for the ice to break out. After lunch a boat went ashore on Jenny Island and we thoroughly enjoyed a 3-hour walk. The island is precipitous on three sides, with steep scree slopes. Round the western side it is possible to climb the 1,200 foot peak, but I didn't leave sufficient time for this. We found evidence of an old FIDS camp site. What a rapturous view we had today. The panorama of Marguerite Bay is breathtaking. Alexander Island stood out beautifully some 150 miles to the southwest. The fast ice was littered with seals (someone counted 62). The scene was paradise!

The rate of the break-up of fast ice depends on wind and currents rather than temperatures, a factor which often causes an unseasonal break-out of the ice and has often ruined plans for sea journeys, and indeed has caused loss of life. Less than three years earlier, in May 1958, three sledgers from Horseshoe Island, who were travelling across the bay ice to visit the emperor penguin rookery on the Dion Islands, were caught when the ice broke up, and were lost. High

100

temperatures inevitably have a long-term effect on the ice but they are not the prime cause of the break-up. Generally, the break-up takes the form of a movement of huge rafts of ice, which hinge along a line of weakness in the fast ice and drift out to sea. The effect of the swell in creating the lines of weakness can be seen anywhere near the edge of a belt of ice which breaths rhythmically up and down as if somnolent before lazily shedding a great floe. Sometimes, the bay ice breaks out in one huge body, perhaps a higher than usual tide works on the tide crack, so that in the space of a few hours, ice from horizon to horizon gives way to completely open water. On May 22nd 1960, whilst we were at Deception Island, a severe earthquake in Chile caused tsunamis to develop across the Pacific Ocean which hit Hawaii and Japan; there was also a noticeable effect to the south which caused disturbances in the ice and would have had an effect on the tide cracks.

For several days the *John Biscoe* waited, and we on board watched. Unfortunately, the weather was calm and there was no swell, so the break-up was very slow, with just an occasional raft of ice floating silently away, eventually to be churned into brash ice and then melt. Captain Johnston set the might of the ship against the ice, and long charges were made which threw the ship into, or even onto, the ice, before it slid slowly back into the water to join the seething ice shattered from its parent body. Though the weight of the ship carried it far, and though great stretches of ice yielded, the general resistance of the ice would have made the battle interminably long; reluctantly, therefore, it was decided to abandon Rothera Point for the base site and investigate the possibility of establishing the base on the south-west corner of Adelaide Island.

Those responsible for choosing the sites for new bases had to bear in mind several factors:

Firstly, the base had to be accessible to ships, often a difficult factor in the days when submerged rocks had not been charted.

Secondly, the base site had to be situated with safety in mind, away from the threat of avalanches, for example, and above the level of even exceptionally high tides (in 1946 the old BGLE hut on the Argentine Islands was completely washed away by a tsunami).

101

Thirdly there must be adequate space for the base to function properly; sledging bases required a large area for spanning the dogs; the impending use of aircraft necessitated large areas for runways, either on rock or on ash (as at Deception Island), or on suitable glacier or shelf ice (as had been used at Stonington Island and at Halley Bay).

Fourthly, and of huge importance, the base had to have reasonable access to the area in which field work was planned, often a difficult problem on a coast whose ice and snow spilled into the sea by way of crevassed glaciers or precipitous ice cliffs.

All of these factors had to be taken into account. There had been examples in the past when the judgment was made purely on accessibility for the ship and the suitability of the site for building purposes. Thus the bases at Danco Island and Detaille Island were both opened in 1956 and both closed in 1959, whilst the base at Prospect Point only operated for two years, from 1957 to 1959; all because access to the main areas of work was impracticable.

With such factors as these in the mind of John Green, SecFids, who with others had to make the decision, the *John Biscoe* abandoned the edge of the fast ice and moved tentatively along the coast. On the way, the opportunity was taken to land on the islets of Guebriand and Dion, where we built cairns on the highest spots, on which the surveyors from Adelaide Island would be able to fix their theodolites.

A small rock promontory on the coast of Adelaide Island several miles to the south-east of Cape Adriasola and facing the Henkes Islets, a long trail of small rocky islands, was visited on February 1st. It apparently satisfied the conditions necessary for building a base, but the possibility of a route inland was unknown. The following day, therefore, John Green and some of the Fids who would be based at the new location went ashore to prospect a route. The way proved unimaginably easy as the rocks were backed by a gently sloping ice piedmont whose crevasse-free surface afforded an easy route towards the mountains. Furthermore, it was certain that aircraft could land and take off in safety. A brief hydrographic survey was made, the decision taken, and the *John Biscoe* moved slowly landwards, anchoring as close to the shore as the submarine contours permitted. Work was soon under way:

February 3rd. Cloudless, calm, beautiful. But we worked really hard today unloading stores for Base T. The landing place is very bad and given any sort of (bad) weather it would be quite unapproachable. So all day long, scow load and lifeboat load continually passed from ship to shore ... I worked in the hold during the morning and afternoon. Sand, shingle, wood, food, nutrican, coal etc provided an endless task. 21 of the dogs went ashore too.

The first cargo to go ashore was mainly made up of building materials, so that a small building party could set to work immediately. The FIDS huts were prefabricated, so the site work consisted of laying the foundations then putting the sections together. Within a few days gangs of cement mixers had joined the builders and the foundations were set, and the hut began to take shape. Other gangs spent many hours bringing the loads of cargo ashore, loads on which the life of the base would depend. Supplies sufficient for two years were taken in, so as to offset the problems caused in the case of a failure to relieve the base. Food, coal, other fuel, sledging food for men and dogs, extra clothing, medical supplies, radios and radio spares, and general electrical equipment, all had to be carefully thought about by staff in London, long before the ships sailed. Soon, sufficient advance had been made to enable twenty-one of the huskies, and the pups, to be taken ashore. They certainly took delight in the clean snow in which they could roll, after so many days on the hard wooden or iron decks of the ship which they could not help but foul.

Before the *John Biscoe* was finally able to anchor, and before we would be overwhelmed with the work of establishing a base, a group of Fids were given the opportunity to go on the ship's jolly boat to visit nearby Avian Island. We wended our way between icebergs which had recently calved from the ice front a few hundred yards away. What a paradise we discovered! For several hours we wandered amongst many thousands of adelie penguins, who breed there. Along the beaches scores of seals of all varieties slept in the summer sun, whilst in the dark waters close by, leopard seals were on the look-out for the first penguins to jump in, leaving the safety of the rocks and the little gaggle with whom they had been standing. Inland, I met up with Brian Sparke, destined for Stonington Island as the base doctor, sitting at the edge of a clear pond whose still water reflected a group of adelies marching resolutely along, just like ducks round a farmyard pond. Amongst some higher rocks we found giant petrel chicks, whose irate parents hissed at our intrusion, whilst scrawny young

103

Dominican gulls wandered to the edge of the rocks to peer at us. At a rocky face we looked at a large number of blue-eyed cormorants and their young. As usual, the skuas wheeled back and forth, either threatening us or carrying their spoils from their depredations of the penguin rookeries. Trying to justify our incursion into this wildlife paradise, Brian and I helped Jeff Stokes and Howard Chapman complete their survey cairn at the highest point.

The excellence of the weather and the speed of the work caused such a quick advancement of the new base that it was decided to cross Marguerite Bay towards Stonington Island, to see if work could be started on the relief of that base, where a new hut was also to be built to replace the aging structure already there. Before we left, however, the two Otters flew down from Deception Island and landed easily on the sloping runway of the ice piedmont. The original aircraft had first been off-loaded at Deception Island on January 27th 1960; it took well over a year before the first flight could be made from Deception to a properly checked, marked-out and semi-permanent runway on February 9th 1961; progress indeed!

We spent five days away from Base T. The ice enabled us to get to within twenty miles of Stonington, but no nearer. We had struggled through a few miles of large floes until we came to the edge of the fast ice, which barred the approach to the whole coast; we were halted at Latitude 68°06′S and Longitude 67°45′W. Longingly some of us looked towards Horseshoe Island, a few miles to the north-east, whose obvious attractions the ice had already caused some of us to forgo; would we ever see it? We could see Pourquoi Pas Island and the red rocks of Red Rock Ridge, and we could see Millerand Island and Neny Island, behind whose bulk lay our destination. Frustration began to set in. Once more we watched the ice, especially whenever a length broke off and drifted away as though it had all the time in the world – we wanted to give it a good kick, such was our impatience. Although the ice was breaking up, it was obviously going to take many days to go. Such days are extremely valuable in a season limited to a month at most, so plans were reformulated to make the most of the time. As part of the Stonington Island programme of work, a field hut was to be established in King George VI Sound from which scientific work would at last begin on Alexander Island and on the southern extensions of Graham Land. Originally, the hut was to have been flown in from Stonington Island, but as the airfield was already in commission at Adelaide Island, this part of the programme could be carried out from there, whilst giving the ice which now frustrated us even more time to break away.

At this time, now that the base at Fossil Bluff was about to be established, we started to mull over the disposition of the Fids. Fourteen of us were to be based at Stonington, but inevitably some would be deployed further south at the new base. Various rumours passed through the Fidary – how many would go?, who?, would there be dogs? etc. Eventually on February 19th, John Cunningham, the base leader, informed me that, along with John Smith and Brian Taylor, I would be part of the first wintering party on Alexander Island at Fossil Bluff. I had mixed feelings at the news. It would certainly be an exciting venture, and a new experience. I hankered, however, for the chance to run a dog team, and that was unlikely to be possible at Fossil Bluff, given the difficulty of transporting the dogs and their food and the sledges; in any case, there were several dog experts already in the party. Also, Stonington Island was a place of such history that I wanted to be a part of it. These mixed thoughts were in my mind in the days ahead.

Also in the minds of all of us at that time was the terrible news that came to us from Signy Island (South Orkneys), where Roger Filer had been killed in an accident whilst bird watching. Roger was a meteorologist who had been with us for training, at Stanmore, and who was a popular colleague. It served to remind us all that the Antarctic was a place of danger; Roger was the sixth Fid to lose his life in the three years 1958, 1959 and 1960.

We sailed back to Adelaide Island. The hut was now really beginning to be properly established and comfortable as a result of the hard work of the six men there. More unloading commenced. The dogs were put to work and the equipment and materials for Fossil Bluff were laboriously pulled up the piedmont to the aircraft. There was a whole hut to be loaded, in sections, together with all the food, fuel, generator, kitchen range and multiplicity of other equipment that would support life at Fossil Bluff. Superb weather enabled the two Otters to each make two flights a day to Fossil Bluff, piloted by Ron Lord, Paddy English and Bob Bond.

It was at Adelaide Island that we first had the chance to see one of the new Muskegs at work in the Antarctic. The Bombardier Muskeg was a tracked vehicle specifically designed for work in wilderness areas. The haulage work necessary to move the supplies from the shore to the airstrip was being carried out by the untiring dogs. However, the work involved so many trips by the drivers and the dogs that only with the greatest of efforts could supplies keep up with the demands of the two Otters. One of the Muskegs was therefore taken ashore. This proved extremely difficult for Brian Bowler (down to the Antarctic specifically to take charge of the Muskegs), who had to drive it quickly from a platform which had been rigged up over the top of a ballasted scow, then straight up the steep ice slope near the landing ground. The transition from the platform to the land, as the weight of the Muskeg tilted the scow, was worrying, but the transition went as planned, fortunately, and the Muskeg was safely ashore. The machine, with its remarkable power and manoeuvrability, made a dramatic impact on the work in hand. It was able to pull the cargo sledge carrying well over a ton of stores up the slope. Within a few trips, the job was done, a great triumph for machine over dogs, especially when the Muskeg later made a quick inland trip of some thirty miles to lay depots for future field parties. This was the first time that FIDS had used Muskegs down the Graham Land peninsula, and it may be that this was the first moment when the most probable method of future travel was suddenly recognised. Husky dogs were not suitable for mass haulage; their contribution was in getting field parties to areas too remote for land machines.

When the pilots flew to Fossil Bluff they needed company in the plane. Lots of Fids therefore travelled with them and all of them brought back reports on the state of the ice west of Stonington Island. Great rafts of ice were continually breaking away and drifting off into the Bellingshausen Sea. From the air, too, a great stream of icebergs trailing round the southern point of Adelaide Island from Laubeuf Fiord was observed. These bergs gave many of us on board the ship some distinctly uncomfortable moments; the nature of the anchorage made a quick repositioning of the ship very difficult, and the endless number which trundled along the deep water channels seemed to take a liking to giving the ship a hearty nudge. On one of the 'nights of terror' which we later laughed about, a corner of a berg elbowed its way through a porthole of the cabin in which Arthur Fraser was peacefully sleeping, spilling ice everywhere and twisting the door frame. On another occasion, while I was on night meteorological duty at 3.00 a.m., I peered out to see an iceberg whose height was level with the bridge. The night watchman too leaned over the side, deliberating on whether or not to call the mate. Too late; before he could move, the berg gently touched the side of the ship, dislodged some of the lumps of ice it was carrying, became unbalanced, and started to roll. As the huge mass rolled, its deep submarine foot levered the ship upwards; great cataracts of water rushed from its sides as they were snatched up in its roll. It scratched deeply many plates, spilled fragments from its huge mass, each weighing several hundredweight, one of which peeled away a section of the hand rails, and continued to roll drunkenly in the water. As worried Fids appeared on deck, it was good to know that the basic roll had been away from the ship and not towards it.

'Iceberg corner' gave us many such nights of terror and many times Captain Johnston moved the ship; it was always a gamble, however, as to which bergs were hazardous and which would pass peacefully by.

By February 28th, well over half of the flights necessary to establish Fossil Bluff had been made. The season was well advanced, and Stonington had still not been relieved. For the second time, the *John Biscoe* headed towards the south-east. This time we were able to get to within four or five miles of Neny Island, a total distance of up to seven miles from the base. Time was pressing, and once more the ship was thrown at the ice edge, nibbling away bits of it over several hours. We gained several hundred yards, but really not enough to justify a continuation of this action. We anchored at the ice edge with large ice anchors. Once more the Muskegs were called on, the ice, some six to eight feet thick, offering a good surface. Both Muskegs were carefully lowered onto the ice and their sledges loaded up. After a first, light load had been secured, a cautious drive was made to the base. The route proved admirable. Apart from a few tide cracks, the surface was exactly what was needed, so a start on the task of relieving Base E was made in earnest. Then followed several days of immense effort, as a result of which Stonington Island was relieved for the first time since 1958.

In February 2000, exactly forty years on, there were, naturally, many changes to be seen. The base at Port Lockroy is in pristine condition, thanks to the endeavours of Ben Hodges and others, and is occupied during the summer season. The big difference is that it is now a fascinating museum, with each room reflecting the past: generator room, radio shack, dark room, kitchen, bunk room, with lots of memorabilia from old food boxes to anoraks and skis. Approximately 7,000 visitors came to the port in the millennium summer – though not all were able to go ashore.

Base T at Adelaide Island, which we built during that summer of 1961, is still a base, but not a British one. It was closed in March 1977, due to problems with crevasses on the runway, and was handed over to Chile, who renamed it Carvajal. The huts that we built were still in excellent condition. Around the base, however, there had been a massive retreat of the ice piedmont with the consequent exposure of much larger areas of rock than forty years earlier. We had a zodiac ride to Avian Island, but the big change is that it is now protected under the 1991 Protocol on Environmental Protection and is no longer accessible to us mere tourists! From our viewpoint, low down in the zodiac, however, there seemed to be just as rich a variety of wildlife as ever.

On February 13th 2000 we were able to reach Rothera Point, our prime objective in both 1960 and 1961, our failure in those years resulting in the establishment of the base near Cape Adriasola. It was quite obvious to us as we looked at Rothera, with its long rock runway, a proper quay for ships to tie up to, a very large area for a variety of base buildings and aircraft facilities, that this was a very superior site (provided that ice doesn't prevent its relief too frequently). Of course, Rothera has developed into an ultra-modern scientific base of the highest calibre. Rothera was the last base to have husky dogs; obviously we saw none at all, anywhere. We did see plenty of evidence of the army of machines that has taken their place.

In the garages of the houses in which I had lived in Worcestershire and Cornwall for twenty years, I had a large trunk addressed to C.J. PEARCE BASE Y HORSESHOE ISLAND. I had lugged it around for over two years (1960 to 1962) without setting foot on the island. Now at last on February 11th 2000, I managed to reach the base. Even though it was late in the evening, and twilight, the visit was magical. The base had closed in August 1960 when the four sledgers moved down to Stonington Island. Because of its inaccessibility it had been virtually untouched by visitors, and entering the hut was a visit back to the past – all the paraphernalia of the working base remained – once more in a scenically magic setting.

As for Stonington Island, our final prize eluded us. For although we reached 68°14′S and 67°02′W, and there was something approaching a three-tenths covering of pack ice, the captain of the *Lyubov Orlova* was concerned about safety, and declined to sail the last few miles. We could see the environs, and the huge North East Glacier (which flows from the plateau and formerly linked Stonington Island to the mainland), and Red

108

Rock Ridge, and poignantly the sad memorial to two base members who died in a blizzard in 1966, but we could not visit the island. We took pleasure, however, in knowing that our location was the furthest south ever made by a cruise ship.

12

Stonington at Last – and Further Southwards

Stonington Island shares with Hope Bay a history of polar research, travel and incident which has given them an aura of romanticism. Apart from being the starting point for sledging journeys of immense distances and duration, both had periods around the middle of the 20th century when the land around their bases was shared by expeditions from other countries – the cause of particularly interesting events. In the case of Hope Bay, the other nationals present were Argentinians, in the case of Stonington Island they were from the USA. The most important international event at Hope Bay came three years after the hut had been burned down (resulting in the tragic deaths of two of the base members), and the base had been closed. When the ship carrying a British team arrived in 1952 to establish a new base, the Argentinians had already established their own base – Esperanza – and they fired shots over the heads of the landing party who were bringing the first supplies ashore. The Fids were sent back to the ship (an older *John Biscoe*) at gun point. Order was restored when *HMS Burghead Bay* arrived, since when harmonious relations have prevailed.

Stonington Island was first occupied by Americans in 1940 to 1941, one of two bases – the other was at Little America – set up as part of the United States Antarctic Service Expedition whose commanding officer was Rear Admiral Byrd. Captain Richard Black was in charge at East Base (Stonington Island), with Finn Ronne also being assigned there. During that expedition Ronne and Carl Eklund sledged to the southern extremities of King George VI Sound on one of the most famous pioneering journeys in this whole region.

Finn Ronne led his own expedition back to Stonington Island for the year from March 1947 to March 1948. When the Ronne Antarctic Research Expedition arrived in mid-March, they were greeted by Major Pierce-Butler, the British base commander. Stonington Island had been established as a British base in 1946 and was then in the second year of its operation. Relationships were very difficult to begin

111

with; the 1940 American base, which Finn Ronne was to use, had been badly damaged during the intervening years by visiting sailors, and Ronne thought that the Britons might have been responsible. Finn Ronne had major leadership and personality difficulties in running the base and he was later very critical of members of his team in his published account of the expedition. He also had with him the first women to winter in the Antarctic, his wife Edith, and Jenny Darlington, wife of Harry Darlington. The stories of that year – of how the American base members fraternised more and more with the Brits, of 'disciplinary' measures taken by Ronne (who formally relieved Darlington, his third in command, of his position and all his flying duties), of shared sledge journeys, of major joint achievements, of crevasse rescues, and mutual help to each other – were set out in two books. Finn Ronne retold the story of his expedition in *Antarctic Conquest*; Kevin Walton recorded the year from the British viewpoint in his book, *Two Years in the Antarctic*; both were compulsive reading for all Fids, as indeed was a third book on the expedition, *My Antarctic Honeymoon* by Jenny Darlington.

Stonington Island continued to be occupied by members of FIDS until February 1950, when it was closed after there had been major problems in relieving it. The ship was unable to relieve the base in 1949, so three members who had gone to the base in 1947 for two years were forced to remain for three. The base reopened again in March 1958, with six men. Once again fast ice prevented access at the end of their year, and the men had to sledge up to Horseshoe Island, where helicopters from an American icebreaker flew them out. Our failure to relieve the base in early 1960 has already been described; however, the four men who had been flown in to Horseshoe Island in March 1960 sledged down to Stonington and reopened it in August of that year. Now, on March 1st 1961, we were almost there, certainly near enough to commence the unloading. We had an understandable sense of elation!

The island, named Stonington after the home port of American whalers in Connecticut, USA, is situated at 68°11'S, 67°00'W, on the eastern shore of Marguerite Bay. It is a tiny island, a few hundred yards in length, but it had a major attraction in being linked to the mainland by a huge glacier, the North East Glacier, whose mass of ice spills into the sea to the north and south of the island. It was this glacier that afforded access inland to the plateau, and over to the eastern coast of Graham Land, which enabled innumerable surveyors and geologists, with their supporting teams, to map and carry out detailed geological studies in the vast hinterland. The seaward panorama from the base is interrupted by the mass of Neny Island, whose scree-covered slopes reach an altitude of 2,216 feet. To the south, the snow and ice-covered coastline extends limbs to the sea at Roman Four and Red Rock Ridge, whilst to the north Millerand Island, with an altitude of 3,179 feet, looks ruggedly out towards the vastness of the Bellingshausen Sea.

My own arrival at Stonington Island was by way of the Muskeg. The trip was exhilarating as the Muskeg trundled over the thick sea ice, passing to the south of Neny Island, before making the run northwards to the base. The loaded sledges, each capable of carrying two tons of stores, slid easily over the ice as the wide tracks of the vehicle sped along. When we reached the tide crack, the loose ice creaked unwillingly, and the Muskeg hauled its cargo rapidly up the slope towards the growing pile of equipment, building materials and other stores. I was at Stonington at last, and like all other Fids new to a base, my immediate desire was to have a look inside the hut.

Under a rapidly encroaching snow drift, I found the door and entered. In the small habitable portion of the hut, Peter Forster and Peter Grimley had already prepared a welcome brew of tea. They, with Charlie LeFeuvre and Dr Tony Davies, had been flown into Horseshoe Island in March of 1960. After wintering at the more comfortable base to the north, in August they had sledged down to Stonington Island, from where their field work could be centred. During the part of the year which was left to them, they had been able to carry out considerable geological and survey work on the eastern flank of Graham Land. As the summer advanced, and the ship drew near, they spent more time at the base, or what remained of it. The thirteen-year-old hut was in a poor state of repair. During the years when it had been unoccupied, snow and ice had filled the majority of the rooms. However, one small room had been triumphantly reclaimed, in which the four men had lived, almost on top of one another. It was in this room that we sipped tea and had a meal cooked from the last remnants of food taken in when the base had last been relieved in March of 1958.

We wandered around the island. The dogs were typically excitable, but the difficulties of providing seal meat, when so few were able to come up through the ice, had given them a slightly emaciated appearance, though the ship would soon be bringing in a supply on which they would soon fatten up.

The American huts were now completely iced in and impossible to access. It needs but a small hole through which snow can blow to cause a room, or a hut, to ice up. The powdery snow covers the floor, melts and refreezes, and gradually the thickness of the ice deepens so that the doors cannot be opened, and eventually the buildings are reclaimed by the elements they were designed to withstand. Old snow vehicles lay rusted and forgotten; the tide gauge hung precariously over the waters of Back Bay, lots of wood and lengths of cable lay scattered about, there was even the skeleton of a dead dog which could be seen in one of the rooms, all providing a mute testimony to previous endeavours by man.

Work was carried on at a frantic pace. From as early as 6.00 a.m. to after 11.00 p.m. the Muskegs toiled backwards and forwards between the ship and the base, speeding (in their own way) across the ice as if it was a great concrete highway. They carried supplies for a new hut, food and fuel sufficient for at least two years, as well as all the personal belongings for the base men. The thirty dogs who had been on the ship since January 26th were run to the base in teams, a joyful affair after sixty days on board. Cracks appeared in the highway from time to time, and eventually the whole highway drifted out to sea, though by the time that had happened the Muskegs were ashore, not to venture onto the sea ice again until they were prepared for the journey to Fossil Bluff.

John Smith, Brian Taylor and I were not present to witness the final break-out of the ice. Before unloading operations had got very far, our minds turned to other preparations. We were to fly to Fossil Bluff as soon as possible, to spend the winter there before joining in the summer sledging programme, when the dogs would arrive with the Muskegs and men from Stonington Island. We had learned of our deployment on February 19th; now, twelve days later, we would soon be on our way – not a lot of time to prepare and adjust to a distinctly unusual posting! The food for a year had already been flown in, together with the materials for the field hut, coal and fuel. The food

114

needed a certain amount of augmentation, and we needed many other things to enable us to live with a reasonable degree of comfort and to travel about the icy environment safely. John and Brian and I spent as much time as we could in collecting a great assortment of supplies from the existing base, greatly helped by Peter Forster, whose two Antarctic seasons enabled him to suggest all kinds of items which we might not otherwise have taken. The shortness of time in planning for the base at Fossil Bluff meant that the type of food and other supplies was not as fully thought through as was normally the case; this was to give us some difficulties later on! We had expected to leave on March 3rd, but cloudy conditions ruled out flying on that day, so we had to wait until the next day.

Saturday March 4th dawned brilliantly sunny and crisp. The sun on the snowy hills dazzled our eyes, and the nip in the air sharpened our awareness of the environment as we looked appreciatively at the majestic world around us. We moved down to the airstrip, an area of thick ice a few yards away from an ice cliff on the southern side of Neny Island. We sat on our piles of luggage and awaited the Otters arrival from the piedmont airstrip at Adelaide Island. A Muskeg came out from the base along the highway, lifting the powdery snow as dust. A group of passengers clambered down to wish us well before they carried on down the road and disappeared round the end of Neny Island, making for the ship. Suddenly we heard the noise of the aircraft humming their way over the ice. They hove into view and made a circuit of the airstrip, passing in front of Roman Four; how small they looked against such a background! The weather was so absolutely perfect that it was hard to realise that this was the Antarctic.

The planes landed, and we loaded our gear before climbing aboard; John and Brian in the first plane, piloted by Ron Lord, and myself in the second, piloted by Bob Bond. All was ready and I watched the other Otter take off. Then our conversation became lost under the noise of the engine. The plane accelerated down the runway, stumbling over the occasional irregularity. Soon the bumpiness stopped and we felt the smoothness of the still air as the ice fell away beneath us. Out towards the ice edge we sped, glancing down at the little red ship that was the *John Biscoe*, hugging the ice edge. We turned southwards and gained altitude. The ice below us was sharp-edged and contrasted sharply with the blackness of the waters. Some distance off, a mosaic of ice floes drifted further out to sea. Elsewhere icebergs, recently freed from imprisonment in the fast ice, were beginning their peregrinations northwards.

We flew towards Cape Berteaux, crossing once more the edge of the fast ice which extended north of the Terra Firma Islands, small outcrops of security gratefully named by members of the British Graham Land Expedition, who found themselves on the ice in this area when it was breaking up. We crossed the almost unobtrusive boundary where the snow drifts on the sea ice merged with the ice face of the Wordie Ice Shelf; we looked down on this crevasse-scarred mass of ice, crevasses whose defining edges showed black and gaping from our position high above.

We passed close to Mount Edgell, a rocky nunatak sticking up out of the ice and reaching almost 6,000 feet above sea level, and as we moved on, the great white highway of King George VI Sound was revealed. Some half an hour later, the immensity of our new environment was obscured by a veil of stratus cloud, until we suddenly emerged over Succession Cliffs. Bob pointed to the wooden hut, a minute speck at the foot of the scree at Fossil Bluff. After one hour and fifty minutes we landed, followed a few minutes later by the second Otter, which had flown by a slightly different route. We entered our new home and made a hasty cup of tea for the four airmen. Soon Ron and Tom, and Bob and Roy climbed back into the planes. The engines spluttered to life, the planes moved over the ice and lifted. We watched as they became diminishing specks to the northern horizon and the hum of their engines faded away into the silence of the Sound. The sun shone over Graham Land, nothing stirred; we were truly on our own ...

So we three went inside the hut, sat down and considered.

In October 2001, some thirty ancient FIDS/BAS and Ronne Antarctic Research Expedition men and women, together with other friends and relations, met together in Mystic, Connecticut for a Marguerite Bay reunion. Central to our programme was a visit to Stonington village, the home port of the whaling captain Nathaniel Palmer. Palmer is credited by Americans with the discovery of Antarctica in November 1820, when – having sailed his forty-seven-foot sloop *Hero* some 10,000 nautical miles from Stonington port to Deception Island – he crossed the strait (now known as Bransfield Strait) to Trinity Island, close to the peninsula which, from then on, bore his name on American maps. (Great Britain stuck with the name of Graham Land, after Sir James Graham, the First Lord of the Admiralty at the time of John Biscoe's voyage of discovery in 1832.) Within a few months Palmer had sailed almost the full length of the peninsula to within a few miles of Stonington Island. It was therefore very appropriate for the Americans to give the island the name Stonington when they first occupied it in 1940.

In the garden of the magnificent early 19th century house built by Palmer, three members each from the 1947 FIDS/RARE base groups exchanged memories of that year. Jackie Ronne, wife of Finn Ronne, enjoyed her 83rd birthday with us and she explained how the great tract of ice shelf at the southern shore of the Weddell Sea, named for her by Finn, had been changed. Originally it was known as Edith Ronne Land. Edith had always been known as Jackie and did not like the formality of the name. Eventually it was agreed to remove her forename and it now appears simply as Ronne Ice Shelf. Jackie shared the distinction with Jenny Darlington of being the first women to winter in Antarctica; Jenny was the first woman to become pregnant there.

13

Alexander Island and King George VI Sound

South of Latitude 69°S, the high plateau of Graham Land widens gradually, until between 75°S and 76°S it apparently joins the main mass of the Antarctic continent, though hidden under the huge mantle of ice. West Antarctica is really a huge archipelago, with Graham Land extending approximately 1,000 miles to the north. A cross-section along Latitude 71°S shows that Graham Land is approximately 625 miles from west to east. From its western side, the land rises well over 7,000 feet towards the interior plateau and reaches heights as much as 7,200 feet in the Batterbee Mountains to the west, and over 11,700 feet at Mount Andrew Jackson to the east. Coastal ranges are exposed along the western edge where it overlooks King George VI Sound, though each range is almost overwhelmed by ice moving down from the collecting grounds of the interior. As the land rises steadily towards the plateau, the amount of exposed rock decreases under the canopy of ice and snow. For hundreds of miles the surface is almost flat, with just a few crinkles on it. Occasionally, a small area of arcuate crevasses and an undulation in the surface betoken a rock mass below, and even more occasionally, a black island of rock, a nunatak, rises triumphantly above the landscape of eternal frigidity. Inland Graham Land is like this; even more dramatic, therefore, is the immensity of upland ice rising from this area southwards to the pole and beyond – well in excess of 10,000 feet and with mountains, such as the Vinson Massif, protruding through the ice to a height of over 16,000 feet.

The eastern flank of Graham Land slopes down to the Larsen Ice Shelf, whose vast reservoirs of thick ice are the spawning grounds for many of the itinerant icebergs which emerge from the Weddell Sea. Parts of this area had been surveyed by the joint American and British sledge parties from Stonington Island in 1947; Finn Ronne had also carried out a massive aerial survey of this area.

Within the curve by which Graham Land bends westward towards the Robert English and Eights coast, is situated the large mass of

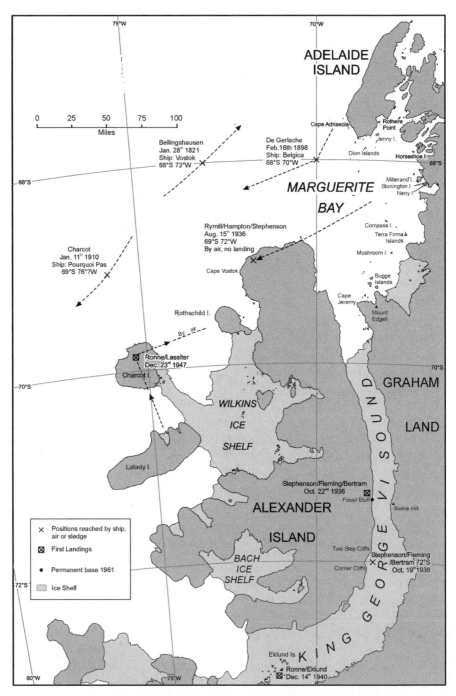

ALEXANDER ISLAND/CHARCOT ISLAND
First sightings and landings
(place names given are as used in 1962)

120

Alexander Island. The first navigator to see the island was a Russian, Thaddeus von Bellingshausen, on January 28th 1821. It was he who gave the island its name in honour of Tsar Alexander. On November 22nd 1893, Captain Evenson in the sealing ship *Hertha*, part of the Larsen Whaling/Sealing Expedition, also saw it and apparently approached the island more closely than had Bellingshausen. Probably other whaling captains saw the island but the most significant sighting after Bellingshausen was made by the crew of the *Belgica*, under the command of Adrien de Gerlache. He sailed into this area, reaching within twenty miles of the coast on February 16th 1898 before, a week or two later, the ship was caught in the ice for over a year. Lecointe, second in command to de Gerlache, charted the north coast of the island on the official map of the Belgian Antarctic Expedition. Jean Baptist Charcot in the *Français*, glimpsed the island on January 13th 1905, and he returned with the *Pourquoi Pas* in 1910. On January 10th of that year he saw the island very clearly, and he also went on to be the first to see Charcot Island, immediately west of Alexander Island, which he named for his father.

The next huge advances were made by the British Graham Land Expedition from their Marguerite Bay base at the Debenham Islands. On August 15th 1936, and on several occasions during the following days, members of the BGLE flew over parts of the island and the Sound, which they named for King George VI. During the period from September to November 1936, three members of the BGLE (Alfred Stephenson, Launcelot Fleming and Colin Bertram) carried out an epic sledge journey as far as 72°S down the Sound. They camped on the coast of Alexander Island, and were the first people ever to set foot on it. Later, in 1940, Finn Ronne and Carl Eklund, sledging from Stonington Island, followed the Sound to the west, south of 72°S, thereby proving that Alexander Island was an island. Finally, Vivian Fuchs and Raymond Adie made another long journey down the Sound in 1949. Fuchs, who was Commander of the whole of the FIDS operation, obviously felt that this area was a most fruitful region for further exploration, and he was able to instigate this next stage in opening up the island by establishing the permanent field station at Fossil Bluff in 1961, and by installing the first residents to live on this island. John, Brian and I were selected for this undertaking; it was a prospect we viewed with excitement and interest.

Alexander Island is some 275 miles from north to south, and between approximately 145 and 150 miles at its broadest in the southern area, and 40 miles at its narrowest, in the north. To the north-west are the islands of Rothschild, Charcot and Latady, all of them connected to the main island by an ice shelf approximately 80 miles across and 90 miles in length, another measure of the hugeness of features in this region. The eastern side of the island has a remarkably straight coastline which rises steeply to the vast Douglas Range, whose peaks reach a highest point of over 10,000 feet at Mount Stephenson, and which extends at great height for 100 miles southwards. Issuing eastwards into the Sound are a great number of large glaciers, those to the south all being named after the planets: Neptune, Uranus, Pluto etc. On the western side of the island the ice slopes steadily down to a coast entirely hidden under a great thickness of ice which, if it melted, would certainly expose a series of islands whose peaks currently appear as nunataks emerging above the ice. In this western area over fifty features are named after composers from Bartok, Beethoven and Boccherini through the alphabet to Vivaldi and Walton. Dvorak is remembered by a small ice rise!

Between the two great land masses of Graham Land and Alexander Island, opening to Marguerite Bay in the north and to the Bellingshausen Sea in the south-west, lies King George VI Sound. It extends for some 300 miles from one entrance to the other, the most northerly 40 miles being an arm of the sea. The shelf itself appears as a great white highway some 150 feet above sea level, a huge mass of ice varying in width between 15 and 20 miles for most of the length ,but extending to over 40 miles in the far south. Obviously the ice descends for hundreds of feet into the depths of the sea below, being certainly grounded in some areas. The shelf ice is fed, apart from the direct sources of precipitation and accumulation, by the scores of glaciers which issue into it from both sides, and whose effects frequently crumple the ice far out into the Sound. It is a grand highway, with some excellent surfaces away from the disturbances caused by the glaciers. In summer time, much of the surface becomes flooded, for the heat of the twenty-four-hour sun for several weeks, even if low on the horizon, melts a considerable amount of snow and sends melt streams along the surface to create melt water lakes which litter the surface. The weight of the ice, suspended by the sea, spreads its mass gradually outwards to the north and to the south and eventually the south-west, and as the leading edges of the ice shelf

122

reach the sea, they break off and drift away, immediately becoming dying icebergs, though they may persist for several years. The ice front has receded considerably over the years.

Standing in the middle of the Sound, at almost any point along it, one can see a marked contrast between the coasts of Alexander Island to the west and Graham Land to the east, although they both share one feature in common: the remarkable straightness of the coasts. Eastwards, the mountains tend to be more jagged and there is no element of uniformity in them. To the west, however, mile after mile of very clearly marked level beds predominate. Sometimes the beds dip or curve; sometimes a great gash has been cut into the land by the work of the glaciers, which trail moraines along their sides and on their surfaces, often dumping the material out into the Sound as their carrying power diminishes. Yet the general impression is one of very even table lands, where bed upon bed has been accumulated in vast thicknesses. Closer inspection shows that there are other differences; to the east colours can frequently be seen where there is a concentration of minerals, patches of blue or green for example, with great black intrusions being quite common. To the west, rocks along the Alexander Island coast contain a high number of well-preserved fossils, indicating a very different mode of formation. Running down the Sound are the major faults which help to explain the reason for this Rift Valley feature.

The differences on the surface reflect the geological history of this area, and these differences imply igneous activity, metamorphism, sedimentation, earthquake, faulting and glaciation. There is also evidence of a profusion of life, and therefore evidence of climatic change as well as of continental drift.

Around the area of Fossil Bluff the whole region is one of sedimentary rocks, and this type of rock extends for approximately fifty miles north and fifty miles south of the Bluff. Apparently there were large areas of shallow water sediments, in and around which a large variety of flora and fauna flourished; we used to visit a nearby valley in which there were layers and layers of belemnites. Brian, our geologist, amassed large collections of ammonites, brachiopods, bivalves, plant remains and other fossil evidence, sometimes only tracks, sometimes a mould, occasionally coprolites, fossil dung; we even acquired some coal during the year. It is therefore possible to visualise a period when, in this area, in shallow waters surrounded by trees and a variety of other plants, submarine molluscs such as pecten and pinna lived with aucellina and inoceramus, fish swam – their black teeth surviving as fossils – and annelids tunnelled under the sands. In between periods of quiescence there must have been periods of dramatic activity, with outpourings of volcanic material, the intrusion of dykes into the sediments, pyroclastic flows, and inevitably uplift, since the fossils can be found high upon the slopes. This, then, was the landscape in the range of our experiences, though to the north and west of Alexander Island the rocks change from sedimentary to volcanic.

Across King George VI Sound, the rocks were very different, being plutonic in origin, with pink granite very much in evidence at Swine Hill. We also found mineral samples in this area, particularly azurite, an attractive green-blue mineral.

King George VI Sound, therefore acts as an incredibly clearly defined division between the two types of land form. Inevitably, with climatic change, both areas were subjected to the same forces of glaciation which have produced similar features on the contrasting rock; ice-worked peaks, arete ridges, U-shaped valleys, lateral moraines, and medial moraines appear everywhere. Also at the time of our occupation of the base, there was much evidence to show that the ice sheets and the glaciers that flowed from them were in retreat.

I spent many days of recreation in studying the nature of 'Hollow Valley', a glaciated valley whose entrance was a mile and a quarter from the base hut. The valley was just over one mile long from its feeding snowfield to the point where it joined the Eros Glacier, the tongue of its own small glacier being 830 yards up the valley. The valley was deep, 500 to 800 feet, and was clearly U-shaped, though scree had disguised the valley profile in part. The side walls, where exposed through the screes, showed evidence of truncation by the movement of the glacier. On the south-east corner, above the confluence of the valley with the Eros Glacier, the profile was markedly stepped, and had a degree of truncation and considerable smoothening, but much of this was disguised by frost shattering. In the valley floor, there was an immense amount of material, some of which consisted of very large blocks of rock which could not have been moved by water, the season of melt being far too short and the size of the stream far too small. The terminal moraine was very high and was almost separated from its glacier; it suggested a long period where the glacier was stationary, followed by retreat. It was quite obvious that the glacier had earlier filled this valley, and had carved it, and was now retreating; it was for this reason that we called the valley 'Hollow Valley'.

On the other side of the Sound, I well remember huge boulders lying around, obviously glacial erratic blocks which had been carried far from their source of origin, having fallen from the hill sides onto the slowly moving glaciers, then dumped when the ice melted. Certainly there was incontrovertible evidence that the ice was in retreat.

The geographical and geological setting for our own hut was impressive. The hut was built on a lateral moraine at a point where the Fossil Bluff Glacier issued into King George VI Sound. Immediately behind the base, scree-covered slopes rose steeply to 1,200 feet, whilst close by the short Fossil Bluff Glacier, about a mile long, came down from beneath the triangular peak which we called 'Pyramid'. The base hut was about 200 feet above sea level, and perhaps 40 or 50 feet above the level of the Sound. To the north, we looked across the Eros Glacier to Succession Cliffs; looking to the east, across the Sound, was a vast panorama of Graham Land with the Batterbee Mountains – Mounts Ness, Cadbury and Bagshawe – reaching to heights over 7,000 feet, and providing us with views of great beauty.

Behind our base, hidden from the great white highway, were mountains and glaciers on which man had never set foot; inevitably it was an exciting prospect for us all, Brian the first geologist to really study the rocks in detail, and John and I – apart from our meteorological programme – supporting Brian and carrying out our own investigations. Interestingly, and for the obvious reason that no one had been there, we had no maps at all, so we were at that time unable to relate the features we saw into the general context; we had to make up our own!

14

Settling In

It was very quiet in the hut on March 4th after the planes flew off. Outside there were piles of completely unsorted equipment and supplies, all jumbled together on the scree slopes below the hut: boxes of ordinary food and boxes of sledging food, other boxes of nutrican (for the dogs when they came), drums of fuel for the aircraft, sacks of anthracite, lengths of timber and plywood panels, rolls of linoleum, shovels, and sledges. A few yards away were the two tents, still up, which the building party had used for ten days. On a rocky platform adjacent to the hut was a Petter generator, securely sited by Mike Tween but lacking any covering building, and with no wires leading from it!

We intuitively established our priorities:

Firstly we had to build a generator shed and connect up the generator and instal lights; the power was also needed for our radio.

Secondly we had to sort out the parts of the Rayburn stove, assemble and fix them, and test them for our heating and cooking.

Thirdly we had to take in and sort out the food.

Fourthly we had to decide how to use the space within the hut.

In between these major priorities there were other important tasks; Brian naturally wanted to get a look at the slopes before they became snowed over, in order to plan his geological work; I wanted to establish a meteorological station; and there were interior furnishings, cupboards and work benches, for example, to erect.

That first evening we sorted out our own personal gear, and over a first cup of tea together we studied our hut. It had been constructed by a building party under the direction of John Cunningham, the overall base leader of our parent base at Stonington Island. The plan

127

of the hut was simple, a rectangular structure measuring 19 feet 8 inches in length and 14 feet in width. Insulated, prefabricated walls in a framework of iron girders formed the shell. The roof was securely held down by cables anchored into concrete. A very heavy door opened into a minute, curtained porch whose side wall formed part of a partition which acted as a radio shack. Opposite the door a small room was partitioned off to act as a WC, though we preferred to make other arrangements for our toilet, so we adapted this area to be a food cupboard. The main living space, 13 feet by 14 feet, in whose confines the three of us would spend twenty-two out of twenty-four hours for three months, was dominated by the stove, whose warmth provided the means for heating the hut, melting the blocks of snow for water, and for our cooking. Along one side of the living space was a narrow writing table which Brian used for his geological notes and reports. The solid table in the centre was used for dining and for John's artistic endeavours, whilst I always used the bench in the radio shack for whatever I was doing. We had a side cupboard, usually littered with rock fragments, and we had a bookshelf which supported our meagre library. Each night we retired to our sleeping bags, using three of the four bunks arranged in two tiers along the end wall. On the opposite end wall was a large working bench for heavy work. We had no chairs, so we had to find the most comfortable boxes, and we had no proper washing facilities apart from some small plastic hand bowls, but the tins in which boxes of cornflakes had been packed enabled us to have a stand-up strip wash when we felt so inclined!

Our first night was very cold as we had no heating and the temperature dropped to 2°F. We rose early and worked solidly from 10.00 a.m. to 10.00 p.m. on priority number one.

March 5th. A cloudy, calm day with temperatures about 25°F gave us good opportunities to work outside and we started the generator shed. We are all complete novices but our effort – starting from a desultory piece of 4 × 2 wood nailed onto the side of the hut – gradually developed into a really sturdy and nice-looking hut.

Within three days we had completed the exterior, double-walled, insulated with fibre glass, and with two windows. A day or two later we had finished constructing a roof and had improved the floor with a layer of gravel. On the 11th I commenced wiring the hut, installed the switchboard and ran the generator for three hours; it worked! By the next day we had five lights and the 119 radio set all functioning.

Once we had reached the stage where I could carry on with the generator on my own, John set to work on the Rayburn stove. We had been using a very poor Uruguayan portable stove and we needed to get the main stove in operation. John started on this work also on the 11th. It needed assembling and cementing, and two days later we were enjoying its warmth and cooking space.

During our last few days at Stonington Island, I had rushed around putting together a basic set of meteorological instruments so that we could carry out regular observations of the weather; unfortunately, most of the new equipment was deep down in the hold of the *John Biscoe*, and was therefore inaccessible. By the time our weather station had been set up, we had almost all of the necessary instruments. A marine barometer was installed in the hut, alongside a barograph. A maximum, a minimum, and an ordinary thermometer were installed in a crate which had been adapted to function as a screen by drilling holes in the ends and making rudimentary louvres. The screen had the attributes of good ventilation and correct height, though we only had aluminium paint so that there was some error. This was set up on the fourth day after our arrival and regular observations were made from March 8th throughout the entire time we spent at the base.

Whilst I worked on the electrics and weather station, John worked on getting the radio working. We used a 119 set, and John was soon able to make contact with Stonington Island. Until we could link it to the general power supplies it was necessary for one or other of us to crank a small generator by hand.

Once we had heating and lighting within the hut, we turned our attention to sorting out the food which had accumulated outside the hut during the many flights which had taken place before we arrived. Normally the supplies for a base are carefully thought about so as to ensure an adequate quantity, quality and diversity. Because of the sudden rush to establish Fossil Bluff, our supplies did not always meet these requirements. We were immediately satisfied that the boxes of sledging rations were sufficient for any journeys we needed to make during the year (these were boxes with food for two men for ten days, suitable for carrying on sledges). What concerned us, however, was the quantity and variety of the rest of the food, our basic source of sustenance. The weight factor in carrying our supplies in the aircraft resulted in our having a limited, but we thought adequate, supply of food.

We soon became aware of problems. It was unfortunate that the crates of vinegar and piccalilli, which quickly froze and shattered, had wasted valuable cargo space. We were perturbed to discover that five boxes which should have contained sugar contained tinned tomatoes. There were insufficient tins of vegetables, and persistent freezing rendered the sprouts and the few tins of potatoes into a soggy mass. We also had very little flour and hardly any dried egg. But we were well provided with some interesting ingredients, including caraway seeds, glacé cherries, and peppercorns! Nevertheless, despite these shortages, we felt that we had most of the necessities to provide for a reasonable diet. Meat figured high on the menu, and we had a good supply of dehydrated meat produced by the Ministry of Agriculture and Fisheries in Aberdeen. This provided us with beef steaks, pork chops and lamb. We also had excellent-quality dehydrated fish. MAFF also produced dehydrated fruit which proved excellent; however, because we only had limited supplies of sugar, taken from the sledge boxes, we rarely used them. We also had good supplies of tinned fruit. By some strange chance we were overwhelmed by dehydrated runner beans, which appeared at virtually every meal for the whole year, after a few months taking the place of potatoes. We also had some boxes of ascorbic acid pills. As we sorted through our supplies we carried them and stored them under the work bench, and filled the shelves of the store cupboard with our immediate requirements. We had one flagon of rum, in a basket, and a few bottles of sherry and wine; our alcohol took up very little space.

Inside the hut, Brian and John put together various cupboards and work benches so that gradually we had a suitably clear living space.

We sorted out the other supplies; we left the dog food, nutrican, outside; things such as the linoleum we carried inside so that it would soften in the warmth before we attempted to lay it. We stacked up the sacks of coal, moved the fuel drums and arranged the surplus timbers so that we knew where to look for them should they drift over. Within two weeks of our arrival we could begin to turn our attention to other matters. Brian had already spent time, sometimes whole days, up on the slopes, and he was anxious to really get stuck into his work before the light failed and the snows came.

130

By now we were getting to know each other really well.

John Smith was twenty-eight, from Kent, and he had already spent two winters in the Antarctic. He had now returned for a third season and it was natural, therefore, that he was designated as officer in charge, whilst John Cunningham (the base leader) was at Stonington Island. John was a meteorologist but he had used his leisure time to produce many beautiful paintings of Antarctic scenes as he had seen them at Deception Island in 1956, and at Detaille Island (just south of the Antarctic Circle on the Graham Land coast) during 1957. John had the distinction of being on cook at Detaille Island on the occasion of the visit of HRH Prince Philip to the base when on his world tour. John was unusual amongst the fids in that he had recently been married – to Frances.

Brian Taylor was twenty-four, and was the geologist. He was a graduate from Swansea, University of Wales, and I had first met him during his preparatory work at Birmingham University in 1959. He had made the long journey on the *Kista Dan* as a cabin mate of mine, so we had already spent 110 days in close proximity. He had returned home after the unsuccessful bid to reach Stonington Island in the previous year.

I was twenty-five years old, and had graduated with a degree in geography and economics, as well as a teaching qualification from the University College of North Staffordshire (Keele University), followed by a year of teaching in Hertfordshire.

We soon organised ourselves. In such a small base one man could do all the basic jobs, so after the first few days we each undertook, a week at a time, to do all the duties. These included keeping the fire going, bringing in the coal, collecting and melting down the ice/snow blocks, keeping the hut reasonably clean, and – perhaps most important of all – doing our best to create culinary masterpieces from the available supplies. The other two weeks in the cycle we had complete freedom to do whatever we wanted to do.

All of us wanted to spend as much time outside as possible and we explored various places in close proximity to the hut. On March 14th, the weather was favourable for John and me to make what we believed to be the first ascent of the mountain behind the hut, which we estimated to be about 2,500 feet above the base, and which we named 'Pyramid' because of its perfect shape. We made a false start, ending up at the bottom of some difficult scree slopes, before finding a way up the 'Gulley', and on to a ridge which led to the top. It only took us an hour or so, but we enjoyed a view that no one else had seen. We were so pleased with ourselves that when I got back to the hut I decided to make the first bread at Fossil Bluff. I found certain difficulties in this because we had no scales, no bowls (except for plastic washing-up bowls) and no baking tins. The loaves were very successful, however, though an unusual shape.

The absolute silence, broken only by occasional bangs caused by the ice settling, took some getting used to, as did the complete absence of any moving creature, other than ourselves. We were positively thrilled, therefore, when on March 18th two skuas appeared. John and I rushed outside with all sorts of food to attract them, so delighted were we to see life! Unfortunately, they only stayed around for ten minutes and didn't partake of our offerings. It was six months before we saw another living creature.

When we decided not to use the facilities provided in the hut for toilet purposes, we had to arrange an alternative facility. We therefore started to chip down through the ice with our axes to carve out a 'bogloo'. It was an excellent form of physical exercise and we worked on it for many days, eventually producing a stepped shaft which led down to a long corridor, off which we constructed cubicles with proper seats spanning deep holes. We all found the use of our bogloo a delightful experience after the cold squattings on the ice!

One day when I was on cook late in March, I decided to look again at our sad pile of broken bottles of frozen vinegar and piccalilli. After much melting, and removing the bits of glass, I rescued one full bottle of vinegar and three bottles of piccalilli, a very satisfactory outcome!

By the end of March, we had become attuned to our environment and we were well settled into our base. Meanwhile the days were shortening and it was getting colder; the autumn season was well advanced.

15

April – an Autumn Journey

As our domestic duties eased, all of us spent more and more time outside. Brian never failed to get out onto the slopes whenever there was the slightest possibility of his being able to work. John and I investigated the area, sometimes on our own, sometimes together. On April 3rd we used the Nansen sledge for the first time, taking it out onto the Sound. We tied ourselves to the sledge and headed away from the Bluff, before turning north in order to pass around the area of disturbance caused by the Eros Glacier as its ice issued into the Sound. We reached the southern part of Succession Cliffs and climbed the scree slopes looking for fossils. We estimated that we had walked ten miles in all and enjoyed every minute of it:

> *April 3rd.* What fantastic delights there are to behold. Graham Land looked magnificent. A mirage effect was prominent to north and south. The snow crystals themselves gave forth the colours of the spectrum, a most beautiful collection of reds, blues and greens. Whenever we stopped we heard the pressure cracking the ice with whip-like sounds. We prodded for crevasses and found several, only a foot wide but very deep.

One evening we had a discussion on danger, prompted by recalling a talk on the subject by Sir Vivian Fuchs which had been given to all Fids on board the *Kista Dan* when we were beset. Brian thought his warnings very much over-dramatised; John and I thought them perfectly reasonable. I felt it was a serious omission in our preparations before we had gone south that there was never any training for working on glaciers and ice shelves. It really was a matter of 'on the job training'. Brian was always prepared to assume that nothing would go wrong, although the sad catalogue of crevasse accidents over the years suggested otherwise. John and I spent several days in trying out our own crevasse rescue techniques, using the deep hole we had already hacked into the ice.

As early as April 10th we began to be concerned about our stores. We were beginning to identify serious shortages in supplies of toilet paper, sugar (only available from the sledge boxes), and coal, so that severe rationing had to be introduced. We counted eighty-one sacks of coal, enough for a sack every other day to take us to September, but what then? Even if our colleagues from Stonington Island were able to sledge down early in the spring, they would not be able to carry coal. We therefore started letting the fire die down overnight, and on some days we let the fire out all day and did the cooking on Primus stoves.

With the sun getting ever lower in the sky, John and I decided to make a short autumn journey across the Sound to Graham Land, Brian preferring to use the last few days of light to carry on with his work. It is just fifteen miles as the skua flies – though these birds were so rare, I doubt if any of them ever did it – and it is entirely on the shelf ice. We wanted to go just for the experience, but also to collect some igneous rocks and minerals, a complete contrast to those around our own base. We were ready to leave on April 14th, having collected together the necessary gear: a pyramid tent, fuel, food, pots and pans, a Primus stove, cooking utensils, sleeping bags and spare clothing. We also thought about our safety, for there is always the possibility of crevasses lurking beneath the surface, especially where glaciers from both sides of the Sound issue into it. We therefore took some ropes and karabiners (a metal coupling link to secure us to the ropes) in case we needed them. We were ready soon after 1.00 p.m.

We adjusted our man-hauling harnesses, secured them to the sledge ropes, stepped into our ski binders and pulled down our goggles. A last glance at the thermometer showed a temperature of –0.5°F. We bade farewell to Brian, jerked the sledge and moved away, our load of approximately 400 lbs sliding smoothly down the slope from the hut on a good surface. There was no cloud, no wind, no noise other than that which resulted from our breathing, our skis and our groaning load. We moved swiftly down the slope to the shelf ice of the Sound. We soon had, once more, the thrill which is always the reward for the traveller here when first he sets out on a journey. After a few minutes we struck a pace of about 2 m.p.h. The surface was hard and frosty though occasionally we met with two-foot-high sastrugi (ridges of hard-packed snow aligned parallel to the prevailing wind), which caused some bumpiness for the sledge.

It was a strange world. Many would say that there was nothing to see; we were on ubiquitous ice, devoid of all trace of organic life, travelling to – and away from – never-changing scenery. Yet there was much to wonder at. The mountains took on a new beauty with changing perspective; the ice and snow reflected colours such as one never imagined would be seen down south, each crystal producing exquisite colours according to which facet caught our eye in passing. There was a quiet magnificence about it all, though the keen air gave to the whole a unique vitality.

Our immediate impressions gradually faded into the background as we focussed our eyes on the yard of snow ever ahead and pulled hard as the weight of the load gradually made itself felt. Although the air was cold, our movement and the little warmth from the weak rays of the sun soon caused us to remove our sweaters. In fact, conditions were extremely comfortable, and as the mountains were left further behind, we were, once more, amazed by the vastness of pure open space that characterises the Antarctic. We travelled on for nearly four hours until the sun began to disappear behind the western mountains. Our progress had been good – over seven miles – so we made camp with a sense of contentment. We pitched our tent facing north so that we could watch the sunset, covered the tent valance with blocks of snow to hold it down should a wind get up, and climbed into the tent by way of the long sleeve. The air temperature had dropped to $-10°F$, so we were glad to be inside. We slipped into our sleeping bags, arranged along the sides of the tent with our sledge box and Primus stove down the middle. Soon the Primus stove was set up and lit, the first job being to melt the snow which would rehydrate and cook our meat bar. We dined on soup, meat bar, cheese and biscuits (with lots of butter), followed by Nescafé. Later we had a cup of cocoa. It was cold in the tent once the Primus was out, and very rapidly the moisture within the tent condensed on the tent sides to produce a covering of frost; outside it was $-12°F$. We lit the paraffin lamp and trapped the remaining warmth in our sleeping bags, one gloved hand and our heads remaining free so that we could read for a while.

We were preparing to go to sleep when John, peering from the tent, glimpsed light to the south. He thought it might be an auroral display, so we rapidly scrambled outside. We forgot the cold as we gazed southwards and marvelled as the great curtains of green and rose swished silently over the Sound. Sometimes the curtains apparently moved overhead then faded, the darkened sky soon lighting up

135

as another curtain rose on the southern horizon and hung mysteriously from Graham Land to Alexander Island. Overhead great shafts of light appeared; to the west a diffuse red light predominated. It was our first witness of the aurora australis, a spectacle which later had us out from our hut on several cold nights, though perhaps, as in many aspects of life, the first experience out-sparkles all others, in nostalgic memory if not in fact!

Morning came, prematurely to us who were very cold, bringing with it its trials and its beauties. The temperature had fallen to −14.5°F, 46.5° of frost, so the first trial consisted of trying to avoid touching the tent, for the inside was covered in hoar frost ready to descend on us at the lightest touch. The second trial arose from touching the Primus stove, so cold that our fingers stuck to it; we soon remembered to keep our gloves on until we had got it going and the air had warmed up a little! Breakfast over (porridge, biscuits, butter and Marmite, with lots of coffee), we were in time to see the pale sun rise, promising another glorious day. The low sastrugi, evidence of recent northerly winds, cast long shadows to the south from their lowly eminences. The feathery flakes of hoar frost epitomised the sense of coldness, dropping off the tent guys at a fairy touch. A low mist between us and the sun produced a brilliant halo whose colours once again proved that in the midst of the white desert, the purest and most brilliant colours are to be seen.

Apart from Brian, a few miles away near the base, our nearest neighbours were some 230 miles away to the north. There in the middle of the Sound, our sense of isolation and self-dependence was absolute, and entrancing.

We dismantled the tent and reloaded the sledge. Harnessing up and adjusting our clothes took a long time in the low temperatures, with our thick gloves feeling hopelessly for our waist loops and karabiners. We trudged on, thankful for the sun and the beauty, but conscious of the thickening ice mass on our beards. We travelled slowly but surely, the only speck of animation on the whole of this huge ice shelf, mindful of the fact that we were almost 200 feet above sea level, on ice well over 1,000 feet thick. Only the vicious crevasses that we could see on the glaciers ahead reminded us of the true nature of our highway. We reached the mid-point of the Sound and carried on until we had travelled 6.2 miles. We came now within striking distance of our objective. The sun was already casting pink shadows around us, and we began to feel hungry and tired, so we camped. We pitched our tent facing south, hoping for another display of aurora, ate our meal, read and had a last look out; but there was no repeat of the celestial firework display, so we went to sleep.

Overnight the noise of a light wind temporarily awakened us. In the morning the ice inside the tent had gone, and we felt distinctly less uncomfortable on stirring from our bags. The temperature had increased to $+10°F$, $25°F$ warmer than the night before. The sky had clouded over and the view around the Sound was not nearly as attractive; we were prepared to sacrifice the view, however, for some warmth. As we were now close to the Graham Land coast, we decided to leave the tent and continue with the sledge, some food and the safety equipment. It took us exactly two miles to reach the cliffs at Swine Hill. A 1956 map shows that Vivian Fuchs and Raymond Adie reached this point on December 19th/20th in 1948, and they presumably were responsible for the name. As we approached the rocks, a big surprise was in store for us, for, as we ascended the final elevation of the ice, we suddenly found ourselves overlooking a twenty-foot incline at whose base was a large lake. The sight of such a pool of water at this time in the season was remarkable. As we got closer we could hear the noise of cracking ice, and as we looked, rafts of ice slid over one another. We tried various explanations; could the lake have derived as a result of huge pressures from nearby glaciers, or might it be something to do with tidal cracks and slight movements of the shelf ice? Fuchs noted it on his map and he probably gave it the name, Gadarene Lake. Certainly it seemed to be a permanent feature, given the extremely low temperatures that had occurred over the past few days.

We enjoyed getting onto the slopes of Swine Hill. There were lots of colours to be seen in the rocks: reds, large bands of black intrusions and green stains were all prominent. We spent much of the day collecting samples, including superbly coloured blue minerals (azurite), pink granite, and black igneous rocks. Unfortunately there were no gemstones (so far as we were aware), but it was always a part of our excitement that nobody knew, because nobody had looked! We also found a few scraps of lichen, a triumph of living in such hostile surroundings.

We had so many interesting specimens to take back to Brian for identification and we planned in the ensuing days to obtain more by going back to explore the screes slightly to the south, climb the hill and traverse the slope along the side of the glacier. The weather now turned against us, however, and the next day dawned sullen and murky:

April 17th. Dear dear! The weather in the Sound has deserted us, and at 3.00 a.m. we awoke to a northerly wind, 15–20 knots blowing, accompanied by snow. At dawn these conditions still held. John took a temperature of $+17°F$, which was pleasing. Still 8 oktas stratus, snow and wind confined us to the tent all morning. I started to read *The Odyssey* by Homer, and we kept our ears on the wind. At 1.00 p.m. the cloud had lifted and the snow ceased. By 2.00 p.m. we were pulling the sledge the 2 miles to the Graham Land rocks. Visibility was questionable, so we staked our route every 3/10ths of a mile, to find the tent in bad visibility out here would have been impossible. I walked in snow boots, but the snow, 12 inches or so, made the going heavy. We had 90 minutes to gather pieces ... We returned to the tent after the sun fell below Alexander Island. What a beautiful green light shone on the snowy silhouettes of mountains over there, whilst Graham Land threw up pink light. The temperature at 6.00 p.m. was $+20°F$.

Our plans for journeying further south were reviewed. It was only ever intended as a short trip, and overnight winds and high temperatures, accompanied by very low cloud, suggested the passage of a depression, which would bring a spell of bad weather. We therefore decided to make our way westwards again when conditions improved, so we spent the morning reading, drinking, and peering out of the tent. After lunch the cloud began to rise, enabling us to see across the great white highway. We decamped quickly and prepared to move. The wind was blowing at perhaps, twenty knots, and aided by the cloud cover, the mercury rose to over $20°F$, so we were very warm.

We had four hours of light left, so we hurried, mindful for the first time of the pedometer which ticked slowly away on the sledge wheel, measuring the distance we had travelled. A fog bow appeared to our left, a great white arc cutting into the mist. Drift whipped along our track, though because it was below waist height it enhanced the immediate scene rather than adding to our discomfort. If we stopped for a bite of chocolate, the paper wrapping snaked away too, joining the flurry southwards. Our minds were on the distant scene as we plodded rhythmically along, with our ski sticks making tracks of little round holes and our skis swishing along in front of the sledge. The cloud lifted from time to time and we caught glimpses of the imaginatively named Alexander Island coast, Waitabit Cliffs, Uranus Glacier, and our destination, Fossil Bluff.

We had made good progress at 2.5 miles an hour when we decided that it was time to camp. We had advanced by 8.2 miles, so the following day would be easy. The light was failing as we set up the tent and cooked the meal; soup, beef curry and rice bar, with biscuits and coffee. The higher temperatures, up to 29°F during the day, had made our clothes, sleeping bags and tent very wet and this made the night very uncomfortable. Next morning, April 19th, started off with very cloudy skies, but by the time we were ready to depart, conditions were good. The sun broke through the gloom and gave us another perfect fog bow to admire as we set out on the last five miles. Soon we were pulling the sledge up the last slope, and Brian came out to welcome us. Back in base, a cup of orange juice and a hot meal made us appreciate the comforts of 'home'. In the evening our rocks and minerals were set out on the table and the reference books came out. We were pleased with our trip; it had whetted our appetite for the summer journeys to come.

16

Winter Comes to Fossil Bluff

As soon as we had settled into the base hut again, Brian gave us some bad news: the diesel generator had stopped working! We had had a preliminary warning of some sort of problem on April 12th, before our departure on the journey across the Sound. On that day, smoke poured out of the exhaust pipe, and I had stopped the engine. On the following day, I spent some time trying to solve the problem, and eventually the generator started and kept going for five hours without trouble. Because of our concerns we only ever used the engine after darkness had fallen. When John and I departed, therefore, I was hopeful that the engine would continue to work. When I discovered that it had failed during our absence therefore, I was extremely worried:

April 19th. The diesel has really gone wrong now, so I spent the afternoon trying to locate the trouble – fuel, rocker box, and air intake – but to no avail. The engine won't start, and cranking it causes black smoke to belch forth. I have asked Mike (at Stonington) for advice.

I worked on the engine for many days. On the 21st I replaced the fuel injector but with no luck. I took the cylinder head off, decoked the top of the piston and had a look at the piston rings, again with no luck. I dismantled the rocker valve assembly to see if the valves were sticking, but it made no difference. I wondered if I would ever get it to go, for not only was the use of Tilley lamp lighting inconvenient, it was a blow to my prestige! On the 23rd, I noted a gross looseness where the piston joined the main bearing, and thought that this may have been the cause of the problem. On April 29th, I made one last, long, effort to solve the problem, but failed. From the 20th on, we had only Tilley lamps for our lighting, and any use we made of the radio was possible only by hand cranking the generator. Yet the generator had worked for just over a month, at approximately five

141

hours a day, so I took comfort from the fact that the fault might be in the generator, rather than in my incompetence, and this was confirmed when Mike Tween was able to look at it more than eight months later.

During mid-April, snow fell on the slopes immediately behind the base. After five weeks of diligent work on the rock outcrops, Brian's immediate geological plans were in abeyance. To make use of the last days of sunlight, therefore, he and John planned a journey to the south, during which time he hoped to take a preliminary look at the rocks further down the Sound. I stayed behind; we had just started the meteorological observations and, in any case, a third man would have required a disproportionate amount of supplies to carry, notably a second tent.

It was a glorious day as they left on April 28th. The sun shone through a suspended layer of ice particles at glacier level, producing a brilliant partial halo apparently a few yards away from us, its intense colours hanging in the air like a diaphanous veil. My two colleagues disappeared over the snow crest and I climbed the slopes of the Bluff to watch them become imperceptible specks – the only life (except for some poor mosses and lichens) within hundreds of miles of me. Nothing stirred; nothing; nothing in the sky; nothing on the mute snow; nothing in the air; all was a great silence, broken occasionally by the portentous whip crack of the contracting ice.

I re-entered the hut and busied myself with clearing up and cooking a meal with the help of light from the Tilley lamps. At 9.00 p.m. I was surprised to see that the temperature was below –12°F; there was no cloud, and the almost full moon cast a beautiful light. The campers had a flare and I waved the Tilley lamp, so contact was established at three or four miles' distance. They were in for a cold night. During the next two days of clear calm weather, the temperatures steadily dropped to –20°F then further down to –26.2°F, 58.2°F of frost. The sun was now rising at 10.50 a.m. and was setting at 3.05 p.m. so the days were getting really short. One evening I read a line from D.H. Lawrence which aptly described the scene: '... and I noticed that up above the snow, frail in the bluish sky, a frail moon had put forth, like a thin, scalloped film of ice floated on the current of the coming night'.

It was very cold in the hut. I cooked a penguin egg omelette for

142

breakfast; the egg was still edible despite a long period of storage, and was delicious after the dried egg which we were using. I spent time on baking bread and mince pies, on analysing the meteorological statistics for March, reading a lot, and managing to pick up some BBC news on the radio. If I was cold in the hut, what was it like in the Sound? I began to wonder if John and Brian might be forced to make an early return.

The next day, my anticipations were fulfilled. Soon after lunch I happened to glance out to the Sound and I detected my two colleagues slowly dragging their burden back to base. I hurriedly put some food in the oven, then skied out a mile or so to help them up the last incline, a tedious end to a journey. The surface was soft, and as I neared I could see that John was pulling, whilst Brian was pushing from behind, without skis. John had a mask of ice covering his beard; we exchanged a few cheery greetings and John told me that Brian had a badly frostbitten toe. We were soon inside the warm hut, where Brian removed his mukluks (knee-length canvas boots which normally have several pairs of socks inside), and socks. He exposed a nasty-looking big toe which had frozen inside his ski boot, which he had preferred to wear instead of the mukluks. They had had temperatures down to –35°F for several days and the discomfort involved made it impossible to continue with the journey. They had travelled a total of twenty-three miles, ten to the south beyond Uranus Glacier, then into the coast at Waitabit Cliffs. Brian's toe took over ten weeks to heal, changing from one colour to another until eventually the purple, dead, cells, along with his nail, sloughed off. This adventure served as a marker between autumn and winter, which was now upon us.

During April and May we spent as much time as possible outside, seeing as much of the novel surroundings as our legs made possible; we really missed not having dogs to help us. Brian worked continuously in his chosen area, keeping to a self-imposed routine with extraordinary powers of tenacity. John and I went out on daily walks or scrambles, which gave us much interest and enjoyment and helped to keep us fit. Occasionally we hitched ourselves to the Nansen sledge and ventured around the fringes of the nearby Eros Glacier which separated us from the beckoning rocks of Succession Cliffs. Sometimes I investigated matters of geographical interest: peculiar contortions in the ice of a meltwater lake gave evidence of movement

143

in the shelf ice, misfit glaciers in 'Hollow Valley' and in the Fossil Bluff valley indicated glacial retreat, erratic rocks and pebbles gathered from nearby uplands indicated that they had been carried to their present location by ice that had disappeared. Always, of course, there was the challenge of finding even more perfect specimens of the fossils that were in such abundance.

On May 9th the sun failed to rise above Succession Cliffs and could no longer shine on the hut, though we could see its rays still weakly lighting up the Sound. Next day we went down onto the Sound for a final glimpse of it before it dipped below the horizon for the winter:

May 10th. Very pleasant day – cloudless (or nearly), with temperatures peculiarly varying between –15°F to +7°F. I was up for morning met. and to cook breakfast. John wanted to film the winter sun through icicles which he has patiently made. The sun no longer shines on the base, so I helped him carry them to the sunlit slope. The sun certainly looked huge on the horizon, beautifully orange and casting shadowy pink light everywhere. I don't suppose we shall see it again until spring.

We did not see it again until August 5th, eighty-seven days during which time we inevitably had some periods of low spirits.

It was a pleasant little hut in which to live. During the day, it steadily warmed up to a pleasant temperature. At night we considered ventilation important because of the dangers of carbon monoxide poisoning and left the door ajar overnight. This made the early morning temperatures very cold, the thermometer at my bedside frequently registering zero degrees (32°F of frost). We who were not on weather observations or on cook duty then cringed in our sleeping bags and listened to the curses of the cook as the cold metal of the paraffin lamp stung his fingers, the milk froze in its tin (we had no jugs), and cutting the bread became a tedious process like sawing mahogany with a hack saw. The temperature gradient in the room was very steep, water on the floor usually freezing quickly, whilst at head height we were warm. As long as we wore mukluks we were rarely uncomfortable, and we could always retreat to our sleeping bags if necessary. When we realised that we had insufficient coal supplies we let the fire go out overnight, so we were able to keep the door shut,

144

24. July 29th 1961 - a few days before the sun returned, page 154.

25. The author enjoying the return of the sun, page 154.

Photo courtesy of John Smith

26. The camp on the Glacier looking towards Pyramid and our route to base, page 164.

Photo courtesy of Brian Taylor

27. John cooks a meal outside the tent we alternately shared with Brian for two months, page 164.

Photo courtesy of Brian Taylor

28. Struggling South, Bryan and Bob view the hole made by the sinking Muskeg, page 177.

29. The journey ends - our friends arrive at Fossil Bluff, page 178.

30. Bob Metcalfe, Bryan Bowler and Howard Chapman - 93 days from base, page 178.

31. Sledging in King George VI Sound, page 183.

32. The players enjoy a well-earned rest, page 184.

33. Sledging Rations - two men for ten days, page 184.

34. Our furthest south - Two Step Cliffs, page 185.

35. January 27th 1961, waiting to fly out from Fossil Bluff (L to R Bob Metcalfe, Bill Tracy, Bryan Bowler, Brian Wigglesworth, John Smith, Cliff Pearce), page 194.

36. Fossil Bluff, King George VI Sound Alexander Island (Fossil Bluff glacier in centre, hut built on moraine to right of valley. Fossil Bluff glacier leads up to Pyramid, the small peak, then up to Snow Dome, later named Pearce Dome), page 194.

37. Stonington Island, Marguerite Bay (1961 British base centre, 1947 British base to left, 1940 and 1947 American base to right), page 197.

and this effected a minor, but significant, improvement to our early morning warmth!

The 119 radio set was very important to us. Even when we had the generator working, the amount of interference it caused made it impossible for us to send or receive messages, so we had long grown accustomed to having to crank a small generator. We could usually hear programmes and messages over the air but we had to use Morse code to send messages; John was the only one of us competent in this field, so one of us would crank hard whilst he tapped them out. There were long periods when we were completely unable to contact Stonington Island; from April 29th to May 24th, for example, we never raised them at all. Whenever we wanted to catch up with the world news, we would share out the four headphones between us and hand crank the generator; this was a time of serious world problems: France on the brink of civil war on April 23rd, Cuba hitting the headlines on May 1st, Adolf Eichmann on trial in Israel that month, George Blake given forty-two years' imprisonment for spying, the Americans sending a man into space for fifteen minutes; it all had a worrying effect on us. There were programmes specifically for us, however. *Calling the Antarctic* was a weekly programme put out on the BBC World Service. It had interesting talks, titbits of news, and records, and from time to time carried broadcasts from our own folks. When the *John Biscoe* arrived home on May 30th, Captain Johnston broadcast and sent good wishes to the 'three we left at Fossil Bluff, they must feel out in the cold'. *South Georgia Letter Box* was also a good source of nostalgic pop songs – Connie Francis, Acker Bilk and Roy Rogers. Our radio listening was limited to approximately half an hour a day and we had problems from the weakness of our cranking device, which kept on breaking, presumably through metal fatigue. We managed to effect repairs, however; it was very important to us to keep alive our contact with the world outside.

Our sources of leisure activity were severely restricted. We had no record player. This was a sad omission in view of the fact that we could only listen to the radio whilst pedalling furiously with our hands or feet – it was like listening to a Brahms Symphony whilst riding a bike. Brian and I sometimes shared a cranking session to listen to popular music, but our enthusiasm waned. We had few luxuries to enjoy; John enjoyed smoking a limited number of cigarettes each day and I enjoyed a pipe while the tobacco lasted; we had no beer at all, and our cask of rum ran out just as I had acquired the taste for it. We certainly derived pleasure from unusual sources, the appearance of an ancient Sunday paper I had kept in a parcel for mid-winter providing a whole wealth of conversational topics! Our library was small, limited to a few books that we had each chosen. Nevertheless in late April and May I read *The Brothers Karamazov* by Dostoevsky, over 900 heavy pages in twenty days, which I enjoyed, except for rambling sections on Socialism. I also read *The Last Chronicle of Barset, The Return of the Native, Aku Aku, The Moon and Sixpence* and *The Day of the Triffids* – Trollope, Hardy, Heyerdahl, Maugham and Wyndham – and also some D.H. Lawrence. Such reading was evidence, either that we had wide interests, or a narrow shelf of books, or both! The long words which we frequently stumbled over in these books was a factor in the founding of the Fossil Bluff Vocabularian Society, whose members, whilst on cook duty, had a responsibility to introduce a new word each day, complete with meaning. What solecisms we had at our command! I suppose that a psychologist might interpret our neologistic tendencies as an expression of suppressed pristine concupiscence!

Evidence of the impact of the FBVS appeared from time to time. One day I noted:

> *May 10th.* We had a culture day today in which swearing and 'eructating' were out. The day was not a success from this point of view!

John would often use time for painting; occasionally he would sit at the entrance to the hut and paint the glories of our panorama, though ours was unchanging, unlike the coastal bases where icebergs and wildlife produced ever-varying scenes. He also painted a fine 'dictionary' of over 1200 geographical terms.

Although our excursions were severely restricted by the lack of daylight, we still needed exercise. We had been steadily constructing two pits, one the 'bogloo', and the other a crevasse rescue pit, a few yards apart. One day, we hit on the idea of joining them up. The resultant corridor would then enable us to excavate small niches which could be used to store food, emergency gear and timber, besides acting as a basis for dog shelters should dogs be based at Fossil Bluff over the next winter. Every day for weeks, therefore, we

146

got rid of our surplus energy hacking our way through the *névé*, which proved excellent as a tunnelling material, being easily workable but very safe. The tunnel was nearly fifteen yards long, with the floor about ten to twelve feet below the surface; it eventually afforded us a drift-proof, dry and comfortable passage for a multiplicity of uses. Apart from digging, we continued to take walks when and where possible. Brian also had some hand springs which he and John used regularly. Perhaps our desire for exercise, often on our own, was an important factor in our surviving so well together; we managed to contrive to get away from each other for part of many days.

Our sleeping hours were naturally longer than we enjoyed at home, though not by very much. Every morning one or other of us was up before 9.00 a.m. to carry out the weather observation, and the day began. We usually retired at 11.00 p.m. One might have anticipated trouble from a condition known as 'big eye', which men at polar bases reported gave them difficulty in sleeping. We tended to keep ourselves sufficiently occupied so as to appreciate sleep. Usually we would curl up in our bags and sleep, then over the breakfast table we would entertain one another with tales of our dreams. Most dreams centred on the things we cherished at home, people, green fields etc. Brian often visited the theatre and reported performances of such excitement they had John and me sitting in rapt attention!

When we were on cook duty, and had plenty of time to experiment, all of us made great efforts to produce good meals. At this time we had flour available, and John and I regularly made bread. Our problem was that we had no bread tins so we produced shapeless but palatable lumps. On May 16th, Brian made his first bread and, with a touch of inspiration, he used the flour tin to bake it in, thereby producing high-quality loaves measuring 1 foot × 1 foot × 9 inches in height, it worked splendidly! We dined well during the first three months, with a good variety of meat-based meals. Apart from the dehydrated foods, we had large quantities of tinned, stewed steak; we also had hafnia (a variation on spam), which was delicious but in short supply. We also cooked lots of cakes and pastries, and ate well. Yet it concerned me that we did not organise a systematic programme of food rationing, and the signs existed early on that there would be difficulties ahead:

May 27th. We are running out of many foods – sugar (from sledge boxes), dried egg, bacon, spuds etc.

147

May 28th. Cook week over again! It really is a rotten job, for we have such a limited variety of food now. Vegetables are already very short, but fruit and cereals promise a headache later on. I cooked breakfast ... then baked bread and scones and lunch.

June 9th. [after a mild disagreement with Brian, who thought I was consuming too much milk] It is strange that he should suddenly be like this, for earlier on he cooked breakfasts combining bacon, hafnia and spaghetti etc, which were in short supply. We made gentle hints at the extravagance, but to no effect – until it had all gone, that is!

June 18th. My last day on cook for the time being. It's a rotten job with such limited food to pick from, these days. Still, we eat well and all keep fit.

Yet we still had at least six months to go before the aircraft could replenish our supplies!

More and more we were confined to the hut, so we concentrated on the tasks that we had, or wanted, to do. The fact that Brian had had five weeks of almost unbroken field work during March and April gave him a wealth of work with which to occupy his winter months. His huge collection of fossils entailed a lot of preliminary descriptive work, followed by compiling a station register, and finally beginning the process of packing his collection into crates for transport to Birmingham University. His patient progress up the rocks would provide information on the stratigraphic succession, as well as leading to scientific descriptions of some of the fossilised creatures immortalised in stone.

We were very conscientious in carrying out our meteorological programme. We tried to ensure that our instruments were properly installed and we compared the readings of the various thermometers, including a whirling psychrometer, to establish the extent of any errors. The fact that our screen was painted with an aluminium colour was insignificant in its effects on temperature readings because the sun was not present for much of the time, and we envisaged that a proper screen would be brought down from Stonington Island early in the spring. We had no instruments for wind recording, but John and I had over three years, between us, of experience in observing

148

wind speeds, so we felt competent to make fair estimates. We started observations on March 9th and continued with them until December 31st. Observations were made at 0900, 1500, and 2100 hours, local time. We recorded air temperature, pressure, wind speed and direction, visibility, present weather and optical phenomena. At the end of each month, the observations were written up and analysed. During June, when the new hut had been constructed at Stonington Island and they were sending their observations to Stanley, we sent our own weather messages, once a day, which John tapped out in Morse while Brian or I cranked. It certainly added interest to our work, besides making a contribution from a completely new station in the Antarctic.

The predominant character of the weather at Fossil Bluff was calm and cold. For long periods the air around the base hardly stirred. On May 20th we heard that Hope Bay had experienced winds of 147 knots on the previous day, shattering windows and distributing boxes everywhere. On that day we had light airs; we were always well south of the tracks of the deep depressions which had given Hope Bay a pressure reading of 937 mb! Only rarely did we estimate winds of over thirty knots, and this was usually only for a few hours. In view of our position at Latitude 71°20'S, 68°17'W, and being 200 miles from open water for most of the year, the temperatures, though cold, were less cold than we might have expected. The coldest months were May and June, when the mean temperatures were –0.7°F and –9.8°F respectively, with the lowest temperatures of –37.9°F in June, –36.1°F in July and –35.4°F in August – cold enough, perhaps! At the other extreme the mean temperature for December was +29.6°F. We were surprised at the low incidence of snowfalls for much of the time. In the report for May I noted:

Snow fell on 11 days of the month, though with few exceptions, snowfall was light. The snow was dry and loose, and the accumulation on the slopes behind the hut blew away, leaving the slopes virtually clear.

The level of the snow increased on the ice of the Sound. Twelve inches accumulated under the thermometer screen, but up on the slopes it kept on being blown away until late on in the winter. On my return home I was able to carry out a complete analysis of all of the statistics, which formed the basis for an article which was published in the first edition of the *British Antarctic Survey Bulletin* in June 1963.

Our days, by June, had taken on a familiar routine:

June 3rd. Between –26°F and –38°F today, in clear, calm conditions. I was on met., but we all returned to bed after breakfast – the temperature at my bedside was + 10°F, and –10°F on the floor. We arose at lunchtime, in time for a sked with (Base) E. It was very interesting for the (sea) ice is 9″ thick, and the dogs are in training. They hope to move here as soon as conditions permit, perhaps August. Evidently 70 flights are to be made next year to make Fossil Bluff fully self-supporting for a 14-man wintering party next winter in tents (poor fools!). Seal will be flown in too. Roll on springtime. It was good to have such a newsy sked.

June 4th. –33.8°F at 9.00 a.m., but the sky clouded over during the day, snow fell and the temperature rose to –15°F. Still cold. The extra 20° makes all the difference though and the hut is comfortably warm again. I arose after 11.00 a.m. and did little 'til after lunch. Then I did some typing on my little screed, 'The Return Of The Penguins'. Brian has been geologising in his pit for most of the day; John has been on cook. Life here is very quiet; no life; no music whatsoever; very little variation of food. Still we all keep pretty cheerful and well. Brian's frostbitten toe is looking very black; it's nearly a month now, and the nail still hasn't come off. I heard the evening news by dint of turning the generator by hand – it's well worth it. I retired to bed at 10.00 p.m. to carry on reading *The Last Chronicle of Barset*, which I have started today. P.S. We all feel a bit concupiscent!

Mid-winter approached. At the beginning of June temperatures fell to below –35°F, and after the first week the average was –25°F. We really felt the approach of winter, even though, in the ensuing week or two, temperatures were warmer. On these warmer days, cloud lurked all around, over the mountains of Graham Land, in patches in the Sound, or swirling chaotically about the dull sky. Occasionally to the north we glimpsed the rays of the sun on high cloud, a starved tributary of light from the great flood over the northern hemisphere. As we cranked the generator for news, we would catch a description of the test match at Lord's, where the English batsmen toiled unsuccessfully under an air temperature of almost 80°F, whilst our own reading was 100°F lower. Sometimes, a few hours of wind would lift the soft snow, sending it snaking across the glacier, its writhing coils stinging our faces. Yet calm conditions predominated, exaggerating the atmosphere of sterility which was epitomised by King George VI Sound.

The sun had disappeared on May 10th, and for a few days afterwards we looked to the north, where we could still see a rosy glow above the horizon. Winter brought with it a sunless world, not that we lived entirely in darkness. The apparent trajectory of the sun moves only a few degrees below the horizon from Latitude 71°S. As a result we had a few hours of twilight until mid-winter, when it was sufficiently light for us to walk for about two hours, though when there was cloud it was virtually completely dark. Within the hut, lights were necessary all day for over two months. At times of the full moon, whose movement had a new interest for us, the landscape was uniformly lit by the mellow light from its benign face, and we would go outside and enjoy it.

Mid-winter's day, June 21st, took on a new significance this year. At Deception Island it had been a day of festivities, though we could still have seen the sun for the effort of a few minutes' walk up the hillside. Now, for us, the day really marked a turning point when we could begin to look forward to the return of the sun in just over six weeks' time, with everything that the sun implies: life! John was the cook for the day, and on the 20th I noted in my diary:

> *June 20th.* John has been incredibly busy all day preparing cakes and pastries for tomorrow. In celebration of the event FIDS programme was 45 minutes long and included a talk by Fuchs, who concluded by extending 'a special greeting to the three men at Fossil Bluff' – a very nice gesture by him, we thought.

So, for the great day, John produced some splendid fare. Despite shortages of baking powder, sugar and flavourings, he made cakes and pastries of the highest quality. Our pork loin was delicious, our carrots crisp and tasty, our peas as fresh as from the farm, and our roast potatoes sheer luxury. After Christmas pudding, from somewhere he produced sweets, jellies, trifles and crystallised fruits; we even had some Manikins to smoke. By the time we had consumed our bottles of port and sherry we had a very satisfied glow! It was a peculiar atmosphere for a party. The three of us had lived on top of

151

each other for nearly four months, but the party symbolised the fact that we had got on well together. After dinner, we pushed our boxes-cum-seats under the table, and flaked out on our beds. Later we listened in to the inter-base schedules in order to find out what was going on elsewhere.

Two days later we heard over the radio of a very significant moment in Antarctic history. For on June 23rd 1961, the Antarctic Treaty was ratified by the original twelve signatories: Argentina, Australia, Belgium, Chile, France, Japan, New Zealand, Norway, South Africa, the United Kingdom, the USA and the USSR. Thus it was that we shared with others the distinction of being the last of the Fids, and the first of the new British Antarctic Survey members! We did not register, at that time, the impact the Treaty would have on the Antarctic, mostly for good, in the years ahead.

Mid-winter passed, and we patiently watched the northern horizon. As the spring began to approach, our minds became centred on the summer programme with all of its excitement and interest, and we began to listen ever more intently to the radio messages from Stonington Island. We were in for some major disappointments.

17

Dark, Dark Days

There proved to be 155 days from our mid-winter's day celebration to November 23rd, when our friends finally arrived from Stonington Island. For the first 114 days of this period we were all stuck in the hut, often for twenty-two or twenty-three hours a day. In October, Brian went to work away from the base, so for thirty-four days either John or I stayed with him in support. This, therefore, broke up the perpetual threesome to which we had become accustomed. These were days when our spirits reached their nadir. A variety of factors contrived to bring about this situation. Firstly, it was dark; secondly, our food supplies began to run out; thirdly, we only had work to do which was self-generated; fourthly, the world news was extremely worrying; and fifthly, it was perfectly natural that we should begin to find the faults, if there were faults, in each other's personality. Despite the difficulties, however, there was always lots of evidence of our good will towards one another in our mutual sharing of some degree of hardship, and a large measure of disappointment.

June ended with us all in good spirits. We were well occupied on our various interests and there was time for jesting and vigorous sparring. On the 24th, John thought I had broken his rib, and six days later, because it was still hurting, we had a sked with Dr Brian Sparke at Stonington. I cranked the generator, Brian was the 'doctor', and John stood with his vest off whilst being examined. There was nothing that we could do for him, so rest and care was prescribed. Our health was always excellent. There are no germs in the cold Antarctic air, and the only areas of concern were internal problems such as appendicitis, or injuries arising from accidents, or frostbite. At coastal bases, when the relief ships arrived they usually brought men carrying all sorts of infections which spread to the men on the bases. Soon after they had gone, colds dried up and months of freedom from illnesses followed.

It was very dark right through to the end of July; the two-hour period of twilight around mid-winter very gradually extended, so that by July 20th it was light from 10.00 a.m. to 3.30 p.m., time to get outside for a walk but insufficient to do anything else. The cover of snow would prevent Brian from working for several more weeks. We daily looked towards the heavens, some days boosting our morale considerably:

July 26th. Another fine day. Brian and I spent the whole afternoon skiing ... we are a bit worried about an avalanche ground which overlooks our main slopes. What a superb day. The sun will soon be back, and today it illuminated the clouds a most superb colour – orange to blood orange. A sun pillar was visible for some time. It will soon be here!

August 4th was the probable date for the return of the sun, based on our latitude (though we were unable to ascertain this), but thick cloud prevented us from seeing it at all. On August 5th, however, we were able to celebrate:

the return of the worshipful sun!!! (seen).

Next day, the sun was glorious. It shone on the Pyramid for four hours, and on the hut for ten minutes. We all went out skiing and truly rejoiced at the pinkish light which the sun cast on the snows; this was a great day. There was a feeling amongst us of euphoria; that we had come through the darkness and that we could now look forward to sunlit summer months of intense interest and fulfilment with new colleagues and new programmes of work. The new Muskegs and the well-tried dogs would transform our knowledge of the area by making possible travel far beyond the limit of our own man-hauling powers. We were buoyed up with optimism!

It was quite obvious during May that we were going to run out of many types of food. Sugar, dried egg, potatoes, vegetables, fruit, cereals, bacon, hafnia, and spaghetti had all been noted as being in short supply. Yet we had no system for identifying what we had, or for planning its consumption. John did not assert himself in this matter, so each of us merely helped ourselves to what was available. By August 14th, I noted that there was only two weeks' supply left of baked beans, bread (we had little yeast left), sausages and spaghetti. We had no tinned potatoes at all. By the 20th, I was on cook and baked the last bread, with the last of the yeast, together with tarts and cheese straws. By September 2nd we had no flour left, or sausages or sprouts or celery. We carried on during September with declining variety, always relying on dehydrated runner beans to fill out the meal. Then on October 2nd, I remarked that our main breakfast foods were almost finished. John pointed out that our colleagues (who were at that time trying to reach us and had become stranded on Mushroom Island) were in a far worse condition than we were. It was a remark that didn't go down well in view of the fact that we had, perhaps, three months to go! The next day I noted:

October 3rd. I have been on cook for three days; our supplies are very restricted now and we are making use of things like pea flour, caraway seeds, sardines and tons of corned beef!

By the 7th we had no sweets, no bread, no tinned vegetables; only a few tins of fruit. Three days later, John declared that there was a milk shortage, and this provoked an argument about food rationing, which Brian and I had been pushing for over many weeks. It must be said, however, that no amount of food rationing could have made up for the shortages in which we found ourselves. Later on, when we were camping with Brian for several weeks, we discovered many inadequacies in the sledging boxes, which caused further problems. When I was alone at the base for twelve days in October I resorted to currants, (from lots of tins which we had), and desiccated coconut to add a bit extra to poor meals. By November 19th, just before we had five extra mouths to help feed, we were really in difficulties:

November 19th. The base food is really telling on our guts these days. We (partly) subsist on pea flour omelettes, currants, corned beef and runner beans with a few extras. The first two items have caused Brian and me to spend the whole time farting!

This was about the time when we were making jellies from gelatine to which we added cocoa. Certainly there was decreasing pleasure to be derived from being on cook duty at this time when we could not express our normal culinary brilliance!

Other shortages began to figure prominently in our minds, notably our coal supplies. On August 8th we were down to thirty-nine sacks out of the eighty-one which we had counted on April 11th, yet we had been careful in our use, with the Rayburn stove commonly allowed to go out overnight. At that rate of consumption we would run out by the end of November, yet our water supplies, cooking and heat depended on the stove. We had no wish to have to use Primus stoves all of the time. Of course, the extreme possibility of our not being relieved was not entertained, yet what if things went as wrong as they had in 1960? On September 22nd we discovered shortages of a more personal kind for there were only two complete toilet rolls left, and two packets of Persil – this with three months to go!

Much less serious, but with an impact on our general morale, was the shortage of tobacco. John smoked a few cigarettes a day and I enjoyed having a pipe. It was soon obvious that the few tins of tobacco I had grabbed up would not last very long, so I put dates on each of the tins to indicate when I could open them. In July I ran out of tobacco two days before the new supply was due; in August it was four days early. On September 2nd I smoked my last pipeful. I knew that I had insufficient to last a year, but I was sorry when it finally ran out altogether. John, meanwhile, was down to a few tins of cigarettes. Neither of us was addicted to tobacco, fortunately, but it was another small pleasure removed from us.

Despite all of our shortages, when my twenty-sixth birthday arrived on August 18th, Brian was on cook duty and he managed to produce a meat pie with the figures 26, made with pastry on the top, served with runner beans, followed by strawberries and custard, peaches, jelly and Ideal milk; he also produced half a bottle of sherry and some nuts. Celebrations indeed!

For well over four months we were effectively trapped within the hut. The darkness and the covering of snow inevitably prevented Brian from working outside, but he was able to work with incredible commitment on his geological researches at his bench (or sometimes in his bed) inside the hut. For John and me, one or other of us was committed to weather observations, but that only took a few minutes three times a day, every other day. Our base duties were also minimal. One person could do everything that was needed to run the base, for the only duties were collecting snow/ice for the water tank, clearing up the hut, keeping the stove going, and cooking, a duty which took increasingly less time as our options ran out. John and I had both served at bases where helping to look after dogs, building work and sharing major duties with other colleagues occupied much of each day. At Fossil Bluff, everything could be done properly and there were still many hours to spare. We therefore had to find other 'tasks' to occupy ourselves, and in this we each showed a good sense of discipline. I spent much time on analysing the meteorological statistics each month, and I spent many hours in writing for my own pleasure, mostly about our time down south. We used to discuss suitable titles for a book about Fossil Bluff and concluded that *The Silent Sound* was probably the best; certainly those three words absolutely described the world on which we looked day after day during those winter months. John worked regularly and expertly at his painting and his dictionary. An important matter in our self-discipline was that we continued to have a structured day, even if on many occasions it did not start until we got up at 11.00 a.m. We never played cards and we had no board games, so we really were on our own.

One recreational-cum-functional activity that we could enjoy was in extending our ice diggings. Each of us, sometimes on our own, often together, would really work hard in tunnelling. By August 27th we had a tunnel about eighteen yards long, fourteen feet below the snow surface, with a crevasse practice pit, two large store areas, a comfortable toilet and two entrances. We later dug a very deep pit for all of our rubbish so that we kept the ground surface clear. This activity was an excellent facility for us to resort to if we were feeling down and wanted to get away from our mates; axing ice is a good form of catharsis!

Our library was small but we each brought some books with us, twenty-one in my case. During the dark months we read a lot, and I got through some of the old classics very quickly; *War and Peace* by Tolstoy in three weeks (about which I was very complimentary), *Sherlock Holmes* by Conan Doyle, *Pickwick Papers* by Dickens, *Eastern Approaches* by Fitzroy Maclean, *Histories* by Herodotus and Boswell's *The Life of Samuel Johnson*. I also tried to read *Festus Merriman* by Eric Linklater and an Erle Stanley Gardner story but I enjoyed neither!

It was paradoxical that the radio, which gave us so much pleasure, with messages from home and colleagues, and with a few minutes of classical or popular music when we chose to crank the generator, should also have been the cause of much anguish amongst us.

Perhaps because of our isolation, we were unable to take a balanced view of the news we were getting. Before mid-winter we were already receiving bad news from France, Cuba, Israel and America; now bad news became a regular feature of our life. In July we heard reports that Russia was rearming furiously, and insisting on a peace treaty with East Germany before the end of the year; the USA responded by saying that this was the first step towards mobilisation. By August 4th, Russia was threatening Berlin; by the 23rd the Western powers had tanks and armoured cars facing the East Germans, 300 yards from their fence which was later to become the Berlin Wall. Early in September, Macmillan and Kennedy sent notes to Khruschev asking him to stop the bomb tests, then America sent 40,000 troops to Germany, and Britain spoke of 500,000 reservists. Dag Hammarskjold, UN Secretary General, was killed on the 18th in suspicious circumstances, and there were reports of genocide in Tibet later on. By October the news was of a Russian fifty-megaton bomb test on the 17th, and a forty-ton bomb explosion on the 23rd, with machine guns along the border in East Germany. Even Tristan da Cunha was not safe, for their volcano erupted and the 280 islanders had to be evacuated. The effect of this news on us was depressing; we all had families at home, and we all wanted to return home, yet we began to wonder what was going to happen, would there in fact be a home to go to? These stories certainly played on our minds and were a major topic of conversation for a long time.

By July 3rd, the three of us had spent four months in very close proximity to each other, much of the time without daylight, with increasingly poor food, with too few formal duties to carry out, and in the atmosphere of a very uncertain future for the world. It was natural, therefore, that any irritations we had with each other might have a considerable impact on our relationships.

A variety of matters created difficulties from time to time. The news gave us concrete matters for discussion and the Russian threat to peace showed major differences of opinion between us which caused extremely heated arguments one evening. Interestingly, the next day we had a further, more reasoned, discussion and we also talked about the value of 'whingeing' in general, especially in our own particular circumstances. We were probably each guilty of having infuriating habits. Sometimes, when we ran out of things to talk about, for

158

example, John would repeat snippets of news from Stonington, ad nauseam; he also liked to give running commentaries on radio plays, which were very intrusive to whatever we others were doing. Brian and I probably had similarly annoying habits, though one is obviously unaware of what constitutes an annoyance. Brian and I were concerned that no food rationing scheme had been agreed on, and this caused a few unpleasant remarks from time to time. We also had different attitudes to cooking and cleaning up afterwards. Perhaps in my own case I was too intolerant of other people outside of our base, and said so; John and Brian were both less critical of others. We always had to try to hide our feelings for our mutual benefit, and it was very hard to do. Inevitably there was a degree of tension between us because, for all of the good qualities we shared, we couldn't get away from each other except by taking our ice axe to the bogloo and bashing away at the ice for a couple of hours.

Matters became even more difficult once our colleagues from Stonington Island, who had set out on August 23rd to join us, began to run into serious difficulties. When the dog sledges left the base, followed shortly after by the Muskegs, our corporate morale rose dramatically. We suddenly had a revived sense of purpose and we all looked forward to three or four weeks when we would be working on wider projects as part of a larger team. On September 10th, a 'Mayday' call went out from Brian Bowler (in charge of the Muskegs) at Compass Islet to say that the ice had all broken up and that they were stuck. Every radio schedule from then on brought generally bad news, until on September 21st we heard that the 'summer programme is off'. We were extremely disappointed and frustrated with this news and it had a demoralising effect on all of us. It was to be ninety-three days from the day they had set out on their journey from Stonington Island to the date when the five men arrived and a little of the summer programme could be saved.

The months passed slowly.

July 19th. We all felt a bit depressed today; the weather has been cloudy for almost two weeks now. I did go for a walk this morning, but visibility was atrocious and conditions unenjoyable ... How nice to think of armchairs and a roaring fire; a classical music background and company at home!

159

July 28th. The sky cleared at night so I took several moonlight shots. The hut is attractive on such a night and I gazed in awe at this incredible world that I always feel privileged to look on.

July 29th. A most incredible dawn. The sun shone on some alto-cumulus cloud and produced a flame red, then all sorts of colours, finally brightening to white. It really was beautiful and we all photographed it. The day being so beautiful, we all went out; Brian up the Pyramid; John along to Uranus Glacier and me to Hollow Valley.

August 13th. Brian finished his cook week in his usual excellent way, handing the job over to me with everything in perfect condition. Yet the things to cook now are very short.

August 16th. Returning to the hut (from a visit to the Sound to examine strand cracks), the bleakness of the Bluff was most striking. The layered beds with snow all over them looked like iced cake. Drift was scurrying across the ice and the sun was shining to the north. All very splendid.

August 17th. Cold, high pressure, windy and gloriously sunny. Temperature –20°F to –31°F. John and Brian skied down the Sound. I had a miniature 'bath' in a cornflakes tin! They *are* starting from E next week, so three weeks should see them here. It promises to be a very interesting summer and the time should fly.

September 3rd. I saw a bird today!!! The day was magnificently sunny, so after breakfast I skied up the glacier then walked up 'The Gulley' towards the Pyramid. The sun was hot, the scenery superb, and as I walked towards the Pyramid a beautiful white bird – presumably a snow petrel – rose above the Pyramid and flew off to the north. What a grand sight to behold after nearly six months. I returned from the excursion for lunch. Temperatures have been from zero to –12°F. Every so often I have been out to peer at the majesty around us ...

The sight of the single bird meant much to us all, and we all kept a close look out for more, so I recorded three on September 9th, two on the 15th, four on the 16th, all snow petrels, but really very few. It is an interesting circumstance that causes one to record, and indeed to

160

look for, every single appearance of living creatures in an area so inimical to any life at all.

We also looked for the various optical phenomena which brightened our lives: fantastic haloes, sun pillars, mock suns, parhelions and parhelic circles (particularly brilliant on September 30th). Auroral displays were occasionally seen but never with such brilliance as that first display on April 14th.

There was a need, given the uncertainties surrounding the travellers from Stonington Island, for us to get involved in more purposeful activity. By early October the light was good for many hours and the snow had cleared from many slopes as a result of the wind. In any case we were getting through our books too quickly, three days to read Hardy's *Tess of the D'Urbervilles*, and three days to read *The Mayor of Casterbridge*, both in the same week!

The new sense of purpose arose from Brian, who was anxious to start on field work again in a different area. He wanted to set up a camp for several weeks at the bottom of a 2,000-foot scree slope at the back of the Bluff. On October 8th, John reconnoitred a route but returned after he had found it impossible. All three of us traipsed along to Uranus Glacier, to the south of the Bluff, hoping to cross a small glacier, get round the end of the Bluff then work our way along the side of the Uranus Glacier to the chosen site under the west-facing slope of the Pyramid. After taking an hour to climb a 200-foot ice/snow slope, we came to an area that was cut by evil crevasses; so we retreated. On the next day we went up to the Pyramid to see if there was a way down from there, and John and Brian roped up and pioneered a route down the long, steep, icy slope. It was impracticable to take a normal tent down, so we would have to settle for the very small pup tent. On the 13th, we all carried equipment back to the top and they slowly made their way to the new camp site, (Camp 1). John would spend the next twelve days with Brian, I would follow in support for the next twenty-two.

Meanwhile the men from Stonington Island whom we had expected to greet towards the end of September were still trapped in Marguerite Bay.

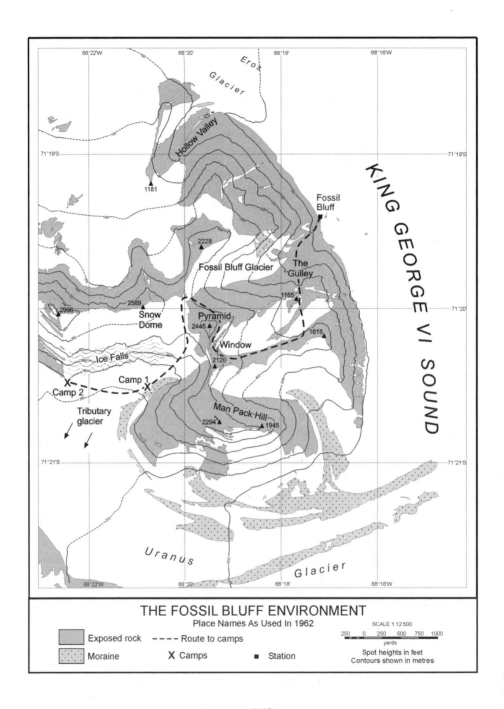

THE FOSSIL BLUFF ENVIRONMENT
Place Names As Used In 1962

SCALE 1:12 500

| Exposed rock | - - - - Route to camps |
| Moraine | X Camps | ■ Station |

Spot heights in feet
Contours shown in metres

162

18

The Camp by the Glacier

I returned to the silent hut in the silent Sound. I thought it particularly important, whilst I was alone, to keep busy, so, after making the weather observations, I started work on bringing all the food into the hut and sorting it out. In the evening I listened in to the Stonington Island radio schedule with the sledgers in Marguerite Bay; even if I had been proficient at Morse I could not have participated, because turning the pedal with one hand whilst tapping out messages with the other was a very difficult process – though John later secured the pedals to a base board which enabled him to use his feet, thus freeing both his hands for this task. Just before I retired to bed, I read the thermometer, then showing –18°F, and I thought of Brian and John in the pup tent.

I had a strong feeling of loneliness on the following day; we had no radio communication between the hut and the camp, so there was a real sense of isolation. I was determined to lead a busy life, so I had proper meals at the correct times and busied myself with lots of writing, reading and outside activities. I also consumed almost half a tin of currants, and the resultant stomach ache gave me a slight touch of hypochondria; doctors were a long way away!

October 15th and 16th were days of cloud and wind, the 16th having winds from the north-east which I estimated at forty knots, with temperatures rising to +33°F. The campers must have found these conditions very uncomfortable; at Stonington Island the temperature rose to +42°F, a real heatwave! I spent much time in philosophising during this time. I continued to be depressed by the world news and this prompted me to dwell on the theme of using whatever time I had, fully. It also made me feel creative, so I wrote a poem called *The Snow Petrel*! In fact the loneliness and isolation produced extremes of mood, a touch of hypochondria, easily dispatched, a sense of depression from the world news, not so easily dispatched, then lots of positive thinking on planning for the future with great optimism.

One day John suddenly appeared. Brian was planning to take another twenty-five days in his work, so more supplies were required, and I agreed to relieve John in a few days' time. He reported that it was 'boring and uncomfortable' in the pup tent. The next few days passed quietly by, and on the 24th I spent much time in clearing up the hut, even washing the floor, so that it would be in a good condition for John when he returned.

Next day was sunny to start with and I trekked up to the Pyramid. When I reached the top I looked down and could see John cutting steps up the ice field towards me. Just as we met, the paraffin can which he had been carrying fell from his pack and slid down some 200 feet. When we tried to retrieve it, a crevasse was probed so we had to accept its loss. Brian also came up the ice slope, and once John had departed we both went back down to the camp site.

The tiny pup tent had been pitched by Brian and John on a stretch of flat ice at the edge of a tributary ice field feeding into the huge Uranus Glacier some two and a half miles before it issued into King George VI Sound. It was at 1,000 feet above sea level, just over 1,400 feet below the Pyramid. Behind the camp site the layered sedimentary rocks rose very steeply. Opposite the site, across the ice of the glacier, was a huge series of ice falls tumbling very steeply from the peak we called Snow Dome. Shortly after our arrival, Brian returned to his task of working slowly up the rock face. I sorted out my gear and checked the sledge boxes to see what food we had. I was daunted by the smallness of the tent, really only big enough for one person in these conditions, but it had to do. I went out for a preliminary sortie before cooking my first meal in the tent.

We soon settled into a routine. We usually breakfasted before 8.00 a.m., and if there was any prospect of work, Brian would be on his way within an hour. I would clear up the tent and get things organised; this often involved taking out the sheepskins and even the sleeping bags in order to dry them. I would then spend much time wandering up and along the hill sides, always on the look-out for interesting fossils. The range of walks was defined by the edges of the ice; it would have been dangerous to cross any such areas alone. Back at the tent, I would read, or reread some of the books we had with us. Often Brian would stay out for ten hours, so there were long days to fill. Even when there was light snow, or wind and cloud, Brian would valiantly continue with his work, rarely surrendering to the elements and returning early; on only four days during our time together at the camp were we tent-bound for the whole day.

Food was a problem, as ever:

October 28th. A day in the tent. It blew all night and carried on throughout the day. Our food is pathetically short – porridge, 2 biscuits, butter and tea for breakfast; bacon and 3 biscuits for lunch (bacon once every five days), and meat bar stew, 3 biscuits and cocoa for dinner. And one bar of chocolate to see us through the rest of the day.

October 29th. Another day in the tent. Brian set out after 9.30 a.m. but had to return soon after 1.00 p.m. We look forward to eating time on such days as this, but tonight we had pemmican, which is terrible, just like sand. My stomach is still complaining.

November 2nd. ... then arrived the time to prepare the dreaded pemmican. It is foul, like sand. The trouble is that we have a lot of old Base J boxes. In this particular one, the chocolate is bad. Ugh!

The dramatic scenery continued to give us much pleasure, and a few surprises. One day I noted how grand the great ice falls opposite us looked; two days later I had a real fright when there was a great crack, like an explosion from the same falls, and I thought that they were about to collapse and charge across the glacier towards us. Walks up to the tops of the ridges always provided views of breath-taking beauty, either of the majesty of Graham Land, or the infinity of ice stretching southwards towards the pole, or looking towards the western areas of Alexander Island to Mount Ariel and beyond, places that we yearned to travel to but had no prospects of attaining. Close by, when up on the high slopes behind the tent, I could look across at the great mass of Snow Dome, probably over 2,500 feet high, with its south face plastered in snow and ice, and its blue/white-coloured, treacherous ice falls tumbling down from its side. I also enjoyed experiencing a phenomenon called 'Glory' one day, as I was walking along a very narrow ridge. Suddenly my shadow appeared on the clouds below me, phantom-like and surrounded by a red-coloured halo; a really dramatic effect, which I have never seen again.

We were completely out of contact with anybody so we lacked any news on the progress of the sledging party. When I had been back at the base on my own, I regularly listened in to the radio schedules and was able to track the various movements of the Stonington men, obviously our most important consideration. One evening, a week after my arrival at the camp, we were particularly pleased to see John, who had trekked over with some new food supplies. He also brought news that the sledgers were at Cape Jeremy, so there was a real prospect that they would be arriving soon. It is amazing how, in our circumstances, such information gave us a wealth of conversational topics to discuss and to mull over; human conversation is important to morale! Brian and I spent a great many hours within the tent when the weather was too bad even for him to work. Conversation played a great part in our life and we enjoyed a great many discussions. Brian and I always found plenty of things to talk about; one day it was caving, camping, university scholarships, and teachers' pay; another we compared the courses at Swansea and Keele Universities; we had discussions on the state of the world, we also discussed books, especially professional books such as a geology masterpiece by Krumbein and Schloss! We were always able to chat about anything; I always found Brian excellent company.

We had major problems with wetness. With the temperatures rising we often found that the heat of our bodies had melted the snow/ice under the tent, and depressions would appear underneath us which filled in with melted water. So on October 30th, and on November 3rd, we had to take everything out of the tent and lay things out to dry. We also had to move the tent in order to be able to sleep on a new flat area.

By November 4th the sun was rising as early as 4.00 a.m. and setting at 11.00 p.m., so Brian was able to remain out at work for even longer. Back in the tent for several hours a day, I soon read the four books that we had, a Margery Allingham detective story, *Festus Merriman* (again), Trevelyan's *History of England*, and *The Human Species* by Anthony Barnett; but time hung heavy.

Occasionally, on a fine day I would make the journey back to base, partly for exercise, partly to take rocks and bring back new supplies:

November 5th. A most glorious day – and something to show for it. Soon after Brian had left after 9.15 a.m., I decided to go back

166

to base. Apart from the 5 hours it would take, Brian's specimens have to go back, we wanted some food, and there might be interesting news. I left at 10.30 a.m. with 80 lbs of rocks, a ski stick and an ice axe. I made my way along the side of the moraine, across the dreaded ice slope – which was extremely easy today – under the tier of the Pyramid, down the ramp and the Gulley, then to the base. It took 2 hours 20 minutes. The hut was in a chaotic state, of course, though in fairness to John, he is painting it and it looks good. However, he stood the precious one and a half gallons of meths on a snow lump and the wind blew it over. Result, one cocoa tin of meths left! The sledges are still around Cape Jeremy in deep, soft snow ... I had lunch and lots of tea, then set out at 2.10 p.m. for another 2 hour 20 minute walk. The sun shone fiercely, a wind blew; it was gloriously exhilarating. I brought back 4 tins of meat bar, 1 corned beef and 1 raspberries – luxuries indeed! Such days make Antarctica intensely satisfying.

On November 7th, we experienced a severe gale and were stuck inside the tent for many hours. For obvious reasons it was sometimes necessary to use a 'pee can' within the tent if conditions were really bad. On this occasion, as Brian opened the tent door to empty the can, he noticed that our food box – with all our food in it, had disappeared. 'I say, Pearce, have you seen our sledge box? Bloody thing must have blown away in the gale,' he called out. He dressed, and searched for it in winds of perhaps fifty-plus knots with visibility of fifteen to twenty yards, a real blizzard, but to no avail. Next day he recovered it on the moraine a quarter of a mile away. Our problem was that the tent was too small to accommodate the box whilst we were sleeping, but we ensured that it was properly secured with big rocks for the rest of the time. On that same day, the weather abated but it was still impossible for Brian to work, so he returned to the base to take rocks back and to bring more food supplies. He brought back with him a Medical Research Council food box. When we opened it, we found a week's supply of HF5 (like pemmican), which displeased us, but we found some good food – two bars of chocolate, a small fruit bar, cheese, pumpernickel and lemonade, all of which really pleased us.

As summer approached we began to see more and more snow petrels, as many as eight and ten on consecutive days in the middle of the month. The only other bird we recognised, however, was a South Georgian teal, presumably way off course; there were no skuas.

We still had some very demoralising times at the camp on the glacier, wetness being the all-pervasive attribute of camp life, yet there was always a positive side to things:

November 10th. When things are at their worst, then suddenly comes an incredible change. That was how we felt at 11.00 a.m. this morning. All night long the wind had shrieked and snow had fallen. About 7.00 a.m., I awoke to find myself lying in a puddled hollow; my bag was soaked all over, and I later tipped out a panful of water from the sheepskin. I cooked the breakfast and then ventured outside, determined to do something about it. But the wind still howled and sent drift everywhere. I returned to the tent and sat for a hopeless hour. Then at 11.00 a.m., the wind dropped and the sun shone from clear skies. Very soon we had everything out on the slopes; we moved the tent and sorted out our gear. The weather held and we rejoiced in the warmth. At 4.00 p.m. the sun had so worked on the snow that Brian decided to go up the slope to get 4 hours of work in!

What a difference a drying day makes!

By November 12th, Brian had spent more than thirty days working his way meticulously up a thousand or more feet of exposures, though with some days lost to bad weather, and with some time spent looking at other exposures. By mid-November he was beginning to want to move elsewhere. We therefore commenced the process of withdrawing from the camp. On the 14th, while Brian was still working, I loaded a box containing sixty to seventy pounds of rock and slowly made my way back up to the Pyramid tier. The surface was generally deep with soft snow, which made conditions very unpleasant, and occasionally the ice was exposed and was very slippery and dangerous and, of course, one false step could have had me sliding down hundreds of feet. It therefore took me two and a half hours to reach the top, where I made a depot of the load. I made the same journey next day (whilst Brian was concluding his work), and continued on to the base with the load of rocks and some other equipment which needed to be brought back. I caught up with all the news about the sledgers and returned to camp for the last time, noting that the ice slope had great potential for an avalanche at that

168

time, with deep, wet, slippery snow on silvery steep ice.

On the 16th, Brian and I dismantled the tent and carefully depoted it, together with some other supplies, on some rocks above the edge of the ice. Brian wanted to work further west in future, so it would have been pointless to carry everything home and then have to start again. The slope was hard work as usual and we puffed and sweated our way to the top and made good progress, reaching the hut in two and a half hours. We arrived back earlier than John had expected, so that he had not had time to clear up the hut, perhaps because he had been working hard on painting the outside, though an area of drift had obstructed him in part, so he had painted round it! John had also increased the number of weather observations to five a day, and was transmitting them over the radio to Stonington three times daily, in order to provide the sledgers with as much information as possible.

We were soon enjoying a meal. Cooking, when hunched up over a Primus stove in a tiny tent with the wind shrieking outside, is a very difficult operation, so we enjoyed having so much space and cooking surfaces at our disposal on the Rayburn stove. Soon we had caught up with the news of the sledging teams and all of the frustrations and difficulties they had had and were still experiencing. It was one week later when they finally arrived at Fossil Bluff.

19

Struggling South – from Stonington to Fossil Bluff

The prime objective of establishing Fossil Bluff as a forward base was that it should make possible geological and survey work on Alexander Island and eventually in areas further afield. It was therefore of paramount importance that men and materials and equipment should get to Fossil Bluff as early as possible, preferably during September or early October, when at least three or four months of field work could be carried out. There were eleven men at Stonington who each had a part to play in trying to bring about this main objective:

John Cunningham	– Base Leader
Bryan Bowler	– General Assistant i/c Muskegs
Howard Chapman	– Surveyor
Arthur Fraser	– Geologist
Roger Matthews	– Meteorologist
Bob Metcalfe	– Surveyor
Tony Quinn	– Radio Operator
Brian Sparke	– Medical Officer
Bill Tracy	– General Assistant
Mike Tween	– Diesel Electric Mechanic
Brian Wigglesworth	– Meteorologist

John Cunningham was an outstanding mountaineer who had climbed extensively in the Himalayas, and elsewhere. He was serving the second of three consecutive years down south, all as base leader, the first at Port Lockroy, the latter two at Stonington Island. (Later still, in 1964 he returned to Adelaide Island and led the first ascent of Mount Andrew Jackson, the highest mountain in Graham Land at over 11,700 feet.)

Mike Tween and Tony Quinn spent almost their entire year at the base, apart from short local trips, in order to provide power and to maintain radio communication with other bases and with the various parties that were in the field. This was especially important when things started to go wrong. I had shared a year with Mike, and Roger Matthews, one of the meteorologists, at Deception Island in 1960, so we all knew each other very well.

Brian Wigglesworth had trained in meteorology in Stanmore, with others of us, and had taken on the role of forecaster for the aircraft when he was at the Argentine Islands during 1960.

Arthur Fraser was one of two geologists; Brian Taylor, the other, was already at Fossil Bluff. We three had shared a cabin on the long journey south in the *Kista Dan* in 1960. Arthur was based at Wordie House, Argentine Islands, during 1960 after the failure to relieve Stonington earlier in that year; Brian had returned home after the debacle, and was now back for the first of two years at work on Alexander Island.

Bryan Bowler, on secondment from the army, was responsible for the Muskegs.

Bill Tracy had major responsibilities for the dogs. He had worked at Hope Bay during 1960, so had plenty of appropriate experience.

Dr Brian Sparke had worked at the Argentine Islands during 1960.

Howard Chapman and Bob Metcalfe were the two surveyors, who had major commitments to surveying work when Fossil Bluff was finally reached.

During July the dog drivers started training the dog teams, and the Muskegs were prepared for the great journey south. Thirty dogs had been landed in February and there were already twelve dogs who had sledged down from Horseshoe Island in the previous August so there were sufficient for at least four teams if necessary. Several of the men were trained to drive the two Muskegs under instruction from Bryan Bowler.

At Fossil Bluff we listened on the radio for any signs of movement, and by August 15th we were talking optimistically of lengthening days and of being outside and the arrival of the men from 'Stonners'. By the 17th we had confirmation that they would be starting in the following week and, sure enough, on the 23rd two dog teams, the 'Players' and the 'Spartans' with Bill Tracy and Brian Wigglesworth driving together with Roger Matthews, set out on what was to have been an initial depot laying journey. Four days later they reached Compass Islet about forty miles from Stonington. We felt delighted

172

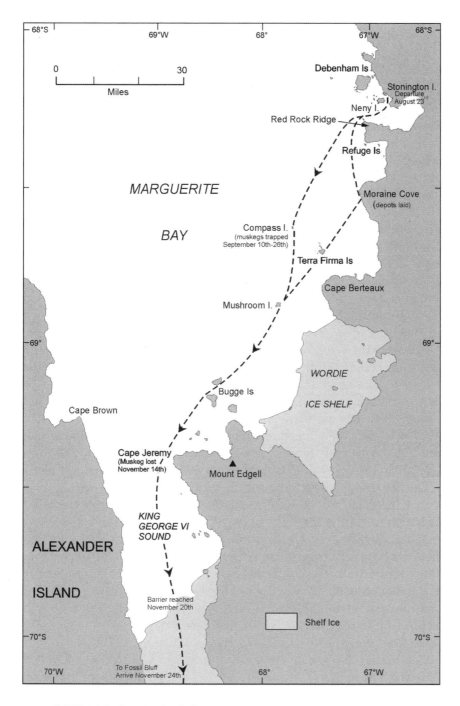

STRUGGLING SOUTH - MAIN DIRECTIONS

that movements were taking place so early! On the 24th the two Muskegs started out with Bryan Bowler, Howard Chapman, Arthur Fraser and Bob Metcalfe. They were towing four well laden sledges, again in order to lay a depot on Mushroom Island, about fifty miles to the south. My diary recorded optimistically:

August 24th. The sledges and Muskegs have started from Stonington and are on their way. Soon our quietness and peace will be shattered, but it promises to be an interesting summer.

During a reconnaissance journey in July it had been observed that the ice closest to the coast was full of consolidated lumps of brash ice and bergy bits which made it unsuitable for the Muskegs. They therefore moved out to the west and, after ten days, including a stop on Compass Islet, they succeeded in reaching Mushroom Island towing two of the four sledges. The next day they returned to Compass Islet to collect the other two sledges. They now laid their depot of supplies of fuel on Mushroom Island. On September 8th they set out northwards for Stonington Island to collect more supplies. As they approached Compass Islet again, a gale blew up and blizzard conditions over many hours caused the ice to break up where they were camping, just off the islet. At Fossil Bluff we heard of their predicament over the radio when we picked up a 'Mayday, Mayday' call, sent out by Bryan Bowler on September 10th. The party found themselves on a large detached ice floe floating amidst a mass of broken ice. Very fortunately for them, the ice floe had been pressed against the islet and they were able to scramble ashore over the few yards where the ice and the shore touched. They had six weeks of food and fuel supplies with them, based on half rations per man. There was a real prospect that they might lose both Muskegs if the ice floe drifted out to sea; in the event, the Muskegs remained on the ice floe for a week. Eventually, with good fortune, they were able to get them ashore to the foot of an ice cliff where they were at least safe, but unusable until the ice formed again.

The dog sledging teams had arrived at Compass Islet on August 27th, but they had been unable to move for a week due mainly to thick cloud at sea level. However, as soon as the opportunity arose on September 3rd, they moved quickly southwards and reached Mushroom Island where once more the weather closed in and they remained there for a week. Another break, however, enabled them to

174

make progress and on the 11th, they reached the Bugge Islands, fifteen miles north of Cape Jeremy.

That same day, John Cunningham at Stonington Island reported eighty-knot winds which had broken the ice and produced leads everywhere, and the outlook became both dangerous and disappointing, for there was no prospect of the Muskegs getting back to Stonington for the rest of their cargoes. At this time, therefore, the Muskegs were marooned on Compass Islet, and the dog teams were well to the south of them. John Cunningham tried to be optimistic, but the outlook in the near future was definitely bleak. Two movements were then set in train:

– the dog sledgers were to attempt to go back from the Bugge Islands to Mushroom, then on to Terra Firma Island to lay a depot; they completed this in five days and went on to reach Compass Islet with some food boxes to supplement the supplies of the marooned men;

– John Cunningham and Brian Sparke were to sledge from Stonington Island to the Refuge Islands, climb to the highest point and study the ice, but they were held up for five days by bad weather. They eventually reached their destination after almost a week.

The Governor of the Falkland Islands, Sir Edwin Arrowsmith, then intervened. On September 14th he issued a statement requesting that the men be withdrawn from Compass Islet as soon as possible, leaving the Muskegs to be picked up by the *John Biscoe* when the summer came. A week later a telegram went to John Cunningham from the SecFids in Port Stanley declaring that the summer programme was OFF. The Muskeg party was to withdraw to the Terra Firma Islands and leave the Muskegs there. The field men were to be deployed back at Stonington Island to do what work they could in that area! At Fossil Bluff, our spirits sank; we wondered, however, whether the dog teams might continue on their way to us as the dogs were naturally able to overcome difficult ice conditions more easily than the Muskegs; we even wondered whether the aircraft might fly down to Fossil Bluff and evacuate us.

Back at Stonington Island, at the centre of conflicting orders and aspirations, John Cunningham was working on a variety of strategies to keep the summer programme alive. He tried to get the two Otters to come down to help. Although they were sorely needed, the aircraft apparently could not be sent down south. On the 25th more new plans emanated from Stanley, and some decisions were made. The two Muskegs were going to make a further attempt to reach Fossil Bluff, but Arthur Fraser was going to return to Stonington Island and work on the Blackwall mountains some five to ten miles from the base, with John Cunningham and Brian Sparke in support. The two dog teams would also try to reach Fossil Bluff, though Roger Matthews would return to Stonington Island to provide weather information. The men actually in the thick of the difficulties were despondent, for it was felt that the plans were being made far away by men not really au fait with the situation – the Muskeg drivers were now being told to get their vehicles to Fossil Bluff at all costs, whilst on the other hand, John Cunningham and Brian Sparke were being told not to try to go to Compass Islet because the ice was too dangerous! John and Brian therefore pushed further south to leave a depot at Moraine Cove by the Bertrand ice piedmont, which they reached on October 4th. When John and Brian finally headed north five days later, they travelled on mushy ice only four inches thick, through which John fell.

In the complicated pattern of journeys which then ensued the following deployments were made:

– Bill Tracy and Brian Wigglesworth with their dog teams travelled the thirty miles to Moraine Cove to pick up the material from the depot and then took their supplies back to Mushroom Island;

– John Cunningham and Brian Sparke made another run with further supplies from Stonington to Moraine Cove, where they waited for a day or two for Bill Tracy and his colleagues to return in order to pick up these additional supplies (including mail), to take south. Bill had to stay there for a few days because of snow blindness; meanwhile Roger Matthews returned to Stonington with John and Brian.

It was to be over six frustrating weeks before the sea ice around Compass Islet had frozen sufficiently for the Muskegs to try to move south again on October 24th. At last they were able to make their way to the Wordie Ice Shelf where they eventually linked up with Bill Tracy and Brian Wigglesworth on October 25th.

By the end of October, therefore, matters were becoming clearer – the two Muskegs with three men and four heavy sledges (having had the Moraine Cove depots transferred to them), and the two dog teams with two men, were on their way to Fossil Bluff, and were approaching Cape Jeremy. The rest of the men had returned to Stonington Island. It seemed fairly straightforward for the rest of the journey. By November 2nd the party reached Cape Jeremy and turned south. Progress was slowed as a result of bad weather and it took twelve days to get to a point forty miles from the ice barrier marking the northern end of King George VI Sound. Nevertheless, things were going well and success was at hand when disaster struck on November 10th. The Muskegs were being driven in an area where leads had refrozen and had been covered by snow. Several such areas had been negotiated before, when suddenly the leading Muskeg sank into deep snow and water started trickling into the cab through two small holes in the cab floor. It kept sinking. Bryan Bowler jumped out and cut the sledge free from the Muskeg as it disappeared into the depths below; it took two minutes to do so and took with it Bob Metcalfe's cameras and Howard Chapman's skis. Howard, who was driving the second Muskeg thirty yards behind later remembered the bubbling of the exhaust as it sank into its watery grave with the engine still running, and the tail end of the cut tow rope as it ran across the ice and followed the Muskeg into the depths. They spent a lot of time looking despairingly at the great hole!

Bill Tracy and Brian Wigglesworth, who had moved on well ahead of the others, immediately turned back north to help – an eight day journey. The five of them reorganised the loads, the surviving Muskeg pulling three of the cargo sledges. A few days later, on the 20th, the party finally reached the barrier, where a huge rift in the shelf ice presented great difficulties for them to get round. They only travelled two miles during the next day but achieved their objective, and had climbed nearly 150 feet on to the barrier surface. The road ahead was straight and clear!

By the 22nd, we heard at Fossil Bluff that the party was only thirty-four miles from us, so John and I climbed the slopes above the hut and cleared snow so as to mark the words WELCOME in large letters. We tidied up the front of the base hut and painted the name 'Bluebell Cottage' above the door; we also went down into the Sound and planted a notice, 'Cottage Teas 1.4 miles'. Travelling on the ice of the Sound we knew to be easy, so we were not surprised when the last thirty-four miles were covered in a few hours. Thus it was that at 1.00 p.m. on November 24th they arrived, having travelled approximately 350 miles in all, though the actual distance from Stonington Island to Fossil Bluff was closer to 240 miles. It had taken them ninety-three days, though on seventy-three of these no travel was possible for the Muskeg teams. Amazingly, however, they had covered 100 miles in the last three days. The men, Bill Tracy, Brian Wigglesworth, Bryan Bowler, Howard Chapman and Bob Metcalfe all looked bronzed and fit; the dogs were very tired. During their journey they had no opportunity to have a bath or shower (neither would they enjoy such luxuries now that they had arrived!); they had also spent a great number of days lying up in their tents when it was impossible to move. It was sad to see just one of the two Muskegs which we had unloaded onto the ice from the *John Biscoe* on March 1st, finally making it to Fossil Bluff.

We were naturally thrilled to see them all, the first new faces since March 4th, a total of 263 days. We prepared the very best meal we could, and sat and chatted for many hours, mainly about the journey, and about plans for future work in the short time ahead.

The outcome of the trip was a matter which concerned us all. Only half of the new supplies had been successfully delivered because the Muskegs had been unable to return to Stonington for their second loads; only one Muskeg had reached the base because the second one had sunk; two dog teams had arrived when it might have been three; five men had arrived when it might have been nine. Perhaps the most damaging problem was the lateness in the season, for by the end of December it was certain that the increased temperatures would make the surfaces for dog travelling very difficult, so that any work had to be completed before then in just over five weeks instead of the anticipated thirteen or fourteen.

Obviously the main cause of the problem was the unreliability of the sea ice. The Muskegs appeared to be unsuitable for long journeys over variable sea ice; they were too heavy and once they were in difficulties they were helpless, though in the following year two new Muskegs did successfully make the journey. The dogs, of course, were able to travel on much thinner ice and had the ability to get themselves out of difficult situations; on the other hand their carrying capacity was very low in terms of helping to resupply a base. There was disappointment in the group that the two Otters were not flown down from Deception Island to Adelaide Island and then to the sea ice at Stonington. John Cunningham was informed that there were problems with an oil leak, and that they were needed to help at Hope

Bay. Although the aircraft could not have taken the Muskegs, they might have lifted most of the dogs and general supplies, thus giving the Muskegs an easy run, and getting the whole summer programme off to an early start. (The Muskegs had actually reached Mushroom Island on September 2nd, it was only when they returned north for their second loads that they became trapped on Compass Islet.)

Perhaps also the lines of command were confused. John Cunningham was the leader in the field and he knew better than anyone what needed to be done. However, he had to defer to John Green, SecFids, in Stanley, who was probably getting advice and instruction from Sir Vivian Fuchs in London. Then suddenly, the Governor of the Falkland Islands, Sir Edwin Arrowsmith issued his request/order for the men to be withdrawn immediately from Compass Islet. Eventually, dog teams and men, and ultimately the Muskegs, seemed to be criss-crossing Marguerite Bay in all directions.

Many of us now gathered at Fossil Bluff had been on the *Kista Dan* in the 1960 season and on the *John Biscoe* early in 1961. Now, as we reviewed the recent journey, and its limited degree of success, we began to wonder whether the Falkland Islands Dependencies Survey was more than acceptably accident prone!

20

South with the Dogs

Within a day of the arrival of the men from Stonington Island, we discussed what could be salvaged from the summer programme. Brian Taylor, having completed his work in the area by the camp on the glacier, was now ready to work farther afield. His new area was to be approximately one mile from the previous camp, across the glacier which fed the Uranus Glacier. The great advantage of this was that he could be supported just by men and without the use of the dogs. This left the dog teams available to support the surveyors, Howard and Bob. They wanted to work as far south down King George VI Sound as they could get, using tellurometers to tie in the various survey points in an area that had only been tentatively mapped by sledgers Stephenson, Fleming and Bertram in 1936, Ronne and Eklund in 1940, and Fuchs and Adie in 1949. That was as much as they could hope to achieve at this late stage in the season, but it would be a good contribution as a basis for further work. In order for the surveyors to have sufficient supplies to keep them going for four or five weeks, it was necessary to lay a depot in the area of Latitude 72°S. John and I therefore joined Brian Wigglesworth and Bill Tracy to carry out the first part of this plan.

Before we set out on our journey, we had to get Brian established at his new geological camp. On November 27th we set to work. John, Brian and I, together with Howard, Bob and Bryan Bowler, carried the equipment up to the Pyramid and down the ice slope, then across the glacier for the first time. Because of the necessary relaying of supplies up to, and down from, just below the Pyramid, I made this trip five times during the day, about 9,000 feet of ascent and 10 miles of walking. This was probably the most fatiguing day I ever had down south; it started at 9.00 a.m. and finished at 1.30 a.m.! However, in the space of one day, thanks to a doubling of our labour supply, we had established Brian in a good location for many weeks of work.

We spent the next day preparing for the depot-laying journey, and enjoying new conversations. Howard worked at the Rayburn stove

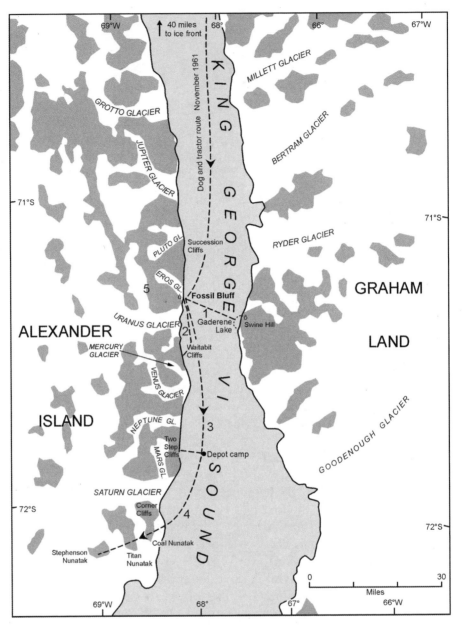

FOSSIL BLUFF JOURNEYS 1961
Place Names As Used In 1962

▭ Ice-free ground

1. Autumn journey (Smith, Pearce)
2. Preliminary geological survey (Taylor,Smith)
3. Depot journey (Smith, Pearce, Tracy, Wigglesworth)
4. Survey journey (Tracy, Wigglesworth, Chapman, Metcalfe)
5. Major area of geological work (Taylor, Smith, Pearce)

and for the evening meal introduced us to a new dish, crabeater seal and emperor penguin steaks; they really were delicious!

We were up at 5.30 a.m. next morning, and away two hours later. It takes a long time to set out on a dog sledge journey. Firstly there were the dogs to be fed and checked. Bill and Brian decided to leave three dogs behind; Tess was ill, Vicar had a broken leg and Pasha was getting too old for much more hard work. The two Greenland sledges were loaded, food for men and dogs, tents, Primus stoves and pots and pans, fuel, the supplies for the depot, skis and ski sticks etc, all very securely tied down onto the sledge. Nothing must be left behind; the best-laid plans will soon be thwarted if the matches are forgotten!

John went with Bill and his seven-dog team, the Players; I joined Brian with his six-dog team, the Spartans. The surface was hard so we soon reached a good speed of between three and four miles an hour. Once we got down into the Sound we put on our skis and allowed ourselves to be pulled along by the dogs. We travelled for nearly four hours, covering fourteen miles, and we made our course about three miles out from the Alexander Island coast so as to avoid any disturbances arising from the inflow of glaciers into the Sound. During the summer months the surface warms up during the morning and makes travel difficult, hence our early start and finish. That day we camped level with Waitabit Cliffs, and immediately spanned out the dogs, with carefully placed ice pickets at each end of the line. Husky dogs like nothing better than a good fight, so spanning and picketing them firmly was a vitally important first task.

We then set to work on erecting the tent. The tents used were always pyramid tents, with four corner supports meeting at a height over six feet. They had a double skin with a gap between the skins of four or five inches. The ground sheet was built into the tent; the entrance consisted of a long sleeve through which we crawled to get inside; this prevented snow from blowing in when conditions were bad. We always brushed the snow from our boots as we clambered inside. There was sufficient room for two men to sleep on either side of the various boxes containing the radio, the food and the Primus stove and cooking pots. Our personal belongings could be stored at our feet. The pyramid tent offered true luxury after our cramped conditions in the pup tent; it also had the great merit that it could be erected in a very short time because it was all part of one structure. One of the tents was white, the usual colour, the other was black.

This was part of an experiment to see if black tents were more conducive to sleep at a time when the sun was above the horizon for all twenty-four hours. Most sledgers were often so tired that they did not need such false darkness to help them get to sleep!

Once the dogs had been spanned and the tent erected, the work was shared between us, one doing the outside work, the other carrying out the work inside the tent. Brian, the 'outside man', passed in the necessary boxes – food, radio and Primus box – through the sleeve, followed by lumps of hard snow to be melted down for water. He then attended to the business of giving each dog a bar of nutrican, and checked that all was well with them. The dogs loved nutrican and often ate it with the paper still on. My job, as 'inside man' on this occasion, was firstly to arrange things on the floor of the tent, then – much later – to start preparing the meal. The Primus stove had to be lit, then a snow-filled saucepan would be placed over the flame so as to melt as quickly as possible. The next task was to select the food for the main meal and cook it. We spent the rest of the day, before having our main meal, in pottering about, reading, and making contact with Howard at Fossil Bluff. We all retired at about 8.00 p.m., knowing that we would have an early start next day.

November 30th. Another splendid day. We arose at 4.00 a.m. in mist. By 6.00 a.m. we were all ready to be off. Bill and John led first away, then Brian and I. The surface was level and the dogs moved well, we moved serenely along on skis. We travelled 18 miles in 5 hours before stopping at 11.00 a.m. We are now at a point immediately south of Neptune Glacier. The coastal ranges of Alexander Island are unchanging – long beds of sediments cut through by glaciers. The Sound really is a great white highway. We camped and dined and slept and skedded with Tony Quinn at E and with Howard at FB. The *Biscoe* left Stanley yesterday, moving southwards, so things might move within a month! Naturally John and I are keen to push on southwards, at least as far as the turn of the Sound to the west. Let us hope conditions stay as they are. We have so little time. The weather is perfect; sunny all the time (after the mist went), warm, comfortable. In fact all is incredibly beautiful and pleasant ...

The next day proved to be somewhat disappointing. We arose again at 4.00 a.m. and were away by 6.00 a.m. The cloud cover was very low and we soon entered fog. We kept going for two and a half hours but the visibility remained poor, so we had to make camp. When there was a break in the cloud we were able to determine our position at a point ten miles south of our overnight camp, and a couple of miles east of Two Step Cliffs. We were then about eight miles north of Latitude 72°S, the point reached by Stephenson, Fleming and Bertram on October 19th 1936, when they had already travelled 295 miles from their base on the Debenham Islands in Marguerite Bay. Conditions at that time of the year enabled them to travel for eight hours up to 5.00 p.m. each day, a fact that confirmed in our minds that we had missed the best of the season. Conditions improved a little later on in the day, so Bill, John and I trekked the long way to the rock exposures which tower up in perfectly marked sedimentary beds at Two Step Cliffs. There were large areas of moraine, and lots of meltwater lakes; we even heard the noise of a sub-glacial meltwater stream. We were close to Saturn Glacier, and could see that the sides of this massive glacier were considerably churned up.

A complete lie-up day followed. We had hoped to take a few dogs and look for a route up the Mars Glacier, a small glacier north of Saturn, but an unpleasant wind arose and blew throughout the rest of the day. Already we had reached a suitable place for the depot to be laid, and though we had hoped to go further we now had to think about returning if Bob and Howard were to have time for their work. On December 4th, we were still unable to head back because of strong winds. However, later on in the morning Bill, John and I took four dogs to find a route behind Two Step Cliffs. It proved to be an easy route with no sign of crevasses. As we looked beyond the Saturn Glacier towards Hyperion Nunataks, we could see extensive melt pools which would preclude much inland travel at this time of the year. We noticed several snow petrels around the cliffs, our old friends from the post-winter period at Fossil Bluff.

Back at the tents, we prepared our food for the evening meal. On sledging trips the food supplies were in boxes which supplied sufficient food for two men for ten days. So four sledge boxes and the equivalent supplies for the dogs could sustain a party of two men in the field for forty days. Each box carried the same supplies, so we had the following meals:

Breakfast – Quaker Oats porridge, with lots of milk and sugar, followed by several plain biscuits with lots of butter and,

185

perhaps, Marmite flavouring. Sometimes if there was no hurry to get under way, we could use a rasher of bacon from our limited supply. This would be followed by plenty of tea.

Lunch – Usually if on the move, a fruit bar or a piece of chocolate was eaten with a handful of melted snow. On a full day of travelling it was impracticable to stop in the middle of the day and unpack the boxes.

Dinner – Meat bar was placed in a pan of melted water, and to this was added a packet of soup, onions, and perhaps a rasher of bacon. Chivers potato powder could be added or prepared separately. In our case we also carried dehydrated runner beans. The whole mixture would be cooked for a long time, with a lot of stirring, and would provide a very palatable meal, to which we added salt. This would be followed with several biscuits spread with lots of butter, and Marmite, and we concluded the repast with chocolate or fruit bar. In the evening we had cocoa or tea – two large tins of powdered milk gave us plenty of milk – and we had sugar. Coffee might be available if someone thought to bring some.

The boxes contained six one-pound tins of butter, so we always used butter generously. It was possible, of course, to bring extra ingredients from the base, but generally we lived on the basic supplies, the only problem being that, however good it was, it was invariably always the same.

Our frustration in being unable to move continued for the whole of the next day. Strong winds again precluded any movement. We were able to listen in to a radio schedule with Tony Quinn at Stonington Island. There seemed to be some difficulties with the aircraft at Deception Island and questions over when, and if, they would fly down to Marguerite Bay and Fossil Bluff. Gossip always being important for isolated groups, we began to imagine sledging from Fossil Bluff to Stonington; certainly, we knew that there were inadequate supplies to support eight of us for more than a few weeks.

December 6th dawned fine and clear, so we arose at 6.00 a.m., checked that the depot was well laid and marked, struck camp and departed northwards two hours later. I went with Bill and the Players while John went with Brian and the Spartans. Dog teams had developed over many years, and many of them had become famous in FIDS dog lore because of the distances they had travelled and various exploits in which they had been involved. The teams all had names, and all tended to be 'owned' by one driver for one or two years. By 1961 some of the more famous teams included the Admirals, the Spartans, the Churchmen (with Vicar, Dean, Monk, Nun, etc), and the Players. Brian was running the Spartans and Bill had the Players – dogs with the names of Younger, Bass, Worthy and Guinness, supported by Leo, Pongo and Taurus. Bill preferred to run the dogs on a fan trace in the Sound because the dogs tended to get bored in such an open area with no particular features, or penguins and seals, to interest them. As usual, the dogs' characters were fascinating; in this team Taurus was a tower of strength. We moved speedily along that morning and within three hours we had covered fifteen miles to Triton Cliffs. Once more, early though it was, the heat of the sun made the surfaces difficult, apart from causing the dogs to get overheated.

December 6th. Oh it is glorious to be down here. The sun has sparkled; Graham Land and Alexander Island have looked grand, and chatting with Bill about Hope Bay, was a real pleasure.

Because of the worsening surfaces we decided to rise at 3.00 a.m. the next morning and do the last thirty-two miles in one session. We travelled between 4.30 a.m. and 11.00 a.m. at an average speed of 5 m.p.h., the dogs pulling splendidly. As usual, at the end of a journey we were welcomed back to the base, where Howard and Bob cooked us a splendid meal, and we sat together and caught up with all the news of ship and aircraft movements.

This journey, just about 100 miles in all, had given me a further taste of dog sledging. It was an unimaginably exhilarating experience, combining the attractiveness of loyal, hard-working dogs with the vast open spaces of beautiful ice scapes where man has hardly set foot. No wonder that the dog men loved their dogs and worked so hard for their welfare; no wonder that there was never any shortage of volunteers to run the teams.

187

21

The Summer Programme Completed: We Leave Fossil Bluff

By December 8th, summer was well advanced. Temperatures on that day rose to 37°F, accompanied by low cloud, wind and sleet. Bryan Bowler and Brian Taylor were still at the new camp across the glacier, and the surveyors were anxious to get going south again as soon as possible. On such a miserable day as this, those of us back at the hut whiled away the time in pleasant discussion and eating. There was one rude interruption to our peace, however, when one of the Players dog team managed to pull out the end picket so that the whole team could move en masse to attack the other dogs. Dog fights invariably caused injury, so swift action had to be taken to restore order.

The two sledge teams left at 6.30 a.m. next morning. They were away for thirty-four days, but had continual problems with the summer surfaces and weather. It took them nine days to get near to Stephenson Nunatak, just south of Latitude 72°S and approximately fifteen miles south of the depot we had laid two weeks earlier. Whilst they were in this area they went inland to the west of the nunatak, and spent some time behind the Titan and Coal Nunataks, from which they brought back some specimens of coal and some bits of petrified wood. Bob and Howard were able to carry out some surveying with tellurometers on good days. On their way back to Fossil Bluff they had been forced to lie up, tent-bound, for nine days. Their journey confirmed the fact that it is difficult to carry out much productive travel in December, January and parts of February. There were extensive areas of meltwater pools, slushy surfaces, and a greater number of exposed crevasses.

As had happened before, it was necessary to leave three dogs behind, Pasha was effectively retired, Vicar had a broken leg and Tess was ill. Tess became very ill during the next few days; she couldn't eat, she hardly drank anything and she lay shivering for much of the time. We feared we might lose her, but didn't want to do so while Bill

189

was away. We kept her lips moistened and tempted her with choice slivers of seal meat, but she continued to get weaker. Surprisingly, after a week of illness she started eating and drinking, and very slowly she picked up. By the time Bill returned from the sledge journey she was up and about and recovered, a survival which gave us much pleasure!

Meanwhile, Brian Taylor was working as hard as ever at the new camp site. John had relieved Bryan Bowler from his supporting role on December 9th and he remained there for ten days until I took over on the 19th. It was interesting to have a new hut mate, and Bryan had a lot of knowledge to impart concerning the Muskegs and their uses, as well as lots of information on life in the army – it had certainly given him a most unusual opportunity to travel!

On December 14th, a beautiful day, I set out to take supplies to the camp. We had started to use a new route directly up the Fossil Bluff Glacier and this saved time compared with our old route up the Gulley. Speeding down the ice slope and across the glacier by our well-marked route, I reached the camp in two and a half hours, with a similarly speedy return carrying some rocks.

December 18th marked the day exactly two years earlier when I had left Southampton on the *Kista Dan*. What a lot of experiences I had had since that day, and now I was packing my rucksack ready to go back to camp in support of Brian for the last time; it was to be for another thirteen days. I made my way by the old familiar route and reached the camp early in the evening. After the many weeks we had spent in the small pup tent, it was a real pleasure to have the benefit of a proper pyramid tent, which had been carried over to the camp when additional manpower was available. Brian had cleaned up the tent splendidly so I felt quickly at home. We soon got into a familiar pattern, though three days of bad weather caused us to lie up for much of the time. Brian, as usual, tried to get out; he wanted to investigate a dyke which had not been covered by the new snow fall, but he was not able to advance in his main area of work. Inevitably we spent much time reading, a new influx of books from the Stonington team giving us new interest. I read *The Loved One* by Evelyn Wa...UGH!, and his *Brideshead Revisited*. We also benefited from having a good little radio, brought by our colleagues, so we could keep up with world news and radio schedules from the bases.

On December 23rd, after Brian had set out for work, I made my way up to the ridge behind the camp and walked along to the highest point at the southern end. The point commanded a magnificent view over Uranus Glacier, horribly scarred with tremendous crevasses. Then I made my way down to the point of confluence between the Uranus Glacier and the small feeding ground near where we were camped. The next day dawned brilliantly clear, and as we had been unable to contact Base E for two days, and were anxious to know about the movements of the ships and aircraft, I returned to base to find out.

Inevitably there was much news. The *John Biscoe* was at Port Lockroy and would stay there over Christmas; the two Otters had at last flown to Adelaide Island and had made one flight to Stonington Island; Professor Lester King was flying down to Fossil Bluff to work with Brian for three weeks at Ablation Point; Arthur Fraser, who had returned to Base E after the sledging problems in Marguerite Bay, had only been able to clock up five days of field work in his alternative area. Having established that there was no immediate plan to fly John and me out, I returned to the camp with the news, and also with some Christmas decorations – one streamer, one hat, and one cracker!

December 25th. Happy Christmas! Surely a most unusual one for anybody. After Brian had left at 9.00 a.m. I lay in my bag reading *Brideshead Revisited* (– a final Ugh!), and *The Proving Flight* by David Beatty. Outside it was windy and drifting, later I went for an hour of rambling.

When Brian returned at 9.30 p.m. we had our Christmas Dinner! We had beef meat bar (and vegetables and biscuits) followed by a cup of dehydrated raspberries, followed by drinking chocolate and one Christmas cracker. A very gay celebration indeed! Still, I do hope the folks back home all had a good time; apparently it was the coldest day at Christmas time this century! Retired at 11.30 p.m., another landmark – or time mark – passes, my third Christmas away from home.

Boxing Day was another day of Antarctic brilliance so I decided to try to do something of significance. Armed with a ski stick and an ice axe, I made my way up the scree to the ridge behind the tent and then turned northwards, rising consistently to the peak, which I estimated to be about 2,800 feet high. I was well aware that this was the first time anyone had stood on this peak and I felt, once more, the sense of privilege which I had had before when out in this huge wilderness. Close by were Snow Dome and Pyramid; to the east the mountains of Graham Land; to the south, ranges of mountains with their blackened north faces; and to the north, ranges of mountains with their whitened southern faces. Out to the west, ice and snow stretched interminably on, pierced by some mountain ranges and many nunataks, towards lands that had never yet been trodden by man. 'It was all very magnificent', I recorded in my diary. Back at the tent I had a feeling of satisfaction and sat down to read *David Copperfield* whilst awaiting Brian.

So day followed day. The 27th was spoiled by one okta of very low cloud settling obstinately on the glacier, where it remained for the whole day. Nevertheless, Brian was able to work for twelve hours, which gave me many quiet hours to fill. The 28th was another day of wonderful weather, the 29th a day of great energy expenditure – by accident. For on that day, I thought I detected a shout from the far off col, and anticipating that the aircraft were coming, I set out hurriedly to go back to the base. I discovered that I had been mistaken! I established that the *John Biscoe* was stuck in the Bellingshausen pack ice (again), and until it could reach Adelaide Island there was only sufficient fuel for one reconnaissance flight to Stonington. So it seemed that we were still several weeks away from relief. December 31st came, an inauspicious end to the year. I took a hundredweight of rocks part of the way home – it was necessary to make two trips – and Brian and I saw in the year of 1962 quietly – we could hardly do anything else in our situation!

We had planned to return to the base on New Year's Day to join the others for a party. For the last time, therefore, I packed my things to depart from the tent; I had spent thirty-five days in tents on each side of the glacier, so I felt that I knew this area pretty well.

January 1st 1962. I packed my things and by 10.15 a.m. we were on our way. It may well be my last time in a FIDS tent; I don't know.

We crossed the glacier – wet snow clogging to our skis – and reached the other side. Brian's rocks were very heavy and we made slow progress up the side of the glacier leading to the snow slope; oh what a drag that slope always is! We roped up and moved slowly up it, having a comedy session en route for I was too close to Brian, and every time he stopped, I bumped my head on an empty fuel drum he carried. We descended the other

192

side and reached base after 3 hours, with plenty of sweating ...
The inside roof of the hut had been painted (most horribly, we
thought). We had a good feed including apricots, spam, tomatoes
and Xmas pudding – luxury indeed. Unfortunately the party was
incomplete for the sledgers have not arrived back yet.

I had promised Brian that I would type out his preliminary geological
report. On the next morning, whilst Bryan (Bowler) and John went
out to move Brian (Taylor's) field base to a new location, I set to
work. It was a long report, twenty-two pages, so it took me the best
part of two days. I also analysed the weather statistics for December
and made a general report to accompany the monthly facts and
figures for depositing in the Stanley archives. John and I kept a close
ear to the radio, and (accidentally, of course!) overheard a gruesome
medical schedule concerning two Fids who seemed to be paying a
penalty for an exciting night out in Montevideo; oh the embarrass-
ment of it all being made so public!

The days of January brought the worst weather of the year.
Temperatures up to 42°F, winds and cloud, caused all of the snow
and ice surfaces to be reduced to a slushy unworkable mess, knee
deep at some times. I went round to Hollow Valley on one occasion,
to find an astonishing number of melt pools and streams which ran
from the valley way down into the Sound where huge lakes had
formed.

At 3.00 a.m. on the morning of January 11th, the three weak dogs
outside the hut started barking, and we knew that their excitement
signified the arrival of the sledgers. Bryan Bowler and I, the only
residents at that time, went out to welcome them and to help them
unload. After nine consecutive lie-up days they were very pleased to be
back. Bryan later cooked them a splendid meal, though by now we
were very nearly reduced to pure sledging rations for virtually all meals.

Every day we listened for information; the *John Biscoe* had been
stuck in the ice by December 29th, and every day that we tuned in,
the story was almost the same, sixty miles from Adelaide Island, forty
miles, no movement etc. It was not until January 13th that it was
finally able to reach Adelaide Island. From that day on, we could
expect to be taken out at short notice, so we went up to the Pyramid
with a flag, a prearranged signal to call John back from the camp
across the glacier immediately. He obviously was not able to see the
flag for he did not return for three days; however, the urgency had

diminished when the *John Biscoe* once more became surrounded by ice. So we waited and chatted and enjoyed each other's company; we even used a bottle of medicinal brandy to celebrate Scott's attainment of the South Pole fifty years earlier. We had also marked our change-over in status from being members of the Falkland Islands Dependency Survey to being members of the British Antarctic Survey, the Antarctic Treaty having already come into force.

Just when everything was ready for flying operations, the weather made any movement impossible. On the 19th, 20th and right on to the end of the month, cloud made flights impossible. On the 23rd, Tony Quinn gloomily reported that Finn Ronne had made only five flights in January and two in February, and only fifteen flights in the whole season; that gave us a good topic of conversation. However, at long last February 1st dawned bright and clear, so the Otters took off from Adelaide Island and arrived at the Bluff mid-morning. It was great to see Ron Lord and Tom Sumner again; they were flying back to Stonington Island, while Bob Bond and Roy Brand were going back to Adelaide Island. So Bob, Howard, John and I piled into the Otter heading for Stonington Island. We had a last look down to the base which had been our home for so long, and the plane sped north-wards, up the Sound, over the Wordie Ice Shelf and Refuge Islands, past Roman Four Mountain, then swept down onto a landing strip on the North East Glacier. John Cunningham, Brian Sparke and Roger Matthews were there with the dog teams to welcome us and to take us down to the base. It was truly wonderful to arrive back at this most magical base!

On June 10th 1998, I received a letter from Sarah Dobson, Secretary of the Antarctic Place-Names Committee, sending me a copy of a paper which had been approved by the committee concerning the naming of features at Fossil Bluff. Nine features had been given names, and much to my surprise the mountain which we had always referred to as Snow Dome was to be named Pearce Dome, 'named after C.J. Pearce, a Falkland Islands Dependencies Survey Meteorologist who spent the first winter (1961) at Fossil Bluff, along with B.J. Taylor and J.P. Smith'. Certainly it was a mountain that I knew very well from my days in the pup tent on the glacier – almost 2,600 feet high (789.3 metres) and with magnificent ice falls clinging to its steep slopes. The final map was published in 2000 and named all of the features we had known so well. (See appendix on Place Names for details).

Brian had been earlier honoured by having 'Taylor Buttresses' named for him in 1977. These buttresses, at Latitude 70°08′S, Longitude 67°23′W rise to an altitude of over 4,600 feet (1,410 metres) east of Mount Pitman in (what was), Graham Land – east of the Sound. It was, perhaps, a little strange that the location for this honour was some seventy miles from the scene of his work, and – as he ruefully commented in an area 'probably made up of igneous and/or metamorphic rocks', rather than on the beloved sedimentaries on which he had spent so much time working in the area of Fossil Bluff!

When we visited Rothera Base in February 2000, I discovered that melting had taken place to such an extent that the hut at Fossil Bluff was in danger of subsiding. A huge balcony had been built around the hut to try to stabilise its movement. New morainic deposits had been exposed in the Sound as the ice cover had decreased. The air strip was now one thousand yards from the hut; in 1961 and 1962 the Otters had taxied to within a few yards of the front door.

After we left, the base was occupied during the winters of 1962, and from 1969 to 1973. It has also been in use as a summer base for many years, linked to Rothera as part of the only active UK Scientific Station on the Antarctic Peninsula.

22

A Month at Stonington Island

As soon as we had greeted the rest of our old friends and unpacked our bags, I immediately wandered outside to take in the atmosphere of this enchanting base. It was a beautiful evening as I peered into the remains of the Finn Ronne huts and I tried to imagine the activities that would have been taking place there fourteen years earlier when Ronne and his expedition were at the end of their eleven-month stay, sharing the island with eleven Britons. What dramas the rocks of Neny Island must have witnessed:

– when Captain Richard Black, who first occupied the island in 1940–41, had welcomed home Ronne and Eklund after their long dog sledging journey to the southern end of King George VI Sound (and had had all of those same dogs killed just before they left the island),

– of the first British Base opening in 1946 under the leadership of Surgeon Commander Bingham, an outstanding Arctic and Antarctic explorer,

– of the cold atmosphere in personal relations that seems to have pervaded the Ronne camp, despite having with them the first two women in Antarctica,

– of the eleven men who couldn't be relieved in 1948, some of whom had to settle for a third year of isolation,

– of the journeys of Fuchs and Adie, and others.

Quarrels, dramatic rescues, heroic sledge journeys, far-reaching flights by Ronne, had all been part of the history of Stonington Island. It was this history that always made the base a magnet for Fids. So I immediately started to read again the books by Finn Ronne, Jenny Darlington and Kevin Walton. In the evening we had superb quality food, the best since we had left the ship a year earlier, and I enjoyed listening to Dvorak's Serenade in E – the first music session for a year without cranking the generator! A wonderful luxury.

The ice conditions this year we regarded as helpful in a negative way. We wanted to have time on the island, and it was fortunate for us that the *John Biscoe* was held up only two miles from Neny Island, so Captain Johnston decided to return to Adelaide Island in order to give the ice time to clear. At this time there were ten of us at the base. Bryan Bowler was still at Fossil Bluff, along with Brian Taylor (who was spending a second year there), and Bill Tracy and Brian Wigglesworth who would bring the dogs back to Adelaide Island by air, and then bring them to their home base by ship.

Sadly, we heard on February 3rd that Bill had had to destroy four of the dogs at Fossil Bluff. Tess, Pasha and Vicar, who had been left behind when the teams went south, had remained at the Bluff throughout December and January, unable to work any more. Tess never really recovered from her illness, Pasha was infirm and Vicar's broken leg never mended since he fractured it on November 19th (indeed he had been carried on a sledge for the last six days of the journey from Stonington Island). Moose, one of the Spartans, had made one last trip down the Sound to Stephenson Nunatak, but had become infirm and there was no possibility of further work. His life was a good example of the life of a typical Fids dog. He was born in 1954 at Arctic Bay, Baffin Island, and was one of three puppies given to the Survey by the Royal Canadian Mounted Police in that year. The puppies went to Hope Bay initially, but Moose's team, the Spartans, were moved to Horseshoe Island from where he worked for several years before his team sledged to Stonington Island in 1960. Moose travelled thousands of miles; in the last five months of his life he helped pull an extremely heavy sledge to Fossil Bluff, then down to the southern area of the Sound and back (twice) – approximately 600 miles. It is easy, therefore, to understand the attachment which the drivers develop for their dogs and their immense sadness when they have to end their lives.

Before the *John Biscoe* set off for Base T, John Cunningham and three others skied out to stay overnight on board and to bring back the mail. We then established a new base routine. My first day as 'gash hand' proved to me the difference between large and small bases, for filling the water tank to supply the needs of ten men took time; then there was coal hauling and maintaining the fires, and cleaning and sweeping up the bunk room and the general living room and kitchen. At Stonington they always spoke of a dreaded wind, 'the fumigator', which blew down from the plateau frequently, so we were not surprised to experience this on our fifth day, with winds of forty to fifty knots and gusts up to sixty-five knots (how nice to have a proper anemometer for accuracy rather than our own estimates).

Whenever possible the two Otters flew from Adelaide Island to Fossil Bluff. At one point there had been talk of up to 100 summer flights but the Antarctic weather precluded that and eventually the Otters made their thirty-seventh and thirty-eighty flights in mid-March, before flying back to Deception Island on March 19th. The dogs at Fossil Bluff were brought out and the new base membership for 1962 comprised Brian Taylor, to complete his work, supported by Jim Shirtcliffe as officer in charge, Sam Blake as radio operator, and Rod Walker, meteorologist.

The *John Biscoe* was always the centre of rumours as Fids picked up messages over the radio. One rumour that caused alarm was that Stonington Island would close again in a year's time, and that three dog teams were to be based at Adelaide Island and then flown down to Fossil Bluff in the spring. It was felt by all of us on the base that it was too soon to rely on the aircraft and that in the event of another failure there would, once again, be a hopelessly late start to any summer programme down the Sound.

The days at Stonington Island passed by in a very pleasant manner. One day Brian Sparke, John Smith and I skied across to Neny Island to do an ice observation; the fast ice was rapidly receding into Neny Fiord. Our route back was safe enough though the ice was black and rotten. Another day I strolled to Flagstaff Hill and surveyed the island. On another day, after we had completed the weekly scrub-out of the hut:

February 10th. After lunch I went photographing and then just sat admiring the breathtaking spectacle. To the SE Roman Four, with Red Rock Ridge several miles away behind it, looked rugged and splendid behind the calm waters of the bay whose icebergs and fast ice gave it real character. To the south, great Neny Island blocked the view; to the SW and NW the sea was filled with crumpled ice from the North East Glacier, and backed by Millerand Island, Adelaide Island (far away) and

Cape Calmette. To the north, the plateau looked superb behind the great ice mass of the glacier. What a wonderful place.

At this time we often went out boating, always being on the look-out for seals. One evening, four of us went out in the dinghy with a Seagull engine, amongst the icebergs. Huge fast ice floes were still blocking the Stonington, Neny and Millerand triangle, but the rest was now open water. The sea was absolutely still; the icebergs were huge, especially from our vantage point in our small boat.

On the 16th, all hands set to work to make the base sparkling, for we had an important visitor, the Governor of the Falkland Islands and its Dependencies, Sir Edwin Arrowsmith. He was airlifted in by a helicopter from *HMS Protector* on its regular patrol in these waters, flying the British flag. We enjoyed a couple of hours of pleasant discussion before he departed.

Now we were coming to the end of our two years down south we had, for the first time, some genuine crevasse rescue training. John Cunningham took several of us onto part of the North East Glacier and found a crevasse some sixty feet deep, of considerable width, and with icicles hanging from its blue sides. Having anchored himself carefully, John plunged over the side and down into the depths. He then demonstrated to us all how to help ourselves in such circumstances, an amazing display, which encouraged some of the watchers to try out their new-found skills, though I personally declined the invitation!

On a large base, being on cook came round less frequently than when there had only been three of us, and we each took three-day stints on the summer schedule. When my turn came I produced Wiener steaks, shepherd's pie and pork loin for the three dinners, each with appropriate vegetables and followed by a variety of puddings. It was a real change to be able to make a genuine choice from attractive supplies, and to be able to bake bread, cakes and pastries again.

By the 24th, the *John Biscoe* was at Horseshoe Island and was spending time catching seals for the dogs at Stonington Island. They needed one hundred to provide sufficient for the dogs, but only managed to kill fourteen on that day. Next day, at just after noon, the *John Biscoe* hove into our view, steaming between Neny and Millerand Islands, then passing round the southern end of Neny Island and anchoring off the base. We had been watching three killer whales swimming near the base only a few minutes before, a most unusual occurrence in that area. We had mixed feelings as the launch came to the jetty; we knew that this truly marked the end of our Antarctic experience, yet we wanted to get home; our welcome was therefore muted!

We soon got into working mode, and shortly after lunch the new Muskegs were brought ashore and loads of coal and fuel were discharged. The hut swarmed with Fids, old friends and new, all interested in looking at the hut and the general environment. In the evening, while we were still working, we were treated to a sunset of great beauty with red, pink and golden colours lighting up the western sky. For the whole of the next day we worked at unloading and completed the whole job in a day and a half. It was typical of Fids that, although there was often a lot of leisure time, when work needed to be done quickly, everyone joined in, inevitably with lots of ribaldry. On the 27th, we sat in the main room enjoying a last chat together. The launch from the ship appeared at about 5.00 p.m., laden with new base men. Only John Cunningham, Bryan Bowler and Bob Metcalfe were staying (apart from Brian at Fossil Bluff), and they were joined by seven new men, together with the three new men at Fossil Bluff, making a total complement of fourteen. The ten of us who were returning home were soon on board with all our luggage; we remained at anchor overnight.

Before the ship finally departed it was planned to carry out two more operations, one to get a supply of seals, the other to place a large depot in the south of Marguerite Bay. March 1st epitomised the variety of endeavours and environments in which we were living and I recorded it in detail that evening:

At free drifting position just inside the belt of pack ice some ten to fifteen miles west of Millerand Island. Position Lat. 68°10'S Long. 67°45'W. The *John Biscoe* started off at 9.00 a.m. The ship moved into Neny Fiord then headed westwards to the open sea. Calm, cloudy conditions prevailed, the water producing mirror images of the mountains. About one-tenth of ice was present, consisting of small bergy bits with occasional trails of brash ice. As the main objective of this day's voyage was to combine sealing with the establishment of a depot of food and fuel on Mushroom Island (Lat. 68°53'S Long. 67°52'W), the ship headed to the south-west after clearing Red Rock Ridge. Several adelie penguins were seen swimming about, and skuas and

201

Wilson's petrels were much in evidence.

A few miles south and west of Red Rock Ridge the frequency of icebergs increased and we came to a wide belt of pack ice. The pack was closed and navigation through it was inadvisable. No leads could be seen, so the *John Biscoe* moved north-eastwards in an attempt to skirt the ice. Later it became known that the aircraft flying from Adelaide Island to Fossil Bluff would be able to carry out an ice reconnaissance for the ship, so the rest of the day was given over to sealing.

Seals spend many hours out of the water and are to be found in any pack ice. The ship therefore nosed into the edge of the ice and it was not long before the first seal was spotted. It was a Weddell seal, recognised by its snub nose, huge eyes and distinctive fur colour. The bosun shot the seal from the foc's'le and then climbed down to gut it. The animal is cut from tail flipper to throat, and the guts are then peeled out en masse by the deft use of a very sharp knife. The whole operation took some two minutes after which time the carcase was hauled up on board. For many hours this task went on. Many Weddells, several crabeaters, two elephant seals and one leopard were caught, a total of almost forty. The sealers become so adroit at this task that often the heart muscles are still working after the body of the owner is on deck! We need at least one hundred to stock the husky larder at Stonington for the next year.

There are large numbers of bergs in this particular belt of pack ice. Two of the tabular bergs we approached today approximated to one mile in length and breadth, and were 50 feet above the water suggesting a depth of ice in excess of 450 feet. It is probable that these have come from the Bertrand Ice Piedmont. Tabular bergs are noted for their flatness and for the sparkling blue caves along their sides. This evening we approached a fantastically shaped berg with a tall spire and arch. This berg is obviously very old and has turned over and over as the waters gradually reduce it to nothing. For the rest, the pack ice consists of floes of variable size and thickness mixed with brash. It would be classified as 9/10ths medium pack.

Skuas have again been ever present predators – especially just after a seal has been gutted – and there have also been a few Arctic terns. The squawk of the adelie penguins is also quite common.

The cloudy conditions of the morning gave way to brighter, sunnier weather in late afternoon. Temperatures remained about 36°F for most of the day.

The ship returned to Stonington for the last time in order to off-load the seals; John Cunningham was very grateful for the supply.

We departed, finally, at 9.00 a.m. on March 3rd, the day before, a year ago, we had taken off from the ice to fly down to Fossil Bluff. Most of us were up on deck as we sailed out round Neny Island and into Marguerite Bay, and most of us hoped that somehow, sometime we might be back.

Stonington Island Base closed in 1975. At the end there were approximately 150 dogs at the base. Chris Edwards, the last base leader, had the awful job of culling 100 of these; 42 went to Adelaide Island. The dogs had been in use continuously since 1961, but they gradually lost in the battle with Skidoos. These snow vehicles could be flown to Alexander Island from Adelaide Island to the exact spot where they were needed, thus saving the scientists much valuable time. Dogs also cost a lot to maintain; the base needed 500 seals a year, which might take a ship three or four days. As the ice strip for aircraft at Adelaide Island deteriorated, the base was closed and all work was transferred to Rothera; its facilities meant that Fossil Bluff could be resupplied from there. In the eighties the configuration of Stonington Island also changed when the North East Glacier receded and no longer linked the island to the mainland, thus there was no longer access to the plateau, and no reason for maintaining the base.

The shooting of the dogs at Fossil Bluff in February 1962 was not to be the last news of them. In the summer of 1999/2000, two men working at Fossil Bluff discovered the mummified bodies of four dogs which had ablated to the surface as the ice had melted. They were in old hessian sacks and had been buried in a hole. Their collars gave their names: Pasha, Vicar, Tess and Moose. They were reburied in a shallow grave on the moraine, marked with a rock cairn.

On the *Lyubov Orlova* in February 2000, Bob Dodson, a member of the Ronne Antarctic Research Expedition, was on board as a lecturer. He had some marvellous tales to tell of that expedition; he himself was involved in a most dramatic crevasse accident, when the British Base members joined with the Americans to save the life of Pete Peterson. Unfortunately for Bob, the *Orlova* was unable to get him, or the rest of us, to the base that most of all we had hoped to revisit.

Sadly four of the men with whom we shared experiences at Stonington Island are no longer with us – John Cunningham, Dr Brian Sparke, Bob Metcalfe and Flight Lieutenant Ron Lord – all good, highly professional colleagues who spread much happiness around them.

Stonington Base has now been conserved under the care of the UK Antarctic Heritage Trust.

23

Northwards to the Falklands

We had stopped overnight in the pack ice, and next morning we picked up some surveyors who had been working on Jenny Island, and then moved to the off-shore anchorage at Adelaide Island. We were to find ourselves here for eighteen days. The base had been growing quickly since we had carried the first building supplies ashore only thirteen months earlier. Four buildings were being erected, a new hut for living in, a meteorological hut, a garage and a diesel shed. It was now the airbase for Marguerite Bay and King George VI Sound, and it had several dog teams. The number of men based there was rising from six in the first year to eleven for 1962, and there were the four aircraft men to accommodate during the whole of the summer season; it had therefore become a major base. As we unloaded vast quantities of supplies the scene was inevitably chaotic, with so much going on.

The second FIDS ship, *Shackleton*, arrived on the 7th, and tied up alongside the *John Biscoe*. Fuel and water and mail were transferred across to us; the crew of the *Shackleton*, like our crew, had been hunting for seals to feed the dogs and, during the day, they transferred ninety-nine seals to the shore. The *Shackleton*, with Captain Turnbull as master, was slightly smaller than the *John Biscoe* and apparently rolled more in stormy seas; nevertheless they were both very comfortable ships to travel in. The arrival of so many men from such far-off places resulted in a whole load of germs amongst us, which produced sore throats, streaming eyes and running noses, a shock to our systems. We were also troubled by large numbers of icebergs which repeatedly followed one another around the south-east corner of Adelaide Island:

March 9th. Overnight, and throughout the day, three large icebergs have been causing the ship some inconvenience. The bergs keep moving towards the ship and nudging it. Since several hundred feet of ice are below the water, the main danger is from

205

overturning, so that the ship must be moved. The largest of the bergs today had been sculptured in a most fantastic way by the water. The berg consisted of a concentric-shaped mass open on one side, with the rim of the crescent reaching from sea level to about 150 feet above sea level. Within the crescent the waves had eroded a perfectly smooth 'shore', with an ice floor several feet below the waves. The water in the bay had a perfect, green colour, and would have made a most admirable swimming pool. But these are no waters for a swim!

The *John Biscoe* helped in the work of the surveyors as much as possible. On one day surveyors were landed with tellurometers on Avian Island, the Guebriands and on one of the Mikkelson Islands in Laubeuf Fiord so that these islands could be accurately tied in to the survey. On another, the ship carried out a hydrographic survey; sometimes geologists would be landed on islands. Sometimes biologists would be landed, Avian Island at this time of the year still had large numbers of chicks, including adelies, giant petrels, skuas and cormorants.

On March 15th, the last flights to Fossil Bluff were made from the runway high up on the ice piedmont. All that remained was to await suitable weather for the long flight northwards to Deception Island. The *John Biscoe* used the time for more hydrographic survey work as far as Isla Cona, a small triangular island some three miles off the Fuchs Ice Piedmont to the north of us. Whilst this was going on I was helping Brian Sparke remove a tooth from Dave Nash, a newly arrived surveyor – my job being to hold his head firmly whilst Brian pulled!

At last, on the 19th, the weather cleared sufficiently for the two Otters to fly north, the *Biscoe* remaining at anchor to act as a radio link for the fliers. Two days later the ship weighed anchor and departed early in the morning, initially to carry out further hydrographic surveys, then finally to head north. The bergs, the whales spouting, and great herds of seals all gave us plenty of interest, and in the evening we enjoyed a clear sky with a full moon shining down on the oily-looking frazil ice – a true harbinger of winter. On the 22nd we crossed the Antarctic Circle again, passed the Biscoe Islands, moved through the French Passage and anchored once more in Meek Channel, off-shore of the Argentine Islands base.

March 23rd. Most of us spent the day ashore for it was a day of clear skies and no wind with temperatures hovering around freezing point. Such conditions are perfect. On Galindez Island we walked up to the ice cap, some 170 feet above sea level. From the top the panorama is one of breath-taking beauty. To the east the coast of Graham Land stretches far to the north and south, an immense wall of mountains with great crevassed glaciers spilling down from the white snow fields. The Argentine Islands are situated from four to ten miles from the mainland, separated from it by the Penola Strait, so called after the sailing ship which carried the members of the BGLE here. Penola Strait and the whole of the sea around the islands is littered with huge icebergs.

Around the islands can be seen large varieties of wildlife. Adelie penguins and gentoos are still here; skuas, pintado petrels, Wilson's petrels, blue-eyed shags (cormorants), and Dominican gulls are here in great numbers, and some giant petrels are seen. Every variety of common seal is present, and provides almost a weekly dish on the menu for the base. In the afternoon while on a launch trip, a killer whale suddenly surfaced about fifty yards from our launch, which was very small beside the dreaded 'Orca'!

In due course the base members came on board for a final, splendid, turkey dinner, and we departed, moving north through Lemaire Channel and passing a closed FIDS base at Danco Island. By March 28th we had arrived back at Deception Island. I was very interested to see how things had progressed during the time we had been away. The hangar was complete and splendid – no more hours of digging out the aircraft as we had done – and there were several improvements in Biscoe House. A bigger bar had been built, there was a new diesel shed, and a library. The dogs were still there to welcome us with lots of barking and tail-wagging. There was a party based at Deception studying 'whistlers' (to do with high-altitude physics), and as they were based in Telefon Bay several of us went in the launch to collect them; Deception Island in the summer is dominated by dreary ash and cinders, and without a covering of snow is never very attractive. On the last day of March, we enjoyed a grand party in the enlarged bar, with lots of music, tomfoolery and chatter, and for those of us who had lived at the base, a large measure of nostalgia.

On April 1st the ship arrived at Hope Bay on the northern end of Graham Land. Like Stonington Island, Hope Bay has a tremendous history and the two of them stand supreme in the annals of exploration in Graham Land. The base is located at Latitude 63°24'S Longitude 56°59'W and stands above Hut Cove, to the east of the embayment of Hope Bay. Behind the base, icy slopes rise up to Mount Flora at 1,393 feet, then higher up to the south-east to the dominant peak of Mount Taylor at 3,274 feet. Several glaciers descend into Hope Bay, and curving round to the east and passing down the eastern side of Tabarin Peninsula, as the main land block is called, is a huge ice piedmont.

The base was the third to be opened by Britain, on February 10th 1945, one year after those at Port Lockroy and Deception Island had been opened. This was not the first time that men had wintered there; that distinction was held by Gunnar Andersson, Lieutenant Duse and Toralf Grunden, who were marooned in 1903 after the *Antarctic*, Nordenskjold's ship, had sunk nearly a hundred miles away to the east of Paulet Island. The small stone hut in which they lived during that first winter still remains. FIDS had wanted to open a base there in 1944, but difficulties with the ice made that impracticable and the venture was delayed until February 1945, when thirteen men under the leadership of Captain Andrew Taylor (Commander of FIDS) established the base. They brought with them twenty-five dogs, which formed the basis of the great tradition of dog sledging for which Hope Bay became famous. As the numbers of dogs increased, so the scale of the journeys became greater, including the memorable journey to Stonington Island in 1947. Tragedy struck in late 1948 when the base burned down with the loss of two lives, and it was closed in February 1949. However, a new era commenced in February 1952, when a new base was established (after some difficulties with the Argentinians, who had themselves opened a base there), and this base was in operation at the time of our call.

We were soon ashore. The Argentine base (Esperanza) was close to the beach, the British base (Trinity House) being a quarter of a mile further up the slope. The hut was small when compared with Biscoe House at Deception Island, but it had the perfect ambience of a sledging base. There were lots of dogs and sledges and sledging tackle, and in the heart of the hut a splendid fifteen-man living-cum-bunk room, with a stove in the middle of the room and a circle of chairs round it. What stories must have been told and retold in that room!

208

It was pleasant to catch up again with Ian Fothergill, Noel Downham and Mike Smith, who I had trained with at Stanmore, and to compare the differences in the experiences we had enjoyed since those far-off days in the late summer of 1959. I was keen to see the dogs; Noel pointed out to me four very superior Greenland huskies which had been sent down by Kai Hindberg, the captain of the *Kista Dan*. We visited the various centres of interest, the 1903 stone hut, the remnants of the destroyed British base, and Esperanza; many of us wished that we could have wintered at such an active base.

That evening on board the *John Biscoe* we all suffered a true 'night of terror'. In the evening a south-easterly wind got up, and soon a large berg came trundling along and thoroughly twisted one of the cabins and tore away a long section of railings. In the middle of the night the wind was shrieking and we soon felt the *Biscoe* dragging its anchors. By 4.00 a.m. we were on the Grunden Rocks with an Argentine beacon twinkling at us from above. The wind gusted to eighty-five knots and held us broadside on; the crunching of the ship's hull plates was distinctly dismaying. Most of the Fids mustered in the saloon, complete with 'escape bags'; we were all very scared. Somehow, eventually, Captain Johnston eased the ship off the rocks and we pressed on towards Signy Island, enduring a miserably rough voyage. For much of the night, once we were clear of land, we hove to. There was a lot of ice about, the seas were very rough and it was dark.

In the morning we were near Gibbs Island and moved from there past Elephant Island, which we could not see, and Clarence Island, which we could – nearly 5,000 feet of black rock descending to Cape Bowles. We were in the area where the three Shackleton boats had struggled to reach land in 1916 and we could not have seen it on a worse day, in terms of the atmosphere of bleak hopelessness that it conveyed. Gradually the sea calmed down as we continued to the east. Five whale catchers appeared during the morning; we could see their vicious harpoons ready for their evil work.

On April 5th, we arrived at Signy Island on the South Orkneys. The first base on the South Orkneys had been built by William Bruce of the Scotia expedition of 1902–1904, at Laurie Island. He gave the base to Argentina in 1903, and it was continuously occupied by them as a weather station thereafter. In 1946 FIDS established a base close by at Cape Geddes, but this was only occupied for one year before the decision was made to open the present base at Signy Island, Latitude 60°43′S Longitude 45°36′W, on March 18th 1947. The base hut was an old one, and showed distinct signs of wear; as usual, however, we were made very welcome by the men at the base. We wandered over to an area known as Elephant Flats to admire the huge seals present in large numbers; the smell was memorable! There was also a large chinstrap penguin rookery; we had hoped to see some fur seals too, but none were ashore. Most sadly, we visited the grave of Roger Filer, another Stanmore colleague, who had been killed in a fall from a cliff in February 1961.

We departed from Signy Island for the run to South Georgia. Soon after lunch we had passed the easternmost point of the South Orkneys and turned to the north-east. A twenty-foot swell caught us beam on, but the *John Biscoe* rode it well. At this time I was reading *Endurance* by Alfred Lansing and spent time trying to visualise the *James Caird*, with Shackleton and his five shipmates battling their way in this great vastness of ocean towards South Georgia – while the rest of his expedition members waited hopefully on Elephant Island.

By April 7th we were beginning to see more and more birds of the South Atlantic, the albatross being particularly thrilling. Very early next morning we reached South Georgia.

The east coast of South Georgia was the location for all of the whaling stations. To the east, the great mountainous spine of South Georgia, reaching up to 9,625 feet at Mount Paget, opens to a series of deep bays, Cumberland Bay being the largest, divided into an east and west bay; Stromness Bay is also of considerable size. It was to Husvik in Stromness Bay that Shackleton and Worsley and Crean had come down, after their epic boat voyage and their climb over the South Georgian mountains from King Haakon Bay on the west coast. The *John Biscoe* entered Stromness Bay on that morning, so we could see the huge backdrop in which the drama had been played out. Then we turned towards the whaling station at Leith and tied up alongside the jetty in order to refuel:

April 8th. Leith really is a dreadful place – pipes, oil tanks, rusty machinery, it all reminded me of Shelton Iron and Steel works. Still, we went ashore and made our way between the buildings and past the jetties where 8–12 catchers were at anchor. Mike Tween and I went past the cemetery and football pitch, and climbed a headland. This gave us a view into Stromness harbour, where Stromness whaling station is located. We made our way to it. En route we passed herds of elephant seals, many gentoos and *one* fur seal. I was particularly pleased to see this seal, with its ears and particularly mobile flippers, knowing of its tragic history. What a ferocious little animal this one was too. We investigated the station – deserted now – and peered into the houses there. All very interesting. Later we returned to Leith via the beach. How superb it was to see green vegetation again, tussock grass, moss and a type of clover. The *Biscoe* cast off from the jetty and anchored in the middle of the three-pronged bay. A 20,000-ton factory ship is due in tomorrow.

The *Southern Harvester* arrived early next morning before we had moved out of Stromness Bay for the voyage round to Cumberland Bay East and to King Edward Point, our anchorage close to Grytviken.

There were about fifteen houses at King Edward Point, all nicely painted white and green and with pink corrugated iron roofs. It looked a splendid little place. We walked round to the whaling station, where there were no whales but we looked at the great mass, and decaying mess, of the station, with off-shore a great number of old whale catchers partially or totally submerged. We visited the chapel and the Grytviken Kino – the cinema. This was the very last year when whale processing was based at this whaling station, with factory ships operating from there, and we saw large numbers of drums of whale oil ready for transport, as evidence of their success.

The great centre of pilgrimage on South Georgia is, inevitably, the grave of Sir Ernest Shackleton, at which several of us paid our respects. We also tried to reach the Nordenskjold Glacier several miles along Cumberland Bay, but were stopped by a great headland. We therefore settled, after our return trip to King Edward Point, for visiting the monument to Shackleton overlooking the bay. In the evening we enjoyed a film in the Grytviken Kino, and we noted two women in the audience, the first we had seen since January 1960 – a cause for comment!

South Georgia, with its evocation of the past, especially its connections with Shackleton, and its intrinsic beauty, was a magical place. However, we were on our way to the Falkland Islands and having picked up some passengers, we sailed early on April 10th.

It took three days for the *John Biscoe* to cross the waters of the Scotia Sea. There was a strong westerly wind for most of the time and this, linked to a heavy swell, caused the ship to pitch and roll for most of the time. On the 12th we crossed the Antarctic convergence, where the cold waters from the south meet the warmer waters from the north. Both the air and sea temperatures on that day were 44°F, so we really had moved into temperate latitudes. Early next morning, we could see the hills of the islands ahead and we were all on deck as the ship made its way through Port William and then passed between the fingers of land that stand on either side of The Narrows, into the shelter of Stanley Harbour.

April 13th. Glorious!! The Falklands hove into view about 10.00 a.m. this morning, a windy but clear and sunny day. Albatrosses, gulls and shags were everywhere. The *Biscoe* crew dressed for the occasion, and by noon we entered the harbour and tied up along- side the jetty.

We had arrived back at the headquarters of the Falkland Islands Dependencies Survey.

The days we spent in Stanley were incredibly enjoyable after over two years of absence. Everything was fresh and new: new landscapes, new vegetation, new people; a busy social programme, long walks and business matters kept us all fully occupied. An hour or two after our arrival several of us walked along the road beside the shore, really noticing in the fine weather the grasses and flowers and even a solitary tree in the shelter of the cathedral, all wonderful to us. To bring home to ourselves the fact that we really were back in civilisa- tion we had a pre-prandial drink in The Ship, and went to the Town Hall to see *Aladdin*!

We took the opportunity to explore the area around the harbour. One day we walked to a fine beach at Yorke Bay, coming across a most unusual pub called The Mon Star; another day I spent hours just enjoying the scene in Stanley Harbour with its many ships. I walked along the Moody Valley past Tumbledown Mountain, and to several bays with lots of jackass and rockhopper penguins to see, as well as steamer ducks, kelp geese and a large variety of other shore and estuary birds. My time at Fossil Bluff in particular had sharpened my interest and enjoyment in all the wildlife and vegetation that we now saw.

212

We enjoyed visits to The Ship and The Rose for drinks, and we went to a number of dances, two shillings and sixpence for three hours at the Town Hall on the Monday, and another organised by the *Biscoe* crew on the Wednesday, also at the Town Hall. At these dances there were lots of partners and lots of waltzing, quick-stepping, and samba-ing, all mixed with old-fashioned valetas, gay gordons and even circassian circles. It was an extraordinary phenomenon that found us all wanting to be involved, and to enjoy the feeling that we were back with normal people!

High on the social agenda was the cocktail party given by the Governor, Sir Edwin Arrowsmith, at Government House. We put on our smartest outfits (another pleasant experience), and enjoyed cocktails with the Governor and his family, and with the FIDS office girls, a return to the world of polite society. On April 21st everyone dressed up in time for the great parade in honour of the Queen's birthday. Unfortunately it was showery, so the Governor took the salute in the gymnasium; he was very formally dressed, complete with cocked hat and sword. The Falkland Islands Defence Force, the Girls' Life Brigade and the Boys' Brigade were in attendance. The *Biscoe* and *Shackleton* were dressed overall for the occasion and a twenty-one-gun salute was fired. It served to remind everyone of the close links between the colony and Britain.

There was a surprising number of business matters to attend to. Apart from signing the ship's articles for the rest of our voyage, I had to renew my passport for a further five years, and get an advance of £20 sterling. It was strange to start using money again after such a long time without. Paying my tax bill, of £74 6s 0d for two and a quarter years was necessary before we could leave; what was more enjoyable, however, was collecting my last pay certificate. For the two years I had amassed the grand total of £1,175, which I felt to be quite good at the time. (Fids never went down south for the money, but for the experience!)

On April 24th, the last visitors left the ship and we drifted out from the jetty and sailed past the *Shackleton*. A little cluster of folks waved us goodbye and Stanley was left behind, though we would always have fond memories of our stay.

By 2001 every base on which we had called on our way northwards in 1962 had closed as a year-round occupied base; only Signy Island had any scientific role at all. The Adelaide Island base is now Chilean; the Argentine Islands base first had its name changed to Faraday and eventually it was handed to the government of the Ukraine, who now run it. Port Lockroy is a high-quality museum celebrating the role of FIDS and BAS over the years; the British base on Deception Island died on February 23rd 1969 as a result of the volcanic eruption. The Hope Bay base is now occupied by Uruguayans. Signy Island still operates as a summer base, so it has the longest continuous record of service of any British base, dating from March 18th 1947.

South Georgia, after the traumas of 1982, had a small military establishment up to 2001, when a new scientific base was opened – a base at Bird Island had already functioned for many years. Whaling ceased in 1962, so the old whaling stations have become more and more derelict. The visit by some Argentinians in 1982 to dismantle them was a precipitating factor in the ensuing war.

The Falklands survived the trauma of the 1982 war; its attachment to Britain remains as close as it was when we witnessed the celebrations for the Queen's birthday in 1962.

24

Homeward Bound

We had picked up some passengers at Stanley, including the Bishop of South America, who had been visiting the Falklands as part of his duties. At that time it was only possible to get to the islands by way of Montevideo (the government of Argentina would not allow direct transit from its territory to Stanley), so FIDS ships occasionally helped out in between the regular runs of the *Darwin*. The voyage to Montevideo was a four-day passage, and we anchored outside the harbour for the night of April 27th. Next day we anchored at the jetty and we all went ashore and into the town.

The first priority was to buy some mementoes for the folks back home, and soon we had acquired a variety of goods made from leather, very cheap in a country with lots of cattle. Six of us then decided to take a taxi ride in order to see a bit more of the town rather than just its centre. I ran into great difficulties at this point. In order to save time, I had offered to go back to the ship to collect cameras for those who wanted them. As I was leaving the dock area with a large number of cameras suspended from my neck, I was stopped by Customs officers who thought I was intending to sell them! Although I tried to explain to them very carefully the real purpose of my mission, before I knew what was happening I was hustled into a jeep at pistol point and taken off for questioning. It took a great deal of explanation, with the help of an elderly woman who could act as translator between us, for me to convince the officers of my good faith. They drove me back to the ship and dumped me, giving me dire warnings concerning my future behaviour! When we had each separately collected our own camera we set out again and visited a series of magnificent beaches, avenues and sculptures; we thought Montevideo a fine city.

Next day we enjoyed more of the town – we walked up the Plaza Independencia and along to the beach, the Playa Pocitos. Cumulus clouds and light breezes, coupled with magnificent panoramas of sea and buildings, made the town a very pleasant place. We attended a football match in the huge stadium used for Uruguay's World Cup matches. After a final spruce-up on the ship, we dined in style at Morinis, a meal based on a huge steak, of course. Most of us eventually boarded ship at 5.30 a.m., having had a good time.

We finally sailed late in the afternoon of the 30th; the next time we would go ashore would be in England. Day followed day with a familiar routine. We all had some minor duties to carry out to help in the running of the ship; we read a lot, and sunbathed a lot. The meals on board the *John Biscoe* were always excellent, combining quality with quantity, and there was always a good supply of bread and cheese for supper. Every evening, right from the day we first boarded the ship at Stonington Island, films were shown and most of us were regular attenders. Steadily we moved north, passing close to Isla de Cabo Frio, along from Rio de Janeiro, and then passing close to Recife. We spent much time watching flying fish moving across the waters; on one occasion one of them flew through the open porthole into the saloon, much to the consternation of the men gathered there. By May 8th we were close to Fernando da Noronha, and beginning the passage across the Atlantic Ocean, crossing the equator a day later, at Longitude 31°17'W.

These were lazy days of great conviviality between the thirty Fids on board and the crew. The Cape Verde Islands appeared, and then fell behind us, Madeira too. By the 21st, we were all busy packing as we crossed the Bay of Biscay and headed up the Channel. Next day we sailed up the Solent towards Southampton and docked in Berth 37. My parents, and all my four brothers and sisters and in-laws, and many nieces and nephews, were there on the dock side to welcome me; it was good to be back home.

216

25

Reflections: The British in the Antarctic 1944–1961

The month in which I sailed from Southampton on the *Kista Dan*, December 1959, was the month in which twelve nations signed the proposals for an Antarctic Treaty. That treaty was ratified and came into force on June 23rd 1961, whilst I was at Fossil Bluff. My period down south, therefore, saw the passing of the old, unowned, but claimed continent, to one that was owned by no one but controlled by everyone. The Treaty also ended all of the territorial claims, including the concept of the Falkland Islands Dependencies, this being the large area of Antarctica which extended, wedge-shaped, from the South Pole to include the whole of Graham Land (after 1964, called the Antarctic Peninsula), and most of the Weddell Sea and South Georgia. For most of the twentieth century, Britain made unquestionably the pre-eminent contribution to the exploration and scientific development of this large area. Elsewhere in the Antarctic many countries, including Britain, produced high-calibre explorers who carried out pioneering work on one or perhaps two expeditions, particularly in the first decade of the century, and several countries established bases that were occupied for many years. In what was regarded as her sphere of influence, however, Britain maintained the greatest number of bases for the longest continuous period of any country. The figures in the accompanying table, which include Halley Bay in the Weddell Sea sector of the British territory, tell the story:

During the FIDS era, therefore, the bases were widespread and astonishingly small. For the most part each base had meteorologists, a geologist, a surveyor, perhaps a glaciologist or a geophysicist, a radio operator, a diesel mechanic, perhaps a doctor, perhaps a general assistant or a mountaineer; very rarely, a cook. One of these men was appointed base leader and given the powers of a magistrate and postmaster.

Small though the bases were, the achievements of the men operating from them gave Britain a good lead in Antarctic research,

POPULATION OF BRITISH BASES 1944–1961

Year	Number of Bases	Number of men	Average Number of men per base
1944	2	14	7
1945	3	21	7
1946	5	30	6
1947	5	33	6.6
1948	7	38	5.4
1949	5	29	5.8
1950	6	26	4.3
1951	5	24	4.8
1952	6	36	6
1953	5	35	7
1954	6	42	7
1955	8	57	7.1
1956	10	76	7.6
1957	11	87	7.9
1958	11	82	7.5
1959	8	78	9.7
1960	9	87	9.7
1961	9	93	10.3

(The figures for 1950 and 1951 include a base at South Georgia; those for 1960 included 12 men who were reallocated from 2 bases which could not be opened at Adelaide and Stonington Islands; had they done so the average would have been almost 7.9 men per base. In 1961, 25 men went to Halley Bay.)

before the days when the modern scientific bases began to develop in the sixties and seventies. The work also covered a large range of disciplines.

On the evidence of their field work, FIDS geologists, working at Birmingham University on their return to England, published innumerable reports on, and maps of, the geology of the peninsula and its off-shore islands, and identified the basic nature of the rocks and minerals and their stratigraphy.

Meteorological observations were carried out on most bases over many years, exceeded only by the Argentinians at Laurie Island in the

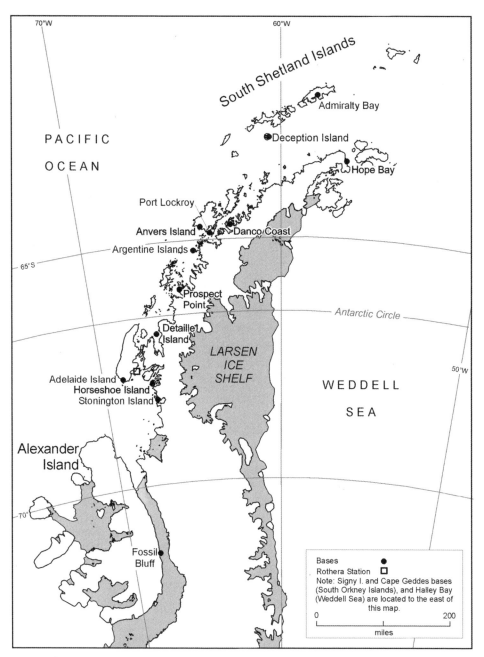

70°W 60°W

South Shetland Islands

● Admiralty Bay

PACIFIC

OCEAN

● Deception Island

● Hope Bay

Port Lockroy

Anvers Island ● ● Danco Coast

Argentine Islands ●

65°S

Prospect
Point ●

Antarctic Circle

Detaille
Island ●

LARSEN
ICE
SHELF

50°W

Adelaide Island ● □
Horseshoe Island ●
Stonington Island ●

WEDDELL

SEA

Alexander
Island

70°

Fossil ●
Bluff

Bases   ●
Rothera Station   □
Note: Signy I. and Cape Geddes bases
(South Orkney Islands), and Halley Bay
(Weddell Sea) are located to the east of
this map.
0   200

miles

F.I.D.S. WINTER BASES
Antarctic Peninsula/Islands 1944–1961

South Orkneys. These records, apart from their immediate use in compiling synoptic charts as a basis for weather forecasting, provided the statistics to determine the climate and weather of the peninsula, the islands and Halley Bay.

Surveyors were on bases right from the start, carrying out initial surveys of lands that had never been mapped. Many of them went on to work at Tolworth in Surrey, where maps were produced by the Directorate of Colonial Surveys. In February 2000, many old Fids (and many not so old BAS men!) were on board the *Lyubov Orlova* on a cruise down to Marguerite Bay, and spent much time on the bridge. It gave us all real pleasure to see that many of the maps used for navigation were FIDS maps of 1957 to 1960 vintage, especially so for Chris Brading, who was at Hope Bay during 1959 and 1960 and could spot the locations of cairns he had set up on some of the South Shetland Islands as survey points made whilst operating from the ships. The FIDS ships all undertook hydrographic surveys, and much of this information found its way into the *Antarctic Pilot* (the navigation handbook for mariners).

Biological work was less well developed on most bases, though a great deal of general work on observing penguins, birds and seals was carried out. Signy Island, however, was to be an exception in this respect for scientific programmes of biological research, both on land and in the sea had been started in the few summer weeks before we had called on the base on our way north, and would make a major contribution in this field.

Programmes of medical research, ionospherics and geophysics, the latter two in their infancy, were all started under FIDS, leading to dramatic discoveries later on.

Within this greater framework it is interesting to identify the specific contribution we made in our own tiny base at Fossil Bluff, despite the catalogue of frustration and disasters set out.

Firstly, we survived the first winter of anyone living on Alexander Island, and therefore had the opportunity to be the first to camp inland and to know a little of a small fragment of the interior. We also almost certainly made the first ascents of what are now called Khufu and Blodwen Peaks, and made the first man-haul crossing of King George VI Sound, short though the journey was.

Secondly, and more importantly, Brian Taylor made a huge contribution to the geology of the island, especially in the field of palaeontology. He published twelve scientific papers over many years (see appendix 3).

Thirdly, John Smith and I made the first continuous set of weather observations from the beginning of March to the end of the year. I later wrote a summary and discussion on these observations, which was published in the first edition of *The British Antarctic Survey Bulletin* in June 1963.

Fourthly, with the use of tellurometers, a start was made on establishing a ground control scheme for King George VI Sound by the surveyors, Howard Chapman and Bob Metcalfe, during the short period of summer travelling that was left to them in 1961.

Fifthly, Fossil Bluff was the first permanent British base to be established entirely by air, and this was important in proving the value of aircraft in extending the work on the survey ever southwards. Fossil Bluff subsequently became a summer base only, with aircraft being essential to its functioning. It has been in continuous use for over forty years.

This small contribution from one of the two smallest bases that FIDS ever opened (there were three men at Signy Island in 1948) added to the mosaic of other contributions which collectively helped to produce a great source of knowledge on this part of the world.

The tremendous record of sustained performance and success from these small bases inevitably resulted from the calibre of the men selected and their ability to get on satisfactorily with their base mates. The adequacy of the preparation and training of the men by the FIDS, was patchy and in some areas inadequate. They tended to appoint professional men who were already trained either in academic fields or as experts in diesel engines, or in radio operating, or as pilots, and assume that other skills would come through experience.

When the bases were first established, because the whole programme was based on a wartime operation called 'Operation Tabarin', they were always led by ex-military men, most of them experienced in action in the war, older than later Fids and with lots of skills and confidence, though not necessarily with scientific qualifications. The 1946 Stonington team of ten men comprised a surgeon commander, a surgeon lieutenant, three majors, two captains and three lieutenants. The assumption seems to have been that men of this experience did not need specific training. Eventually the bases became reliant on civilians and after 1948 very few men from the services were recruited – mainly for their service-based skills in flying, aircraft maintenance or tracked vehicle driving.

The civilian Fids were appointed after advertisement and interview at the Crown Agents in London. Geologists and surveyors were already qualified, though they invariably had some form of familiarisation courses before they sailed. Meteorologists were recruited from a variety of backgrounds, for example having a degree in geography, as in my case, and everyone went on an eight-week course of thorough training, at the Air Ministry in Stanmore. Other scientists were appointed for specific work based on their knowledge and needed no additional training, neither did the radio operators or diesel/electric mechanics. Finally 'general assistants' were appointed who could bring special skills to the base, perhaps in the skills of mountaineering or building.

At the base, therefore, a group of well-qualified and well-motivated men arrived and the programme of work proceeded. This was where some inadequacies in preparation became evident. On virtually all of the bases under the FIDS regime, everyone contributed to all duties, and this had an important positive role in making each base a fully integrated unit. On the other hand there were some who did not enjoy cooking, and they had to learn on the job, though most men responded well to this challenge and it did not seem to cause major problems. There was no training whatever in first aid, and although the bases had well-stocked medical chests with a variety of bandages and splints, and tablets and ampoules of palliative drugs, most of us had no idea of the appropriate use of some of these aids; 'common sense' seemed to be the best form of training!

The greatest inadequacy, however, was in the complete lack of training for travelling in the Antarctic. I had my first real insight into crevasse self-rescue techniques eight days before I boarded the ship to come home, though earlier at Fossil Bluff we had dug a pit in order to try to teach ourselves! Travelling on glaciers, whether getting down the back slope of a corrie, or travelling up the centre of the ice, or crossing it transversely, is a dangerous activity and the large majority of Fids were absolute novices in this field. Crossing sea ice was also a very hazardous occupation because of its propensity to break up without warning; training for this was also a matter of 'common sense'! Yet in 1958, three men died when Marguerite Bay ice blew out whilst they were on it, and in 1959 one man died in a crevasse accident at Admiralty Bay, and another died at the same base from a head injury when he slipped down a difficult snow patch and over a rocky cliff. In the years following our departure, further groups of two and three men were lost on sea ice and several other men were lost in crevasse accidents, including three who died in an accident at Halley Bay when a tractor fell into a crevasse; two other men died in a blizzard near Stonington Island. Travelling in small boats also caused several potentially fatal occurrences, as well as resulting in the loss of life of a man at Signy Island in 1956. There was, however, no boatsmanship training even on bases where travel by small boat was essential, as at Deception Island, Port Lockroy, Horseshoe Island and in fact on most of the bases; I don't remember ever wearing a life jacket!

There have been fires on bases on several occasions; one led to the deaths of two Fids at Hope Bay in 1948. Another Fid lost his life in 1960 when he fell over a cliff at Signy Island. The concept of 'risk assessment' was a long way off at the time, and there were times when I felt that bravado was given more importance in meeting hazardous conditions than was a careful consideration of what was involved.

Perhaps there was too much reliance on the amateur spirit overcoming all difficulties; the diesel/electric mechanic would make a good cook (and they often did), the meteorologist would make a good dog driver (and they usually did), two meteorologists and a geologist at Fossil Bluff would make good diesel/electric mechanics and radio operators (and they only partially did!).

Preparation in terms of supplies was excellent, provided that things went as planned. The quality of the base huts, strong and well-insulated, with a practical design, was good. The base hut at Horse-shoe Island when visited in 2000 was absolutely secure, and dry, more than forty-five years after its construction, even though it had not been in use for the last forty years. The clothing which was issued to us was outstandingly good: plenty of high-quality clothing appro-priate to our various needs. The same was true with respect to foods, all of it pre-packed and boxed in England, including the sensibly packed sledging boxes with their supplies for two men for ten days; I never heard any complaints on this matter. Inevitably when circum-stances necessitated ad hoc arrangements, problems did arise, as was obviously the case at Fossil Bluff when food and fuel was inadequate.

223

Provisions for the husky dogs was also good in terms of boxes of nutrican for travel (seal meat being provided on the bases). There always seemed to be good supplies of sledges and boats and outboard motors.

When the need for new forms of travel emerged in the early sixties, it did seem that the necessary investment was not really forthcoming. By starting off with just two aircraft in 1960, there was too little room for misfortune; thus when the Beaver aircraft was damaged in March, there was no back-up for the Otter and it had to be used sparingly. When the Beaver was lost on September 16th (on its first operational flight after its repair), the whole summer programme involving Adelaide Island had to be abandoned completely. Perhaps too much reliance was placed on the assumption of perfect conditions; the result was that a considerable number of men were unable to carry out the programmes for which they had been employed. In later years at Rothera, the base had many aircraft available, giving adequacy and much needed security.

The actual organisation of the bases was in the hands of the base leaders, some of whom had been appointed at the outset, on the basis of their proven skills or specialities, or after they had worked on bases and their 'qualities' had emerged. After the early years of the Survey, the British bases were largely peopled by civilians. On the bases of other nationalities the structure was often a military one, as in the case of Argentina and Chile. The USA in 1957, for their IGY programme, combined military bases with civilian scientists. The bases on which men were under a service regime, and where they had either been 'posted', or had volunteered for the Antarctic because of the prospects of higher pay, gave rise to problems. A lack of commitment and perhaps motivation by the participants was often expressed in the desire for frequent family radio calls, and in the South American bases at Deception Island, even a reluctance by some men to go outside! In the case of mixed bases with servicemen operating alongside civilian scientists, as described by Finn Ronne at Ellsworth in 1957, it was a disaster involving non-cooperation and even non-communication between the two factions. (This may simply have been a unique occurrence due to the personalities involved.) The British bases worked on a good system of planning and control, provided the base leader was well organised and respected, but it also depended very largely on good will by all in a very large measure. No Fid had joined the Survey to make money; they had all gone south because of a genuine desire to be there, and there was a good degree of mutual support. At Fossil Bluff, there was never any question in our minds that the most important task was to support Brian in his geological work, so John or I stayed with him at his camps on the glacier for sixty-five days and nights between October and December.

As for external control and organisation, we were sometimes aware of different voices making conflicting demands. Obviously the line of command seemed to be straightforward: London – Stanley – bases. However, once the strategic plan had been made, decisions in the light of local conditions needed to be made by the senior person on the spot. We became sceptical concerning chains of command when, after eight weeks at Deception Island, the six of us who had been installed in the Hunting Lodge aerial survey base were suddenly instructed to move into the main base. Although this proved to have great benefits, there was no evidence of discussion with the men actually on the island.

Much more serious was the difficult situation that occurred in Marguerite Bay late in 1961. It seemed to most of us who depended on the correctness of the decisions being made, that John Cunningham, the base leader at Stonington Island, should have been able to call in the aircraft when it became obvious that the Muskegs and sledges were not going to deliver the men and materials to the area where they were to work. Instead John Green, SecFids in Stanley, was giving one set of instructions, presumably coming from Sir Vivian Fuchs in London, then the Governor of the Falkland Islands ordered a withdrawal, and the result was a considerable degree of chaos with the ensuing failure. At least a change was forthcoming, for in 1964 John Cunningham returned as base leader at Adelaide Island with responsibility for coordinating all field operations in Marguerite Bay and further south. So lessons had been learned!

Inevitably there have been many changes in the Antarctic world during the forty years that have passed since 1962, both in the environment and in the manner in which human beings impact on it.

The diminution of the cover of ice has been well documented over the years – sometimes with dramatic photographs of massive icebergs breaking away from the Larsen Ice Shelf or other ice shelves, the enormous Wordie Ice Shelf, over which we had flown to and from Fossil Bluff, has been reduced to a few remnants of ice, and the ice fronts at both ends of King George VI Sound are retreating steadily. At Stonington Island the glacier link to the mainland has gone, at Adelaide Island and Hope Bay large areas of rock have become exposed, at Deception Island the permanent snow cover has retreated ever closer to the tops of the mountains.

There have also been some obvious changes in the flora and fauna. Even the most ordinary, unexcitable Fid of 1962 would have been amazed to find such a huge transformation in the numbers of fur seals on the South Shetlands and on the islands and coastal locations on the peninsula that were evident in 2000. I saw only one fur seal in over two years between 1960 and 1962, and that was at South Georgia; there were a great many at Deception Island in 2000, and hundreds at Half Moon Island and other locations. Another strange phenomenon was to see grass growing amongst the rocks at Cuverville Island in the Gerlache Strait, and many more areas of rich moss than we had ever seen before. We also saw many whales of different species in 2000, perhaps a response to the end of whaling, but maybe it was just an impression that we had that there were more whales than there had been in the middle of the 20th century. Hunting of seals for dog meat has also ended. However, even when there were sledging bases simultaneously working at Hope Bay, Stonington Island and Adelaide Island, well under 1,000 seals were taken each year; the impact on their numbers was therefore insignificant.

The impact of man, arising from the greater interest being taken by many nations in Antarctica, and from the protocols of the Antarctic Treaty, has been dramatic, both for good and bad reasons. Over twenty countries maintained bases in the 1990s, including China, Poland, Ukraine, Korea and Peru; at least nine countries have bases on King George Island in the South Shetlands, where once there was one British base (Admiralty Bay). The United Kingdom, on the other hand, has reduced its permanent bases to Rothera and Halley Bay, with Signy Island and Fossil Bluff operating in summer time only. The average number of people wintering on UK bases has declined from an average of 85.4 men in each of the years 1957 to 1961, to 39.6 men and women in each of the last five winters of the 20th century (excluding those based in South Georgia).

From the growth overall in the number of national bases, with varying standards of environmental awareness, it follows that the amount of rubbish and decaying machinery has also risen dramatically. Set against this is the improvement in care resulting from the Antarctic Treaty. During the years of FIDS, and the early years of BAS, environmental care was almost non-existent. At Deception Island the latrine buckets were tipped into the water at the nearest beach; at many bases, such as at Adelaide Island, all of the base rubbish was systematically tipped straight into the sea. If there was sea ice, at least the refuse could be placed on it, after which it would probably drift far out to sea. Hopefully new policies to clean up the environment are having a positive impact.

The disappearance of dogs also marks a change, and their primacy as a means of transport has been taken over completely by modern machines and aircraft. I suspect that there is no evidence anywhere of the permanent impact of dogs on the environment; in huge numbers of locations, however, there remain thousands of fuel drums scarring the landscape, not to mention a large number of crashed aircraft and dead tractors.

The development of tourism has the potential for a massive impact on the environment, yet the potential for harm may be overplayed. Nearly all tourists are ship-based and through the force of logistics make only fleeting visits to a few accessible areas. Seven thousand tourists visited Port Lockroy in 2000, but large numbers never go ashore, especially from the biggest ships. Guidelines are rigidly enforced by the tour operators with respect to proximity and harassment of wildlife, removing all litter and respecting sensitive areas of moss or grass. In any case, the type of tourist that wants to visit Antarctica is invariably the most environmentally sensitive person. The Antarctic Heritage Trust has established Port Lockroy as a superb museum; the Horseshoe Island base also has the potential to attract tourists, though its limited accessibility probably precludes its development. Certainly, there is tremendous scope for the further development of tourism without detriment to the environment.

Another large change has been in the nature of the new settlements and in the nature of the bases. At Hope Bay, the Argentinians have established a genuine village, Esperanza. The village has many individual houses with resident families. There is a well-equipped school, a church (with its own 'Madonna of the Snows'), a bar and shop as well as scientific buildings. On the Fildes Peninsula on King George Island near to the runway at Marsh base is a Chilean hotel.

The change in the nature of the bases is very marked. British bases are fewer in number, much larger in their complement, especially during the summer, and have significant numbers of women scientists. The bases themselves have become intensely scientific and comprise professional scientists to a very high degree. The days of the multi-talented specialist have also gone: those who shared the cooking, ran a dog team, looked after the boats and scrubbed the floor, in between their geological field work. Visiting the base at Rothera with its well-equipped offices and laboratories, huge accommodation block and 'airport' with many aircraft, it was hard to recognise the seeds from which such splendid centres of scientific research originated! Yet it is a continuation of the tradition established over fifty-seven years in tiny, remote bases. With modern forms of communication and transport I doubt if they are subject to the type of uncertainties which afflicted those who served in earlier times. What we all share, I am certain, is a love for the magic of Antarctica, a magic that enriches our lives.

On board *Lyubov Orlova*, Off Rothera Point, *Feb. 12th 2000*. We had moved overnight from Horseshoe Island to near Millerand Island. Unfortunately there was a bit of broken ice between us and Stonington Island and the captain wouldn't pass through it. We could see the memorial to two lost sledgers, and we could see the North East Glacier. We went a short way past Red Rock Ridge ... our furthest south was 68°14′S. We steamed to the Dion Islands and anchored. Later the weather became incredibly beautiful and we moved past Jenny Island and into Laubeuf Fiord. All around was a landscape of magnificent grandeur – high rocky mountains, severe ridges, glaciers, piedmonts, ice shelves ... Pourquoi Pas Island was particularly superb. As we entered the fiord a red BAS Otter flew over us, going to Rothera – it reminded me of my own trip to Fossil Bluff, those many years ago ...

APPENDIXES

1 Place-Names in Antarctica

Up to the middle of the twentieth century the history of naming places in the Antarctic, arising as it did from the earliest visitors to the continent in search of whales or seals, or for the purposes of discovery and science, was a long saga of confusion, with haphazard duplication and want of regulation.

This text, the story of two years in the British sector of the Antarctic, has used the names in use in that sector in 1962. At that time 'Graham Land' described the whole of the peninsula from the extreme north where it merged into Trinity Peninsula, to the area south of Latitude 71°S (as shown on the map in *Southern Lights, The Story of the British Graham Land Expedition 1934–37*). However, this nomenclature was not accepted by other countries, notably Chile and Argentina, who had bases there, nor by the USA, who claimed primacy in discovery. It was John Biscoe, after his 1832 voyage who named the area 'Graham Land', after Sir James Graham, the First Lord of the Admiralty at that time. The Americans claimed that Nathaniel Palmer had been the first discoverer in 1821, and they used the name 'Palmer Land' on their maps. H.R. Mill, the first major Antarctic historian, in his book *The Siege of the South Pole*, written in 1905, recognised three sections of the peninsula, one of which was named after King Louis Philippe (by Dumont Durville), 'Louis Philippe Land', and another after Emile Danco (by Adrien de Gerlache), 'Danco Land'. The third section, 'Graham Land', extended southwards from Latitude 60°S. Later on 'Tierra San Martin', appeared on Argentine maps, whilst 'Tierra O'Higgins' was preferred by Chile.

The regularisation of place names came together perhaps after 1943 when the US Board on Geographic Names was established, to be followed by the UK Antarctic Place-Names Committee in 1945, and the two groups informally co-operated. Thus in 1964 a final agreement was made to use the term 'Antarctic Peninsula' for the total land mass in this sector, and to sub-divide it into two sections,

229

'Palmer Land', for the southern area, and 'Graham Land' for the northern area, the division being 70°S. Some other changes followed, the most relevant to this work being the change from 'King George VI Sound' to 'George VI Sound'. 'George VI Ice Shelf' is now used for the southern area of the Sound.

These changing names exemplify, in part, the diversity of ways in which place-names in Antarctica have originated. Sir James Graham was a person of importance and influence in Great Britain; Nathaniel Palmer was (perhaps), the first Captain to see Antarctica, Emile Danco died in the course of duty with de Gerlache, Louis Philippe, the King of France, was honoured by his loyal subject d'Urville; General San Martin, and Bernado O'Higgins were heroes of Argentina and Chile.

The diversity of names throughout Antarctica, up to the middle of the twentieth century, derives from the early explorers and most fall into one of the following categories:

- Honouring the head of state of a country
- Recognition of the leaders or members of expeditions
- Remembrance of the ships that were fundamental to the work
- Respect for members of the families of leaders or expedition members
- Appreciation for sponsors of expeditions, or for influential supporters
- Identification of specific, descriptive geographical or geological features

During the late 1940s and '50s, and during the second half of the century, increasing journeys of exploration, and the increase in aerial surveys created a need for large numbers of additional place names and this spawned the use of over forty groups of associated names, which do not fit in to any of the earlier types of classification. Because of the deviation of this group from the traditional order, they have here been grouped together as 'anomalous'. This list includes features named after Greek letters (an early deviation in the late 1920s), and characters from novelists such as Jules Verne (late 1940s), Chaucer and Dickens (both in the mid-1950s). Alexander Island is rich in such associated names with planets, Saxon kings, geologists, and composers and their works, all introduced when maps were being compiled in the mid and late 1950s. Elsewhere in Antarctica such groups include acronyms such as Banzare, Usarp and Anare representing Antarctic work in Britain, Australia, New Zealand and the USA.

Because of their primacy in exploration the names given by the early explorers were invariably confirmed and most appear on Antarctic maps to this day.

Honouring the head of state of a country

Over two dozen heads of state are honoured, with British monarchs being the most numerous. For example, British kings and queens are honoured in Victoria Land, Edward VII Land, George V Land and George VI Sound. King Leopold of Belgium is honoured with Queen Astrid in a long section of coast in Eastern Antarctica. Norwegian Kings Haakon (a huge plain near the South Pole), and Oscar II (part of the east coast of the Antarctic Peninsula), as well as Queen Maud (huge areas of plateau as well as mountains), represent the enormous importance of early Norwegian whalers and explorers such as Amundsen. Other heads of state honoured include Peter I (Island) and Alexander (Island) representing the Russian presence, and Kaiser Wilhelm II of Germany (Wilhelm II Coast). There are very few elected leaders honoured, but the USA remembers Roosevelt (Island), and Andrew Jackson (a mountain in Palmer Land); Bismarck Strait was named by explorer Edward Dallman for Otto von Bismarck.

Recognition of leaders or members of expeditions

This is perhaps, not surprisingly, the largest group of names. Virtually all of the early explorers from whaling captains or owners to expedition leaders are honoured. In the 1820s and 1830s James Weddell (Weddell Sea), William Smith (Smith Island, South Shetlands), Edward Bransfield (Bransfield Strait), Thaddeus von Bellingshausen (Bellingshausen Sea), Nathaniel Palmer (Palmer Land), Henry Foster (Port Foster, Deception Island), and John Biscoe (Biscoe Islands) were all amongst the earliest to penetrate south. Enderby Land (Eastern Antarctica) was named for the owners of the Biscoe ships. Dumont d'Urville (d'Urville Island, Antarctic Peninsula), also had a huge sea area (Dumont d'Urville Sea) named for him. In this era,

Charles Wilkes (Wilkes Land) led the first American expedition to Antarctica and followed the West Antarctic coast for well over a thousand miles.

A thirty year lull in new discoveries was followed by a gradual development of scientific expeditions during the rest of the 19th century. The naming of features, however, continued the tradition of honouring the captains or leaders. Thus the British Naval expedition under Sir James Clark Ross (Ross Sea), the German whaling expedition under Captain Edward Dallman (Dallman Bay), and two voyages by whaling captain Carl Larsen (Larsen Ice Shelf) all added new dimensions to the map.

The list of explorers' names continues into the classic age of discovery: Adrien de Gerlache (Gerlache Strait), Carsten Borchgrevink (Borchgrevink Coast), Eric von Drygalski (Drygalski Ice Tongue), Otto Nordenskjold (Nordenskjold Ice Tongue) – these last three all in the Ross Sea – preceded the first of Robert Falcon Scott's two expeditions, and the three led by Ernest Shackleton. Antarctic maps naturally have many features named after Scott and Shackleton, as is the case with Roald Amundsen. Nobu Shirase (Shirase Coast, Ross Sea), Wilhelm Filchner (Filchner Ice Shelf, Weddell Sea) and Douglas Mawson (a range of features including a glacier, a cape, an escarpment, a coast and a peninsula!), all led expeditions in 1911/1912 contemporaneously with Scott and Amundsen

From the 1920s onwards, the number of private expeditions declined as countries set up their own organisations to investigate Antarctica. Nevertheless naming still continued. Hubert Wilkins (Wilkins Sound), Admiral Richard Byrd (Cape Byrd and others), Lincoln Ellsworth (Ellsworth Range), John Rymill (Rymill Bay), were all honoured. Even Alfred Ritscher, a German aviator whose 1938 Schwabenland expedition laid claim to much of Dronning Maud Land merely by flying over it and dropping aluminium darts, has Ritscherflya Highlands in that area named for him.

Virtually every expedition leader recognised colleagues when they named, or recommended names for features, so there are hundreds of examples.

The map of the Antarctic Peninsula and Palmer Land is strewn with the names of expedition members from the earliest times to the middle of the 20th century. For example, Wiencke Island and Danco Island commemorate two casualties of the *Belgica* Expedition (de Gerlache), Duse Bay (Nordenskjold) remembers Lieutenant Duse,

232

who, with two colleagues, survived a winter at Hope Bay after the expedition ship sank. Further south off Alexander Island, Latady Island and Eklund Island carry the names of Finn Ronne colleagues. Glaciers on the eastern side of George VI Sound carry the names of British Graham Land Expedition men, Millett, Ryder, Bertram and Riley.

Elsewhere on the continent a few examples serve to demonstrate the tradition. Captain Scott's expeditions are represented by large numbers of features named for his scientists or crew. For example, Cape Royds, Cape Barne, Skelton Glacier and Koettlitz Glacier are all named for officers on the *Discovery*; inevitably Bowers (Mountains), Oates (Land) and Wilson (Cape) joined Priestley (Glacier) and Campbell (Glacier) in the list of famous names from the *Terra Nova*. Right through the classical period of exploration and beyond, Shackleton, Mawson and others all had many of their staff recognised in this manner.

Remembrance of the ships that were fundamental to the work

All expedition leaders recognised the supreme importance of their ships, and large numbers of names are a permanent testimony to them. The names of these ships, like the names of the expedition leaders themselves, catalogue the history of exploration. The earliest explorers began the fashion. Dumont d'Urville reached Adelie Land in 1840 with the help of the two ships *Astrolabe* and *Zelee*, whose names were given to two glaciers in Adelie Land. Sir James Clarke Ross in the early 1840s discovered the Ross Sea and named Mounts Erebus and Terror after *Erebus* and *Terror*, his ships. Ernest Shackleton named Nimrod Glacier and Mount Nimrod, after *Nimrod*; Captain Scott named Terra Nova Bay after *Terra Nova*, whilst Aurora Peak commemorates Mawson's ship *Aurora*. Gaussberg was named by Drygalski after *Gauss*; Charcot named Mount Francais on Anvers Island and Pourquoi Pas Island in Marguerite Bay after his two ships *Francais* and *Pourquoi Pas*. In the 1930s, the British Graham Land Expedition used the *Penola* for their successful expedition, and Penola Strait was named for the waters between Graham Land and the Argentine Islands, the site of their first base. Even with the advent of national organisations, the trend continued. In 1945 the Falkland Islands Dependencies were established and Trepassey Bay, near Hope Bay, was named for the very first Falkland Islands Dependency ship in 1945.

Respect for members of the families of leaders or expedition members

Once the leaders and their colleagues had been recognised, many leaders extended the recognition to the members of their families or to the families of their colleagues. This list is not so numerous, but there are good examples. Dumont d'Urville honoured his wife Adelie, both in Adelie Land and in naming the Adelie penguin; Charcot Island was named for his father by Jean Baptiste Charcot and Ronne Entrance was named by Finn Ronne for his family, particularly for his father, Martin, who was with Amundsen in 1910–12. Finn Ronne also named Edith Ronne Land after his wife Edith. The name was subsequently changed, firstly because Mrs Ronne did not like the name Edith (she is always known as Jackie), and secondly because her territory was reclassified from Land to Ice Shelf. Thus on modern maps it appears as Ronne Ice Shelf.

Appreciation for sponsors of expeditions, or for influential supporters

It was natural (and very wise!) for sponsors, or influential supporters of the early expeditions to receive grateful recognition from the expedition leaders.

One of the first explorers to express his appreciation for financial help was Carsten Borchgrevink who was given the huge sum of £40,000 by Sir George Newnes. His generosity was rewarded when Borchgrevink named Newnes Land and Lady Newnes Bay south of Cape Adare after his benefactors.

Captain Scott was very much indebted to Sir Clements Markham for being 'the father of the (*Discovery*) expedition'. On the way back from his farthest south in December 1902, having seen 'this splendid twin-peaked mountain, which even in such a lofty country, seems as a giant among pygmies', he named it Mount Markham! Other wealthy contributors to the expedition included Llewelyn Longstaff (Mount Longstaff) – £25,000.

The Misses Dawson Lambton (Dawson Lambton Glacier) helped Scott with £1,500 and Shackleton with £1,000. Shackleton was also aided by Sir James Caird (Caird Coast and James Caird boat) with the huge sum of £24,000, and by Dame Janet Stancombe-Wills

234

(Stancombe-Wills Glacier and Ice Tongue and Stancombe-Wills boat); she provided money for equipping the *Endurance* and purchasing one of the three boats crucial to their salvation. An interesting benefactor who was recognised by Shackleton was Allan McDonald (Allan McDonald Glacier). He worked hard to raise, within three days, £1,500 from the British Association of Magallanes to charter the ship *Emma*, which was able to make the initial (unsuccessful) run to Elephant Island to save those who were marooned there in 1916.

Douglas Mawson was similarly aided by generous sponsors who received recognition. Samuel Hordern (Cape Hordern) – £2,500, Robert Barr-Smith (Mount Barr-Smith) – £1,000, Roderick Murchison (Mount Murchison) – £1,000 and Lord Strathcona (Mount Strathcona) – £1,000; all of these features are pre-eminent in Queen Mary Land.

Later on, the names of the various supporters of the British Graham Land Expedition, both financial and influential, appeared on maps after the expedition had completed its work. Thus Lord Wakefield (Mount Wakefield – later called Wakefield Highland), Mrs Henry Cadbury (Mount Cadbury), Sir Arthur and Lady Bagshawe (Mount Bagshawe) and Mr William Meek (Meek Channel) are among those recognised. John Rymill, the leader of the BGLE, recognised one of his major supporters and his family in a most unusual way. Professor Frank Debenham had been vital in getting the expedition planned and financed and his name was given to the islands where the southern base hut was built. Subsequently, the tiny islands that make up the Debenham Islands were named after his six children Ann, Audrey, Barbara, Barry, Brian and June.

Probably, of all Antarctic explorers, Finn Ronne was the most generous in bestowing the names of his supporters and friends on a variety of features. In his book on the Ronne Antarctic Research Expedition, following his one year expedition of 1947, he recognised eighty supporters. (This follows his 'modest' claim that despite claims made to land sectors by Great Britain, Argentina and Chile, 'the fact remains however that American expeditions have done the original exploration of practically the entire sector'!) On the east coast of Palmer Land he named large numbers of features after his supporters – Louis Keller of Beaumont, Texas (Keller Inlet), Dr Isaiah Bowman president of Johns Hopkins University, Baltimore (Bowman Peninsula), and Dr John Wright, Director of the American Geographical Society, New York (Wright Inlet), and many others. Inland from the coast, Ronne gobbled up the mountains – Dr Dana Coman of New York (Mount Coman), Mr Knut Vang of Brooklyn (Mount Vang), Professor and Mrs Edward Sweeny (Sweeny Mountains and Mount Edward), to identify just a few. On Alexander Island he named mountains after Lt General Curtis LeMay (LeMay Range) and Colonel R.C. Walton, US Marine Corps, Washington (Walton Mountains). Near Cape Jeremy are the Bugge Islands, after Miss Ruth Bugge of Molde, Norway. Even the owners of the Horne Department Store in Pittsburg (Horne Mountains), and 'the seat of the Kasco Dog Food Company's mills at Waverly, New York' (Waverly Glacier) gained recognition!

Finn Ronne was not averse to pushing areas named for others further away in order to make greater recognition for his own. Maps from the Shackleton era recognised the Filchner Ice Shelf as being very extensive across the southern end of the Weddell Sea. Ronne flew from Graham Land (or Palmer Land!) along this ice shelf front and initially named it Lassiter Ice Shelf after his chief pilot. The area of ice, stretching hundreds of miles inland he named Edith Ronne Land. The Filchner Ice Shelf now covers a much smaller area east of Berkner Island.

Identification of specific geographical/geological features

The naming of features for reasons other than giving personal recognition is much more clear cut and self explanatory. A few examples from the western side of George VI Sound will serve as examples. Tilt Rock, Block Mountain, Belemnite Point, Succession Cliffs, Fossil Bluff, Bandstone Rock, Two Step Cliffs, Corner Cliffs and Coal Nunatak all conjure up images which are easy to visualise and are non-contentious. Large numbers of similarly descriptive terms – Plateaux, Domes, and Pyramids adorn maps of many parts of the continent.

Anomalous names

Alexander Island also has many good examples of names which don't fit into the traditional categories, and have no relevance to explorers, financial backers or supporters, or to geographical features. There are four types of anomalous names on the island; those of composers or their compositions, those named after the planets, a group of Saxon

Kings of England, and those named after British geologists. Over fifty musical names appear; it is somewhat incongruous to see Eroica Peninsula, Corelli Horn, Mozart Ice Piedmont, Chopin Hill, and Monteverdi Peninsula appearing in a world that was completely alien and unknown to most of the composers.

The names of all the planets, apart from Earth, have been given to glaciers issuing from Alexander Island into George VI Sound. Uranus Glacier, the largest, is immediately south of Fossil Bluff, with the Mercury, Venus, Neptune, Mars and Saturn Glaciers increasingly southwards; Pluto and Jupiter are to the north. Other celestial names appear, Planet Heights, Milky Way and Stella Crests, for example.

Finally Antarctica undoubtedly has some of the most boring names ever bestowed on a land, some of them probably a reflection of the American 'military' mind, some perhaps, evidence of the increasing influence of a 'committee' at work. It may be that Admiral Byrd is responsible for some of them, Executive Committee Range in Marie Byrd Land being one example. Support Force Glacier in the area of Dufek Massif probably owes its name to Rear Admiral Dufek. The USARP Mountains and the ANARE Mountains in Oates Land reflect American and Australian interests. The Publications Ice Shelf and the Polar Record Glacier in Eastern Antarctica sound suspiciously British in origin.

It was inevitable that, as the era of private expeditions came to an end and national organisations, whether military or civilian, took over the further exploration of Antarctica, there should be a system of agreed procedures on the naming of places. The Americans had their Board on Geographical Place Names to which Finn Ronne and others had had to apply for approval for their recommended names; by 1945 Britain had formalised its Antarctic Place-Names Committee with responsibility for deciding names in areas in which their scientists were operating. Obviously international agreements and co-operation were necessary in areas where there was overlap.

In Britain the Place-Names Committee meets at least once a year to consider appropriate names for features in areas which are being mapped. The Committee works to a very specific set of principles to achieve consistency and fairness; many compromises have had to be made between claims of priority, or claims by different nations. Inevitably the number of places to be named has risen dramatically as map-making has proceeded and throughout the continent there are vast numbers of features named for men (and for some women), who have worked in Antarctic areas. The Antarctic Place-Names Committee has approved the names of a great number of geologists and surveyors from FIDS/BAS, usually in places where they worked. Other base personnel, meteorologists, diesel mechanics and general assistants have also had places named for them.

A specific example of the working of the Committee can be seen in the case of the area around Fossil Bluff for which names were decided in 1998. A map had been prepared for publication at a scale of 1:1250, and the publication of this map provided the ideal opportunity to formalise place-names in this area. The committee were referred to a paper prepared by present and past members of the British Antarctic Survey. They had looked at various papers and reports, some published and some unpublished, which had been produced over the years, including ones dating back to the first year of occupation. Brian Taylor in particular had produced geological reports which included sketch maps and panoramas in which some unofficial place-names were first used. After 1973, the base was only used during the summer, so that hardly any names were remembered.

The two maps entitled The Fossil Bluff Environment in this text, shown on pages 162 and 239 illustrate the way in which place names are finally made. The map indicating the place names used in 1962, those which we three at Fossil Bluff developed through our familiarity with the landscape, were essentially descriptive, and used only by us. Thus, Hollow Valley had lost most of its glacier and was therefore Hollow. Our route to the camps took us up a well defined Gulley, past a gap in the ridge between two glaciers which acted as a Window, round the huge mountain top called Pyramid, down the treacherous ice slope below Ice Falls and across the Tributary glacier to Camp 2. From Camp 1 and from the slopes above, we looked across at massive Snow Dome. Fossil Bluff Glacier was a self-evident name; Man-Pack Hill was named by Brian Taylor after much man-packing, mostly by him.

The names finally approved by the Place-Names Committee were entirely different. Three Egyptian names, Khufu Peak, Giza Peak and Scarab Bluff, (some more anomalous names!), the first of which was given to Pyramid, had been approved some time before 1998. Presumably there were so many pyramids throughout Antarctica that a unique name was felt to be necessary. Following the Egyptian theme,

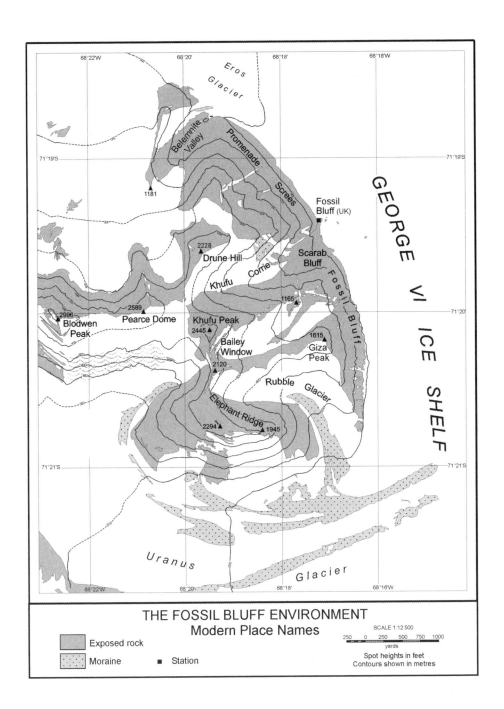

THE FOSSIL BLUFF ENVIRONMENT
Modern Place Names

SCALE 1:12 500
250   0   250   500   750   1000
yards

Spot heights in feet
Contours shown in metres

Exposed rock

Moraine   ■ Station

239

the glacier we referred to as Fossil Bluff Glacier became Khufu Corrie. Belemnite Valley replaced our Hollow Valley; certainly we always enjoyed looking at the vast numbers of Belemnites there, so the name is equally descriptive. Other descriptive names have been added to the map such as Promenade Screes and Rubble Glacier, and Elephant Ridge was preferred to Man-Pack Hill; it is more visually descriptive! Blodwen Peak which we never referred to other than as 2nd Pyramid, was named apparently after a Muskeg which made the journey from Stonington (much later than 1961). The origin of the name Drune Hill is not known – that makes it a very rare phenomenon in Antarctic place names! Finally two of the features were personalised, the name of 'Bailey' prefixed our 'Window' and derives from David Bailey, who was a cook at Fossil Bluff in 1994–1995 and who helped in the topographic survey. Snow Dome became Pearce Dome in recognition of my year at the base with Brian Taylor and John Smith in 1961.

Naming Antarctic features is a continuing process, and, from time to time, new name claims are made. In the 2001–2002 season, a Royal Navy medic attached to *HMS Endurance* noticed a tiny island whilst looking for somewhere to locate a monitoring station for tides along the coast of the Antarctic Peninsula. Mark Robinson landed on the islet, at 64°S and 62°W – highest point twenty feet. The Royal Navy, noticing that it was unnamed, indicated that it would put forward the name Robbie Island to the Antarctic Place-Names Committee for consideration. Perhaps this will be the first of many thousands of claims to name every lump of rock in Antarctica; what an attraction for every tourist first-footer!

2 Falkland Islands Dependencies Bases 1944–1961

This list is chronologically based, with the first date of occupation given. The code letters were given to each base and were used in radio communications and for ease of identification on food boxes and other cargo. Only bases which were occupied for a complete winter are identified.

Base B Deception Island – 62°59′S, 60°34′W. Occupied Feb 3rd 1944.

Base A Port Lockroy – 64°49′S, 63°31′W. Occupied Feb 11th 1944.

Base D Hope Bay – 63°24′S, 56°59′W. Occupied Feb 10th 1945.

Base C Cape Geddes – 60°41′S, 44°34′W. Occupied Jan 18th 1946.

Base E Stonington Island – 68°11′S, 67°00′W. Occupied Feb 24th 1946.

Base F Argentine Islands – 65°15′S, 64°16′W. Occupied Jan 7th 1947.

Base G Admiralty Bay – 62°05′S, 58°25′W. Occupied Jan 25th 1947.

Base H Signy Island – 60°43′S, 45°36′W. Occupied Mar 18th 1947.

Base M King Edward Point, S. Georgia – 57°17′S, 36°30′W. Occupied Jan 1st 1950

Base N Anvers Island – 54°46′S, 64°05′W. Occupied Feb 27th 1955.

Base Y Horseshoe Island – 67°49′S, 67°18′W. Occupied Mar 11th 1955.

Base Z Halley Bay – 75°31′S, 26°37′W. Occupied Jan 6th 1956.

Base W Detaille Island – 66°52′S, 66°48′W. Occupied Feb 21st 1956.

Base O Danco Island – 64°44′S, 62°36′W. Occupied Feb 26th 1956.

Base J Prospect Point – 66°00′S, 65°21′W. Occupied Feb 1st 1957.

Base T Adelaide Island – 67°46′S, 68°55′W. Occupied Feb 2nd 1961

Base KG Fossil Bluff – 71°20′S, 68°17′W. Occupied Feb 20th 1961.

By the end of 1961, the following bases had closed:

Cape Geddes (1947), Admiralty Bay (1961), Prospect Point (1959), King Edward Point (1952, but re-opened later), Anvers Island (1958), Horseshoe Island (1960), Detaille Island (1959) and Danco Island (1959)

Of the other bases all had closed as winter bases before 2000 except for Halley Bay (which still operates). Adelaide Island was replaced by Rothera Base in 1977. Fossil Bluff and Signy Island remain operative as summer bases.

3 A Note on the Weather at Fossil Bluff, March 1961 to January 1962

The main features of the weather at Fossil Bluff during the time of our observations were its comparative mildness, the surprising lack of wind, the rareness in the manifestations of 'weather' (snow, drift, fog etc), and the tendency towards low pressure during many months.

The comparative mildness of conditions during the year was surprising. The monthly mean temperatures (in Fahrenheit), ranged from $+29.6°$ in December, to $-9.8°$ in June, the coldest month, with means of $-0.7°$ for May and $+4.2°$ for July. The highest daily temperatures reached over $40°$ in November, with five of the eleven months having temperatures above freezing point. The lowest temperature, of $-37.9°$, was recorded in June, though temperatures below $-25°$ were recorded in each of the seven months from April to October. In view of its latitudinal position, the main influence on climate might have been expected to be high pressure and polar air. Fossil Bluff was also situated well to the south of the eastward-moving depressions associated with the latitudes further north. Additionally, for twelve weeks of the year twilight or darkness prevailed and the base stood at least 100 miles from open water at all times. During several months the distance from open water probably extended for over 200 miles. Lower temperatures than we recorded were therefore to have been expected.

Factors relating to its position did have a bearing on wind, pressure and 'weather'. Fossil Bluff enjoyed much calm weather. On well over half of the observations from March to June conditions of absolute calm were recorded, with 55%, 63%, 55% and 61% respectively. October saw the most disturbed weather, though even then, 36% of the observations were recorded as calm. Gale force winds were estimated on only three days, one each in March, August and October, and none at all in the other months. Most of the winds blew from the north (almost 70% of observations) or south (23%); this is partially explained by the site of the base which was well sheltered from westerly winds by the mountains of Alexander Island. The topography of George VI Sound, with its corridor effect, tended to channel such winds as blew into a northerly or southerly direction.

243

Approximately 40% of the observations recorded barometric pressures between 960 mbs and 980 mbs, with a slightly higher number between 980 mbs and 1,000 mbs. Only during the four months from June to September did over 25% of the readings show pressures above 1,000 mbs, whilst during four of the other six months pressure never exceeded 1,000 mbs.

Snowfall during the year was astonishingly small, with falls few and often far between. In May, for example, snow fell on eleven days, though, with few exceptions, snowfall was light. The snow was dry and loose and the accumulation on the slopes frequently blew away. Later on, during July and August, more snow fell and accumulation was greater, so that an accumulation at the weather screen of only three inches during the first five months increased by a further eleven inches in August. The hillsides were clear of snow by mid-October. The incidence of 'drift' was low, except around obstacles outside the base hut. December and January (1962) were marked by long periods of cloudy skies with much drizzle and rain.

4 Published Scientific Reports Derived from Fossil Bluff Field Work 1961–1962

Note – Brian Taylor continued his field work at Fossil Bluff for a further year after our first year at the base. His work at the BAS centre at Birmingham University resulted in the publication of the following papers, mostly in the British Antarctic Research Bulletin (BASB):

1. Aptian cirripedes from Alexander Island. BASB, No 7, 1965, pp 37–42.
2. Taxonomy and morphology of Echinodermata from the Aptian of Alexander Island. BASB, No 8, 1966, pp 1–18.
3. Trace Fossils from the Fossil Bluff Series of Alexander Island. BASB, No 13, 1967, pp 1–30.
4. Calcareous concretions in the Lower Cretaceous sediments of south-eastern Alexander Island. BASB, No 21, 1969, pp 19–32, (with R.R. Horne).
5. Small tubiform fossils from the Lower Cretaceous of Alexander Island. BASB, No 21, 1969, pp 71–78.
6. Thallophyte borings in phosphatic fossils from the Lower Cretaceous of south-east Alexander Island, Antarctica. Paleontology, No 14, Pt 2, 1971, pp 294–302.
7. Stratigraphical correlation in south-east Alexander Island (in Adie, R.J. Antarctic geology and geophysics. Oslo, Universitetsforlaget, 1971, pp 149–153).
8. An urdidid isopod from the Lower Cretaceous of south-east Alexander Island. BASB, No 27, 1972, pp 97–103.
9. The cuticle of Cretaceous macrurous decapoda from Alexander and James Ross Islands. BASB, No 35, 1973, pp 91–100.
10. Macrurous decapoda from the Lower Cretaceous of south-east Alexander Island. BAS Scientific Report, No 81, 1979 (39 pages).
11. The geology of the Ablation Point – Keystone Cliffs area, Alexander Island. BAS Scientific Report, No 82, 1979 (65 pages) – with M.A. Thomson & L.E. Willey.
12. Sedimentary dykes, pipes and related structures in the Mesozoic sediments of south-eastern Alexander Island. BASB, No 51, 1981, pp 1–42.

My own paper, 'Meteorological Observations at Fossil Bluff, Alexander Island', C.J. Pearce was published in the British Antarctic Survey Bulletin No 1, June 1963.

John Smith produced a 50-minute film, also called 'The Silent Sound', parts of which have been used in a variety of television programmes, and as part of the training programmes for new recruits to the Survey.

5 Bibliography

Behrendt, J.: *Innocents on the Ice. A Memoir of Antarctic Exploration, 1957.* University Press of Colorado, 1998.

Borchgrevink, C.E.: *First on the Antarctic Continent: Being an Account of the British Antarctic Expedition 1898–1900.* G. Newnes Ltd, London, 1901 (republished by C. Hurst & Co, London, 1980).

Byrd, R.E.: *Discovery: The Story of the Second Byrd Antarctic Expedition.* G.P. Putnam's Sons, New York, 1935.

Charcot, J.: *The Voyage of the Pourquoi Pas: The Journal of the Second French South Polar Expedition, 1908–1910.* Hodder & Stoughton, London, NY and Toronto, 1911.

Cook, F.: *Through the First Antarctic Night, 1898–1899.* William Heinemann, London, 1900.

Darlington, J.: *My Antarctic Honeymoon: A Year at the Bottom of the World.* F. Muller, London, 1957.

Filchner W. (trans William Barr): *To The Sixth Continent. The Second German South Polar Expedition.* Bluntisham Books, Huntingdon, 1994 (translation of original publication by I.M. Verlag, Berlin, 1922).

Fisher, M. & J.: *Shackleton.* James Barrie, London, 1957.

Fuchs, V.: *Of Ice and Men: The Story of the British Antarctic Survey 1943–73.* Anthony Nelson, Oswestry, 1982.

Gerlache de Gomery Adrien de: *Voyage of the Belgica: Fifteen Months in the Antarctic.* Bluntisham Books, Huntingdon, 1998 (translation of original published by J. Lebeque, Brussels, 1902).

Grierson, J.: *Challenge to the Poles: Highlights of Arctic and Antarctic Aviation.* G.T. Foulis & Co, London, 1964.

Grierson, J.: *Sir Hubert Wilkins – Enigma of Exploration.* Robert Hale, London, 1960.

Hattersley-Smith, G.: *The History Of Place Names In The British Antarctic Territory.* British Antarctic Survey Scientific Reports No 113, 1991.

Hayes, J.G.: *The Conquest of the South Pole.* Thornton Butterworth, London, 1932.

Herbert, W.: *A World of Men.* Eyre & Spottiswoode, London, 1968.

Mawson, D.: *The Home of the Blizzard.* William Heinemann, London, 1932.

Mill, H.R.: *The Siege of the South Pole. The Story of Antarctic Exploration.* Alston Rivers, London, 1905.

Mott, P.: *Wings Over Ice: The Falkland Islands Dependencies Aerial Survey Expedition.* Peter Mott, Long Sutton, 1986.

Nordenskjold, O.: *Antarctica or Two Years Amongst the Ice of the South Pole.* C. Hurst & Company, London, 1977.

Ronne, F.: *Antarctic Conquest. The Story of the Ronne Antarctic Research Expedition, 1946–48.* G.P. Putnam's Sons, New York, 1949.

Ronne, F.: *Antarctic Command.* Bobbs-Merrill Inc, Indianapolis/New York, 1961.

Ronne, F.: *Antarctica, My Destiny.* Hastings House Publishers, New York, 1979.

Rymill, J.: *Southern Lights. The Story of the British Graham Land Expedition.* Chatto and Windus, 1938.

Scott, R.F.: *The Voyage of the Discovery.* John Murray, London, 1913.

Scott, R.F. (ed. L. Huxley): *Scott's Last Expedition.* Smith Elder & Co, London, 1913.

Shackleton, Sir E.: *The Heart of the Antarctic: Being the Story of the British Antarctic Expedition, 1907–1909.* W. Heinemann, London, 1909.

Shackleton, Sir E.: *South: The Story of Shackleton's Last Expedition.* W. Heinemann, London, 1920.

Walton, E.W.K.: *Two Years in the Antarctic.* The Knell Press, Upper Colwall, 1982 (reprint of 1955 edition).

Walton, K. and Atkinson, R.: *Of Dogs and Men.* Images Publishing (Malvern) Ltd, 1996.

Other sources of information include:

The Reader's Digest publication *Antarctica: Great Stories from the Frozen Continent,* Surry Hills, NSW, Australia, 1985.
The American Geographical Society.
The Polar Record (Britain).
The British Antarctic Survey Bulletins.

INDEX

251

253

254

South East Point (Deception) 52
Southern Harvester 211
Southern Hunter 39
Southern Ocean 19
South Georgia 16, 37, 65, 92, 93, 210, 211, 214, 217, 218, 226
South Georgia Letterbox 145
South Orkneys 2, 72, 89, 105, 209, 210, 220
South Pacific 45
South Pole 62, 87, 119, 165, 195, 217
South Shetlands 2, 37, 65, 72, 75, 79, 89, 220, 226
Sparke, Dr Brian 103, 104, 153, 171, 172, 175, 176, 194, 199, 204, 206
Sparrow Cove 9
Stanley (Falkland Islands) xiv, 5, 7, 9, 43, 44, 46, 50, 63, 87, 99, 149, 175, 179, 184, 193, 212, 215, 225
Stefansson Strait 81
Stella Creek 98
Stephenson, Alfred 5, 20, 121, 181, 185
Stephenson, Mount 122
Stephenson Nunatak 189, 198
St Helena 92
Stokes, Jeff 104
Stonington Island (Base E) xiii, 13, 27, 28, 31, 39, 43, 54, 60, 62, 81, 89, 94, 99, 102, 103–107, 108, 111–114, 117, 119, 121, 127, 129, 131, 134, 145, 148, 149, 152, 153, 159, 161, 163, 166, 171–178, 181, 186, 191, 192, 194, 197–204, 208, 216, 218, 219, 221, 223, 225, 226, 228, 241, 242
Stonington Village (Connecticut) 112, 116
Stromness Bay 210, 211
Succession Cliffs 116, 125, 133, 143, 144
Sumner, Tom 11, 12, 40, 42, 43, 83, 84, 94, 95, 116, 194
Sweeny, John 62
Swine Hill 124, 137

Tabarin Peninsula 208
Tait, John xiii, 51
Taylor, Brian xv, 2, 28, 87, 105, 114, 115, 121, 123, 125, 127–179, 181, 189–194, 195, 198, 199, 201, 220, 225
Taylor Buttresses 195
Taylor, Capt Andrew 208

Taylor, Mount 208
Telefon Bay 71, 78, 207
Terra Firma Islands 116, 175
Three Slice Nunatak 54
Titan Nunatak 189
Tourism 227
Tracy, Bill 99, 171, 172, 176, 177, 178, 181, 183, 184, 185, 186, 187, 189, 190, 198
Trans-Antarctic Expedition 2, 11
Trinity House 208
Trinity Island 116
Tristan da Cunha 92, 158
Triton Cliffs 187
Tumbledown, Mount 212
Turnbull, Capt 52, 205
Tween, Mike 42, 47, 50, 51, 67, 84, 94, 127, 141, 142, 171, 172, 210
Two Step Cliffs 185

UK Antarctic Heritage Trust 204, 227
Ukraine 21
Uranus Glacier 122, 139, 143, 160, 161, 164, 181, 191
Uruguay 4, 5, 79, 214
Uruguay Island 15, 98
US Antarctic Services Expedition (USASE) 111
USA IGY Bases 224

Vinson Massif 119

Waitabit Cliffs 139, 143, 183
Walker, Rod 199
Walton, Kevin 112, 197
Weddell Sea 1, 19, 54, 72, 89, 92, 93, 117, 119, 217
West Antarctica 119
Westlake, Brian 42, 44, 47, 78, 84, 92, 93, 94
Whalers Bay 10, 11, 35, 44, 55, 72, 74, 82, 89
Whales 10, 16, 27, 49, 200, 206, 207, 226
Whaling 11, 37, 38, 44, 209, 210, 211, 214
Whyte, Fraser 39, 40, 41, 42, 46, 47, 50, 53, 84, 92, 94
Wiencke Island 27
Wigglesworth, Brian 84, 171, 172, 176, 177, 178, 181, 183, 184, 187, 198
Wilkins, Sir Hubert 81
Wilson, Edward 62

255